MY ENEMY, MY SELF

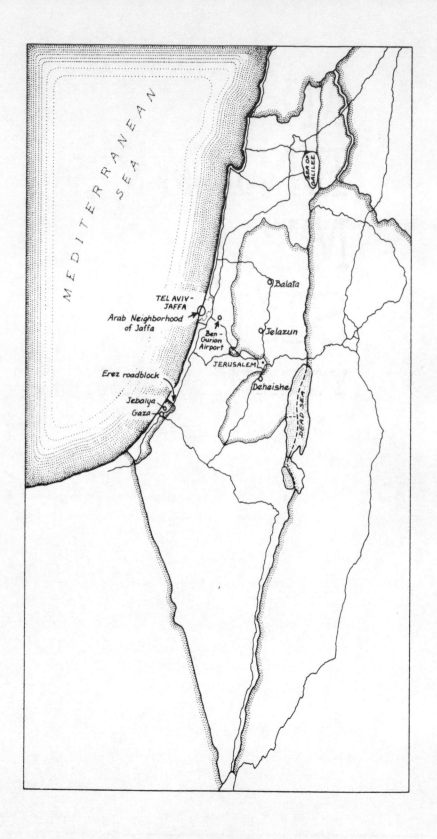

MEDITERRANEAN SEA

SEA OF GALILEE

Balata

TEL AVIV-JAFFA

Arab Neighborhood of Jaffa

Ben-Gurion Airport

Jelazun

JERUSALEM

Erez roadblock

Deheishe

Jebalya

Gaza

DEAD SEA

MY ENEMY, MY SELF.

YORAM BINUR

Doubleday

LONDON · NEW YORK · TORONTO · SYDNEY · AUCKLAND

Translated from the Hebrew by Uriel Grunfeld

TRANSWORLD PUBLISHERS LTD
61-63 Uxbridge Road, London W5 5SA

TRANSWORLD PUBLISHERS (AUSTRALIA) PTY LTD
15-23 Helles Avenue, Moorebank, NSW 2170

TRANSWORLD PUBLISHERS (NZ) LTD
Cnr Moselle and Waipareira Aves,
Henderson, Auckland

Doubleday Canada Ltd
105 Bond Street, Toronto, Ontario M5B 1Y3

Published 1989 by Doubleday
a division of Transworld Publishers Ltd
Copyright © Yoram Binur 1989

British Library Cataloguing in Publication Data

    Binur, Yoram
    My enemy, my self: an Israeli's
    undercover life as an Arab.
    1. Israel. Palestinian Arabs. Social
    control by government
    I. Title
    323.1' 19275694

    ISBN 0-385-268947

Printed and bound in Great Britain by
Mackays of Chatham PLC, Chatham, Kent

I dedicate this book to a better understanding
among the Israelis and Palestinians

ACKNOWLEDGMENTS

I WISH TO THANK all the people without whom this book would never have been completed: Feisal Al Husseini from East Jerusalem, Uriel Grunfeld from Tel Aviv, Amit Harpaz from Rosh Pina, Hassan Jibril from Shati refugee camp in the Gaza Strip, Fat'hi Raban from Jebalya refugee camp in the Gaza Strip, Daoud Kuttab from East Jerusalem, Yisrael Cohen from Tel Aviv, Makram Houri Mahoul from Jaffa, Carol Mann from New York, and many others whose identities I cannot reveal.

PREFACE

ONE YEAR after the events described in this book, twenty years after the Israeli Defense Forces entered the West Bank and the Gaza Strip, a popular uprising sprang into being in the occupied territories. The Palestinians are rebelling against their intolerable position, in which they live under foreign rule and are denied any form of legitimate political expression. It is a desperate struggle. At the time of writing these lines the death toll exceeds two hundred, hundreds of others have been wounded, thousands are under arrest, and there is no end in sight to the turmoil.

I find myself sitting at home, in Jerusalem, completing a book on my exploits as an Arab imposter. The volatile circumstances make it difficult for me to concentrate on the screen of my PC, when it would suit my nature much more to get into my car, throw a keffiyeh across the dashboard, and drive to Jebalya, Shati, Ramallah, Jelazun—wherever the action is—in order to witness the dramatic turn of events from as close as possible. But I force myself to remember that the present situation bears a direct relation to everything I have been trying to convey about my experiences as a Palestinian Arab. If there is anything extraordinary about what is happening today, it is only that it hasn't happened sooner.

At some point the Israeli people will have to express their opinion as to the fate of the occupied territories, whether by means of elections or by means of a public opinion poll. The public should have the best tools available in order to pass an educated and well-informed judgment on the issue, and if my book can contribute even a little toward that end, I will regard it as a success.

CONTENTS

INTRODUCTION

IN 1984 I BEGAN WORKING as a reporter for the local weekly newspaper in Jerusalem, *Kol Ha'ir (The Voice of the City)*. When I started the editor explained that they needed someone to cover the Arab sector of the city, forming contacts and reporting on events that took place there. I agreed to take the Arab "beat," and my first article was about a group of villagers who were hospitalized in an Arab hospital on Mount Scopus. The Israeli army had imposed a curfew in their village and conducted searches during the night, involving rough handling which left many of the inhabitants in need of medical attention. When I requested an official response to the information I had gathered, the spokesman for the Israeli Defense Forces (IDF) denied any wrongdoing on the part of the military. After the article was published, with substantial evidence that the Israeli Defense Forces were indeed responsible for acts of violence, the spokesman was reprimanded by his superiors. (I should note in passing that he accepted his rebuke like a gentleman, and has treated me fairly ever since.)

Within a short time I had extended the boundaries of my assignment and began covering not just East Jerusalem but also most of the West Bank, and occasionally the Gaza Strip as well. My close daily interaction with Arabs from the occupied territories considerably improved my command of spoken Arabic, as well as my knowledge of their etiquette, manners, and gestures.

I first became aware of the degree to which I had absorbed Palestinian culture when I traveled to Nablus with Danny Rubinstein, a seasoned reporter from the newspaper *Davar*, to interview a relative of Abu Nidal, the notorious Palestinian terrorist leader. During our conversation I learned that the interviewee thought I was Rubinstein's Arab guide. On other occasions too, Arabs from the occupied territories mistook me for a compatriot.

This misapprehension, together with the fact that news items on the West Bank tended to be rather dull and routine at that time, led me to suggest to my editor a different approach in my reporting. My idea was to offer a fresh perspective on our relationship with the Palestinians by posing as a Palestinian in a variety of settings within Israeli society, and recording my own feelings as well as the reactions of people toward me. In Jerusalem, where Arabs and Jews live in neighboring quarters of the city, my initiative seemed particularly relevant and the editor approved it.

In order to carry out my project, I first had to give myself the appearance of a typical Palestinian laborer. This was easily accomplished with the aid of suitable clothes and accessories. Near one of the gates in the walls that surround the Old City there is a secondhand-clothes dealer who displays his wares in a supermarket shopping cart. I purchased several pairs of big, very old black pants from him as well as a few patched shirts. My new wardrobe was completed when I took down from the top shelf of my father's closet an old striped jacket which had been worn years before the State of Israel was established.

I also gathered some of the typical paraphernalia of an Arab laborer. First, I borrowed a cheap plastic shopping basket from my mother; the type of basket elderly housewives take with them when they go shopping in the open market, it is also frequently used by Arab workers to carry a few necessities when they go to work. I then bought several copies of the illustrated weekly newspaper *Al Biader Al Siasi*. Even at a distance the newspaper could easily be identified when it lay in my basket or was rolled up in the pocket of my jacket. Finally, I bought three cartons of Farid cigarettes; manufactured in East Jerusalem, they have a strong bitter taste and are never smoked by Jews.

To complete the image, I left my face unshaven and brought along my worn and trusty red keffiyeh, the traditional Arab headdress. The color of a keffiyeh in the occupied territories has a certain significance. The red keffiyeh, for instance, has been converted over the past years into a symbol of the supporters and sympathizers of the PFLP and other leftist organizations in the occupied territories. A black-and-white keffiyeh signifies a supporter of Al Fatah. Sometimes one sees men wearing green-and-white keffiyehs; these are the religious fundamentalists, supporters of the Moslem Brotherhood or the radical group Islamic Jihad. I, however, chose to sport a red keffiyeh out of pragmatic considerations—it was the most eye-catching color among those available.

In addition to their dress, the gestures and body language of the Arabs are also different from those of the majority of Jews. For instance, very few Jews (only those perhaps who were born and raised in other Middle Eastern countries) will grasp a glass of tea by holding the bottom of the glass with four fingers and laying the thumb across its rim. When an Arab rides in an Israeli taxi or bus, he will cross one leg over the other in such a way as to occupy a minimum of space. There are many other, mostly unconscious, physical expressions which I imagine I picked up over time.

Having successfully created the appearance of a Palestinian, I embarked on a series of brief excursions in the center of "Jewish" Jerusalem, engaging in such mundane activities as riding a bus and sitting around in cafés. I also visited several night spots and social clubs, and attempted to rent an apartment together with a female accomplice, presenting ourselves as a racially "mixed" couple. In the article I wrote about the reactions to my "Palestinian" presence in these situations, I concluded that despite the proximity in which Jews and Arabs live in Jerusalem, and the supposed unification of the city, there remained a tangible mental barrier between the two peoples, who continued to regard one another with fear and suspicion.

The project aroused interest and led to the more comprehensive undertaking that is described in this book. Over a period of six months I lived more or less continuously as an Arab in a variety of settings, including a refugee camp in the Gaza Strip, a number of work situations in Tel Aviv, and an interesting experience as a volunteer on a kibbutz. I deliberately chose to avoid Jerusalem this time, because, as I resided there, there was too great a risk of running into acquaintances and being unmasked. Besides, the Arab laborers in Jerusalem go home after work hours and don't remain in the Jewish sector of the city. Tel Aviv, in this respect, offered a wider range of possibilities, such as investigating the living conditions in an illegal boardinghouse in Jaffa.

Generally I sought to involve myself in situations that were typical for the average Palestinian living under Israeli military rule. These included working as a restaurant helper and garage mechanic, lodging with other Arab laborers, and even having a relationship with a Jewish Israeli woman. Sometimes I got involved in situations that were not typical. Volunteering for work on a kibbutz, for instance, was not so much representative as an excellent opportunity to hold up a specific sector of Jewish society to closer scrutiny.

The second project was marked by a greater thoroughness in preparation. I tore off all the tags and labels on my clothes that could arouse suspicion. In a shoe store in the Old City of Jerusalem I purchased a pair of cheap sandals made of plastic designed to simulate brown suede. These sandals are manufactured in Gaza and only Arabs wear them. When I first entered the store, the salesman addressed me in Hebrew, but he immediately switched to Arabic once I told him what I wanted.

The next thing I arranged for was a passable ID, in case I needed to present one to potential employers. A Jordanian ID had in fact fallen into my hands some months earlier in the course of my work. It had belonged to Ali Hussein, who was killed in East Jerusalem. The late owner of the document was born in 1947 and his features roughly resembled my own. In order to avoid unnecessary complications I decided that I would show my Arab ID only on certain occasions—to Israeli employers, for instance, but never to representatives of the Israeli authorities, whether policemen or soldiers. With these I hoped to stretch the game as far as it would go, but if it finally became necessary I would display my own Israeli ID. Presenting a false document could have led to my arrest for obstructing a policeman in the course of his duties, improper use of a document, and other charges that would cause the project to end sooner than I had planned.

Finally, I developed a more or less consistent cover story. As the document gave only the place of birth of its owner and not his current address, I decided to say I was a resident of the Balata refugee camp near Nablus, one of the more militant camps on the West Bank. On many occasions I presented myself not as Ali, as the ID had it, but as Fat'hi, a name I'd already been using for years among my Arab acquaintances, who find it difficult to pronounce my Hebrew name. After consulting with a Palestinian friend I decided on the surname of Awad. The Awads are a small and relatively unknown family in the occupied territories, so the chances of running into people who knew them were negligible.

Still, there was always a chance that a particularly suspicious person might insist on speaking with me at length, eventually uncovering gaps in my familiarity with the local situation, and the truth would be discovered. I decided that whenever necessary I would add to my cover story a chapter of life in the United States, to account for any such gaps. In terms of vocabulary, I took care to steer clear of discussions in Arabic on such subjects as the natural sciences or classical literature, in which my knowledge of the language is inadequate; I took care to remain within the realm of daily life and politics, where I felt much surer of myself.

I needed to hire a photographer in order to have the project documented whenever possible. I interviewed a number of professional photographers who expressed their enthusiasm and willingness to join me, but as I prepared for the project, I came to the conclusion that I needed more than just a photographer —I needed someone who would keep cool in a situation that could become embarrassing and even dangerous, someone who wouldn't be afraid to enter places which are generally out of bounds for Israelis. Most important, I needed someone who would be able to encourage me and urge me on if I ever faltered.

The only person I knew who met all these requirements was Yisrael Cohen. He knew me well, he was aware of my weak points, and he wasn't particularly impressed with my respectable journalist credentials. He had served with me in the army; later we had worked together and traveled together.

Yisrael grew up in one of the toughest neighborhoods in Jerusalem. When I was raising pigeons on the roof of my parents' house, he was hanging out in bars, and when I was nurturing dreams about the prettiest girl in my class, he was already consorting with foreign girls who had come as tourists to see the Holy City. After completing his military service he studied photography; today he has his own studio in Tel Aviv and teaches in a school of photography. As he puts it: "The story of my life is a lot of willpower. According to my background I should have wound up as a waiter or a locksmith."

One memory in particular motivated me to offer the project to Yisrael, and it wasn't a very pleasant or flattering one to me. In 1979 we were traveling across the United States together in an old beat-up car. Somewhere out on the dusty roads of Alabama, I annoyed him so much that he stopped the car in the middle of nowhere and, shaking with anger, ordered me to get out. In the end I persuaded him to calm down and we remained together. I thought that anyone who could have scared me so badly could, without a doubt, guard me both from others and from myself.

Feisal Al Husseini, one of the most important Arab leaders in the occupied territories (who recently spent nine months under administrative detention), listened patiently as I told him what I intended to do. He explained the risk I was running: if the Arabs I contacted suspected me of being an undercover agent working for the Shin Bet (the Israeli secret service, now known as Shabak), my life would be in danger.

Feisal gave me a letter in which he asked that I be given all possible assistance so that I might carry out my journalistic mission without hindrance. Feisal is the son of a famous Palestinian leader and national hero who was killed in a well-known battle during the War of 1948 on the road to Jerusalem, and he is one of the most important figures who support the political line of the PLO. In view of Feisal's uncontested leadership among the populace in the occupied territories, the letter served as a sort of insurance policy; it could save my life in a tight spot—if I had enough time to show it. It was most gracious of Feisal to give me this letter without hesitating. After all, from his point of view, there was always a risk that I was lying, that the letter would be used in order to spy against the Palestinian people. For his trust I am grateful.

MY ENEMY, MY SELF

ONE

Coliseum

IT WAS A SUNDAY MORNING when I first arrived on Yefet Street in Jaffa, in the area known as the "slave market." Wearing a gray T-shirt, ragged jean shorts, and a pair of sandals, I took my position among the others and waited. A quick survey of my surroundings revealed some forty-odd men standing around or sitting on the iron railings that lined the sidewalk. In addition to these men, who hadn't yet found work for the day, there were also a few taxi drivers whose cars bore license plates marked with the Hebrew letter *ayin*, indicating that they came from Gaza.

Two Jews in their fifties were present as well, wearing baggy military uniforms and toting unwieldy Czech rifles which dated back to World War II at least. The soldiers were friendly enough and would occasionally stop to chat in Hebrew with one or another of the Arab men. They were members of the Civil Defense, Israeli reserve soldiers who are posted in the streets of the larger cities and carry out policing activities, in

1

particular keeping an eye out for Arabs who enter Israel from the occupied territories.

Competition for work was fierce and each addition to the pool reduced the others' chances of getting a job. In addition to my being a newcomer, I didn't come from the Gaza Strip, as did most of the others. On my first day I hardly spoke with the other workers and satisfied myself with just an exchange of greetings. *"Asalamu aleikum,"* I would say, and the traditional reply immediately came back: *"Aleikum asalam."* In general, there wasn't much conversation. We were busy keeping a lookout, darting glances off to the sides, to observe the approaching cars. Perhaps it would be a Jewish boss coming to fetch workers at the "slave market."

On the second day I was a little bolder and asked one of the workers, a man of about forty dressed in worn-out work clothes, where he came from.

"Camp Jebalya, in Gaza. And you?"

"I'm also a son of the camps. From Balata."

"Blessed be the sons of the camps," the man responded.

His name was Abdallah. He had no steady job and so every morning he took a taxi from Gaza to try his luck in Tel Aviv. On days when he couldn't find work there, he'd take another taxi, around midday, back to his home in the refugee camp.

Abdallah was introducing me to some of the others when we were interrupted by the arrival of a dark blue police van, which was then discreetly parked in a narrow alley across from where we were standing. A hundred wary eyes fastened on the van. A tall policeman stepped out of it, approached us, and without saying a word, went from one man to the next collecting identification papers. The men responded with an automatic gesture, which was the mark of experience: a worker would send a hand to his upper left shirt pocket, withdraw an orange-colored plastic card, and hand it to the policeman.

"Damn! What the hell did he have to show up for?" I thought nervously. Inevitably, the policeman reached me, and with a blank expression he ordered, *"Hawiya!"* (Arabic for ID card). Now I was faced with a dilemma. In my left-hand pocket I had my Israeli ID and in my right-hand pocket lay the Jordanian one. If I presented the Jordanian ID and the policeman knew what he was doing, he would arrest me for further questioning

2

as soon as he checked the ID number. If, on the other hand, the Arab workers caught sight of the blue Israeli ID card, my cover might be blown.

"*Hawiya!*" The policeman impatiently reminded me that I didn't have much time for reflection. I hastily handed over my Israeli card, more frightened, apparently, of the police than of my fellow workmen.

After collecting IDs from all the men in the street, the policeman returned to the van, carrying the documents with him. We sat and waited while he and a colleague took down the names and numbers on the cards. I hoped they would overlook the oddity of my case, and in fact they failed to react to it. Either the number sequences had lost their meaning due to the sheer quantity of documents that had to be checked, or else the cops simply wanted to get their shift quietly over and done with and wished to avoid initiating a complicated procedure. In any case, after about half an hour, a khaki-sleeved hand was thrust out the window of the van. One of the workers went over and fetched the documents and began calling out names, to return the IDs to their owners. The moment I saw the blue card, I grabbed it and tucked it away. No one seemed to have noticed that something was amiss.

Another day without work went by, and then another. It was now noon of the fifth day and I had given up on finding any work that day as well. Abdallah was there and I decided to ask him if he knew of a place where I could stay overnight in Tel Aviv.

"What do you need to sleep among the Jews for? The police make trouble. If they nab you, you'll be beaten, sent to jail, and fined two thousand shekels," he said.

I explained that it's difficult to catch a taxi from Tel Aviv to Nablus and also that I hadn't enough money, so that it was more convenient for me to find a cheap hostel where "our brethren" were used to lodging. Abdallah obligingly asked around and the general recommendation was that I should approach Abu Rajab. Someone pointed him out to me—a well-dressed elderly man who sat on the side, in the taxi drivers' company.

As I was about to go over to Abu Rajab, a white Subaru rolled into sight. This time I was prepared. Together with the

3

other hapless men who still hadn't gotten a job, I charged wildly at the car. We shoved each other aside as we did our best to grab hold of any protruding object—a fender, a windshield wiper, a door handle. In this way we were dragged along down the road for several dozen yards. The driver finally halted and then he called through the window, in Hebrew: "I'm looking for restaurant workers. There's a chance to sleep on the premises."

We stormed the car and I suddenly found myself in the back seat, squeezed between two sweaty fellows from Gaza. Despite the discomfort, I was greatly relieved to exchange the asphalt sidewalk for a cushioned seat of Japanese manufacture. Abdallah, who sat up in front, next to the driver, conducted the negotiations. The Jew, around thirty-five years of age, dressed in a black leather jacket, was offering 15 shekels ($10) a day for kitchen work that was to begin every day at noon and continue until four o'clock in the morning. We could have as much food as we desired and there was a room in which we could sleep. The pay that the Jew was offering, relative to the required number of working hours, was absurd even by "slave market" standards, and Abdallah argued with him over it. The drawn-out bargaining process apparently wasn't to the Jew's liking and he ordered Abdallah, "You! Out of the car! Scram!" When Abdallah asked why, the answer was curt: "Because I don't like your face!" Abdallah now left after muttering a curse.

We in the back seat decided that, even for a Jew, the man we were dealing with was a mean character, so we all got up together to leave. But just as I put one foot on the ground, Abdallah addressed me. "Fat'hi, you were looking for a place to sleep, so stay with him at least for the night. Never mind how much you'll make, you'll solve your immediate problem." Thus released from the obligation of expressing solidarity with my fellow workingmen, I slid into the front seat of the car, next to the Jew. He looked me over. In contrast to the men of Gaza, who are famous for the glowering looks with which they greet all Jews, I lowered my gaze. My humble reaction, without a doubt, made a favorable impression on the man and he immediately made what seemed on the face of it to be a worthwhile offer: "Want to work on a monthly basis? You'll get five hundred shekels a month. Where do you come from?"

4

I ignored his offer and addressed myself only to his second question, as if that was all I had understood. In broken Hebrew I answered, "I from Nablus, Balata camp."

"What's your name?" he asked.

"My name is Fat'hi. Fat'hi Awad," I replied in Arabic.

The man started the car and turned to look at the other workers as we moved away; his face twisted into a hateful grimace. "The workers from Gaza are a bunch of stinking bastards! But you seem like a good sort. Could you get me some more workers from your place?" I pretended not to understand his Hebrew, and only after he had painstakingly explained himself in a language that was part Hebrew, part pidgin Arabic, did I make a fist and hold it to my ear, as if I were holding a telephone receiver. "In evening I talking with friends want work," I said.

The Jew stopped his car at the back entrance of a large industrial building, located on Ben-Zvi Road in Tel Aviv. On the second floor were the "Coliseum" Halls (not the real name), where I was to work, a place where weddings, receptions, and the like were held. We entered the large hall, which had just been scrubbed clean. The chairs were all raised onto the tables. "Moshe" (as the man in the black leather jacket introduced himself) hustled me to the kitchen in the back. I was the only Arab in the place at that moment, and the other workers all seemed to be gawking at me. They were Russian immigrants: cooks with faces red from standing over steaming pots all day long, and Georgian women with kerchief-covered heads, the skin of their hands cracked from too much dishwashing.

Moshe pointed at an older man of about sixty. "That's my father, "Shmuel." You take orders from him. Do what he tells you." The old man signaled me to follow him. He went up to one of the huge pots that were heating over the fire, filled a bowl with hot soup, and added a few pieces of cheap fatty meat that he took from one of the cooks, who was seasoning it on a cutting board. Then he set the bowl down on a plastic tray and presented it to me, along with a whole loaf of challah and a bottle of orange juice. The steam from the soup rose to my nostrils and reminded me that I hadn't had anything to eat yet that day. Back in the hall, I took two chairs off one of the tables

5

and Shmuel and I sat down, surrounded by a forest of chairs with their legs sticking up in the air.

Shmuel measured me with his stare and said, "Fat'hi, you eat here as much you like. Just eat, work, eat, work . . . you don't need to go out at all, so you won't get in trouble with the police." I nodded blankly, dipped a hunk of challah into the soup, and savored the sweet warm bread as I chewed on it.

My first task was to take down all the chairs and arrange the hall for a wedding that was going to take place there that evening. I fought a losing battle with the hundreds of chairs, covered with imitation brown leather. I could feel the old man's eyes boring holes in my back, down which the sweat was beginning to run, into my shorts and my underwear. After two hours of lifting chairs and setting them down, the hall seemed larger to me than it really was. Another worker, a Jew, was assigned to help me complete the job.

When I had taken down the last chair, I felt a tap on my shoulder. The gold tooth in Shmuel's mouth sparkled as he smiled and indicated, in the peculiar sign language which he had devised in order to communicate with me, that I should follow him back into the kitchem, which was now bustling with activity. We went to the dishwashing corner, where two big stainless-steel sinks awaited me, piled high with huge pots and dirty pans. He poured a strong-smelling liquid soap into a plastic container, diluted it with some tap water, and made a circular motion with his hand, like the old man in *The Karate Kid* explaining to the boy how to wash cars. As he gestured, the old geezer said, "Quickly! Quickly!" and I began scrubbing.

While I scraped away, the cooks sent a constant flow of dirty pots and pans in my direction, at a much faster rate than I could keep up with. One of the cooks, a big Russian, approached me dangling a large, juicy hunk of meat, which he gave to me. I wasn't taken in by his gesture: the tricky bastard simply wanted me to work faster and to give priority to the pots that he needed.

As I was working, the water overflowed in the open sewer beneath the sink. I threw a questioning look at Shmuel, who was standing right behind me like a watchdog, and he pointed to the drain at the end of the canal. There was no way out of it. I got down on my knees in the muck, scooped up the grease

6

and the peelings that were clogging the sewage, and threw them into the garbage pail. My feet, in their cheap sandals, were sticky and slippery from the mixture of soap, filth, and grease.

After eight hours of nonstop work I was barely able to stand. Finally, the cooks completed their work and gave the kitchen a superficial cleaning, and I enjoyed a brief respite. Very brief, for soon there was Shmuel, like some devil, beckoning with his finger. I followed him to where he opened a big refrigerated storeroom, and then stepped back to avoid a wave of cold air that rushed out through the open door. He motioned that I should go in and fetch some crates of beer bottles. I was entirely covered with sweat from working in the heated kitchen, and to enter a refrigerator put me in serious danger of catching pneumonia. The old bastard was aware of the risk, which was why he kept at a safe distance, indicating from afar what he wanted me to take out.

The wedding guests began to arrive, and the Jewish waiters, sporting white shirts and cheap bow ties, scurried to and fro between the kitchen and the hall, carrying trays laden with food. My main task now was to set out the food and drinks for the waiters to serve. The kitchen doors were shut and Shmuel made sure that the guests wouldn't be exposed to a dirty Arab worker. Soon, one of the waiters, a youth of about twenty, addressed me sharply: "Ahmed, bring me two more crates of beer, quick!" Ahmed and Mohammed are common Arab names, and frequently Jews, who don't bother to learn the names of their assistants, address them by one of these two names. Now, it may be that Jews owned the wedding hall, even the entire country, but my name was my own and under no circumstances was I willing to let them take that away as well. Weak with fatigue and trembling from the insult, I forgot my position—the lowliest of workers—and grabbed the waiter by his starched collar. Bringing his face close to mine, I hissed in Arabic, "I'm not Ahmed. I am Fat'hi!" The lad grew pale and dramatically changed his manner: "O.K., let it be Fat'hi, then. Please, could you fetch two crates of beer?"

The average Arab worker would never have dared to do what I had done that evening to the young Jewish waiter. The near-violence of my outburst, which had scared the fellow and

7

caused him to apologize, came as a result of the continuous humiliation I experienced and of the fact that I simply wasn't used to being anyone's slave.

On the few occasions when it became necessary to empty the garbage pail, Shmuel made an exception to the rule that I was not to leave the kitchen. I would go through the corridor leading to the hall, wheeling the garbage cart. The guests passed by me, dressed in their finery, smiling and carrying colorfully wrapped gifts for the newlyweds. It was humiliating and frustrating to confront such complacent, well-fed people and to know that my presence was tolerated only on account of the dirty work that I was performing, at the rate of one lousy shekel an hour. One of the guests who happened to cross my path asked me where the men's room was. I waved indifferently and answered in Arabic, "I don't speak Hebrew."

After a while, two Arab youths arrived to help, and as we worked I briefly made their acquaintance. Their names were Hamdi and Thair and they were both from the Gaza Strip. During the day they worked at a pastry shop that belonged to Moshe, the man who had brought me to work here. In the evenings, for a few extra shekels, he employed them at the wedding hall. Later in the evening, a third youth arrived. His name was Jaber and he was assigned to be my assistant in my current task as porter, carrying things around and organizing the storeroom. Since he spoke a passable Hebrew, Shmuel had him translate directions to me. I spoke little and worked hard, to Shmuel's great satisfaction.

By one in the morning I was completely exhausted. Still, with the aid of Jaber's translation, or else by means of poking a finger in my back and then pointing at a crate that had to be moved, Shmuel relentlessly continued to give me work, as if I were a machine. My arm muscles and back ached terribly, so I asked Jaber to inform Shmuel that I was tired and was going to sleep. Knowing that no other worker would agree to work in a place like this for such a low salary, I was uncompromising. When Shmuel said to Jaber, "Persuade Fat'hi to work another hour or so," I told Jaber to tell the Jewish dog that if he still had a lot of work left he could go get his sister to do it. Jaber modified my message somewhat: "The worker is tired and asks very much to sleep and tomorrow he'll work more." Jaber took advantage of the situation as well and told Shmuel that he needed to sleep because he had "cream puffs to make tomorrow." Shmuel tried to get him to keep on working but finally he handed Jaber a key tied to a shoelace and we left the kitchen.

At the end of the corridor there was a metal door, which Jaber unlocked with the key. The doorframe was fastened by means of a few iron rods that had been driven into the wall and welded. A gaping space above the door seemed to say that there was nothing worth stealing on the other side. As soon as the light in the room went on, a large rat came flying out of one of the corners and disappeared in a crack between the floor and the exposed concrete wall. A three-tiered bunk had been carelessly constructed out of metal shelves, and three more mattresses were spread on the floor, taking up nearly the entire room.

"Hamdi, Thair, and I sleep here, ya Fat'hi," Jaber said, indicating the bunks with the shyness of a youngster who is a little ashamed of having arranged better conditions for himself than for someone who was his senior. The boy already had the manner of one used to a life of work and hardship. "Tomorrow, if Allah be willing, I'm going home and you'll be able to sleep on the bed," he added as if he'd read my mind.

I placed my plastic shopping basket on one of the mattresses, rummaged among the few items in it, retrieved a towel, and went to the bathroom. The staff of Coliseum Halls used the same rest rooms that were available to the guests. Given the facilities, I didn't stand a chance of removing even a fraction of the grime which had stuck to me during the day. Taking a shower was obviously out of the question. As a minimal concession to hygiene I slipped off my sandals and washed my feet with soap in the washbasin. My toenails were black with a layer of filth that no amount of soap could eradicate. "An Arab's feet," I thought. I caught a glimpse of myself in the mirror and realized that this was my first moment alone since I'd come to work. I assessed the situation and tried to make some sense of it. That Hamdi, Thair, and Jaber were going to be sleeping soundly in their bunks while I would have to sleep on the floor was difficult for me to accept and gave me cause for reflection. In 1976 I had served as an officer of the Israeli army in Ramallah, an Arab city near Jerusalem. In those days I used to throw youths like Hamdi, Thair, and Jaber into my jeep with a kick and a good crack on the head. Tonight they were taking sweet revenge on me, though in a small way and without even being aware of it: proper bunks for them, the floor for me.

Shortly after I returned to the room, as I was attempting to cover myself with a dirty blanket, Hamdi and Thair came in. Hamdi treated me to a bunch of grapes and a bottle of juice which he had brought from the kitchen. *"T'fadal,* ya Fat'hi," he said, offering them to me. *"Shukran, amo,"* I thanked him and silently picked at the grapes.

The moment of truth had come. For the first time I was posing as an Arab in the company of Arabs, and the situation was not a comfortable one. We were in a secluded room, the wedding had been over for quite some time, and there wasn't anyone close by who would be able to help me if I was unmasked. Because of the Shin Bet's widespread practice of planting informers among Arabs who come from the occupied territories, these Arabs live in constant fear. The terms *amil, jasus, chain, bishtril* (agent, spy, traitor, co-worker) are in frequent use. Anyone who is suspected of collaborating with the Israeli authorities can expect to be knifed or strangled with a twisted towel, which serves as an improvised rope.

I decided to remain as passive as possible, and to restrict my conversation to concise answers. One unnecessary word on my part, or a mistake in pronunciation, and none of my roommates would believe that all I wanted was to write a book.

The three youths were lying in their bunks now, and Hamdi launched into a detailed description of a girl he'd met in Gaza. "I looked her in the face and could immediately tell that she wasn't one of us. She was so shameless! In Raffah we stick by the Islamic code. Once it was strictly observed in Jebalya as well, but now they've changed for the worse over there." Then he got carried away as he told us about the room he was building for himself in his parents' home in Raffah. "Each of us has a room three by three [meters], but mine is four by four and everything in it is brand-new. There's even a Formica dining counter and the kitchen utensils are new too."

The chill of the floor easily penetrated the thin mattress I

10

was lying on. During Hamdi's monologue it occurred to me that I should measure its thickness. I stuck out a finger and held it against the edge of the mattress with my fingertip touching the floor. The mattress reached one-third the height of my finger, about two centimeters. Surely, even in prison the mattresses are thicker than that.

Jaber addressed me with a question: "How are your girls over in Nablus? They say that you've become like the Jews."

This was it. I'd been called upon to join in the conversation and there was no turning back—I had to do it somehow. Despite my fatigue all my senses were keen. Lines of dialogue ran through my mind, and I decided for the moment not to address myself to the subject of the girls of Nablus. If I had to speak in Arabic, I preferred to discuss a topic in which I was more conversant. "Have the police ever raided this place? Do they know about this room?"

Thair, who'd been quiet up to now, raised himself up on his elbows and exhibited his ignorance with regard to the policies of the Israeli military authorities. "What? You, from Nablus, are also forbidden to sleep here?"

"Of course it's forbidden," I answered. "Last week they caught a cousin of mine who was shacking up in a hostel in Ramleh."

"Yeah, the police know," said Thair. "They were here two weeks ago. That night I was sleeping here with another friend from Raffah. They beat us up real bad and took us to jail. We received an eight-hundred-shekel fine and a jail term on probation."

The youths stirred uneasily. They were clearly frightened by the mere mention of the police. They seemed younger than before, when we were working together. Heartened by my success, I went a step further: "The girls in Nablus really are freer, but among us, in Balata, it's different. We keep to the tradition more strictly than they do."

"Blessed be the sons of the refugee camps who have always suffered at the hands of the Zionists," responded Thair, in whom the mere mention of refugee camps aroused a spark of nationalist fervor.

In answering the youths' questions I elaborated a bit on my "background," at the same time checking my cover story to see

11

if it was sufficiently credible. "I'm a mechanic, but I've also taken some courses at the Bir Zeit University. In Nablus I worked in a garage, mainly with Peugeot and Mercedes cars. Sometimes I also send articles to the newspaper *Al Fajr.*" Fortunately the youths from Gaza weren't well acquainted with what was going on in the West Bank, and I was able to tell them about what we had to endure in Balata.

A few moments after the light was turned off, Thair said, "Ya Fat'hi, I hope a day will come, just one day, when we'll be able to settle accounts with those Jews."

I pulled the blanket tightly over myself as a shiver ran up and down my spine. Those words, precisely because they were delivered in such a dry and matter-of-fact tone, sounded terrifying to me. The day that Thair was alluding to was, in effect, the end of me. I recovered and replied, "*Allahu maa asabirin* [Allah helps those who are patient]. Don't worry, that day will come." And on this note we fell into a deep sleep.

After several days of work at Coliseum Halls, I was in a sorry state. "I need to leave the building in order to meet some friends," I told Shmuel. But the old man couldn't understand what I was saying and Jaber wasn't around to help with the translation.

Shmuel called Moshe over. "What do you have to look for on the outside? The police are likely to arrest you and then they won't let you come back to work. Today there's a large wedding and we're under a lot of pressure here," Moshe explained in his broken Arabic and with noticeable impatience.

"I have friends from my camp who are working not far from here and I want to visit them," I answered with all the determination I could muster.

"For that you have a home. Here you don't need to go visiting friends and getting into trouble. You should work. If there isn't any work this weekend you can take a vacation."

After a long argument and after I had promised Moshe that I would try to find him a cheap worker from among my friends, he granted me permission to leave work for half an hour. "But no more than that. And I'm taking that half hour off your pay, so don't you come complaining either."

I grabbed my basket and took the elevator down two flights

to the street. Cars whizzed by, shops were open, the street was busy—I had almost forgotten what it was like out in the real world. Since my arrival at the industrial building on Ben-Zvi Road, days earlier, I hadn't set foot outside the wedding hall. I felt around in my pockets; thank God, my tokens were still there and now all I needed to find was their complement, a phone booth in working order. I wandered through the nearby streets, which were mostly lined with car repair shops.

I recognized a large, fenced-in building with a forbidding exterior that was set slightly back from the sidewalk. This was the Abu Kabir detention center. A few hundred yards farther on, I came across the Institute for Forensic Medicine. I could almost feel my Jordanian ID card burning a hole in my upper right shirt pocket. Its former owner had visited here, though not alive. It had been his next-to-last stop in this world. Here his body had been slit by a surgeon's knife and the bullets which had killed him were extracted from it. I allowed my imagination to indulge in a pathetic exercise, speculating on how the cuts were crudely stitched and how the stitches clearly marked the corpse; how the man's family hauled his remains onto a pickup truck and brought them to rest in a village somewhere in the arid hills of Judea; how the mourners held palm branches raised high, according to Islamic custom, and the hatred welled in their breasts, mingling with the tense sadness they felt.

I couldn't find a telephone booth. Twenty minutes had already passed since I had left Coliseum and in order for my plan to succeed it was necessary for me to get back on time. I spied a phone on the counter of a diner and entered. The customers stared at me, especially at my basket, with obvious discomfort, as if I had a bomb inside which might bring the ceiling down on their heads at any moment.

From out of nowhere a fat man materialized and planted himself squarely in front of me, looking very much in charge. "I don't have work here," he said in Arabic, without being asked.

"I'd like to make a phone call, if it's possible," I said.

"The phone is out of order. Now move on!" the fat man ordered, bringing our conversation to an abrupt conclusion.

The customers apparently approved of the little scene and

13

enjoyed my discomfort. As I turned away, I could feel their malicious smiles behind my back. "They're improving, they are. Now they know how to use a telephone," I heard someone comment. I tightened my grip on the handles of the plastic basket until my knuckles turned white.

At the next restaurant I asked for a bottle of juice and a pastry cake, and only afterward asked to use the phone. Thank God, Yisrael Cohen, my photographer, was at home! I covered the mouthpiece with my hand as I spoke into the phone. "Come to Coliseum this afternoon, it's a kind of wedding hall." I tried to explain briefly to Yisrael all that had happened to me over the past few days. He wrote down the address and promised to be there.

A few hours after my little excursion I heard a man's voice announce, "I want to be your photographer. I'll come and photograph every wedding and the hall will receive a ten percent commission from my total earnings." The voice invested me with renewed energy, but also with anxiety. I wasn't allowed to leave the kitchen and was afraid that Yisrael wouldn't see me. Apart from our one phone conversation, we hadn't been in touch over the last few days, and he might think there was a mistake in the address I had given him and simply leave. Because of the fatigue and the humiliation I'd been experiencing I couldn't even think of independently quitting the place. I felt that only Yisrael was capable of getting me out of there, and that without him I'd have to stay and keep on working.

My strong desire to put an end to this nightmare led me to take a brave initiative, at least by the standards of a lowly Arab worker. Without being instructed to do so by the old man, I wheeled a hand truck filled with crates of beer out into the corridor. Shmuel was evidently pleased with my action, for he went along with me. And in the corridor, there he was—my savior! When Yisrael caught sight of me the smile on his face froze. However, he immediately recovered and hastened to press the button on his camera, capturing Shmuel and me on film.

"If you want to be a wedding photographer, what did you photograph that Arab for?" the old man asked suspiciously. Fearfully, I held my breath, but Yisrael wasn't the least bit concerned. "One Arab more or less doesn't make a difference.

14

I'll bring you the picture and you'll be pleased," he said. After I emptied the garbage Shmuel returned to the kitchen and I managed to ask Yisrael to come back the next day at four in the morning, in order to pick me up.

Yisrael left and I remained behind, jealous of the privileged status which enabled him to get into a car, start the engine, and drive off to a warm house and a wife. I overheard part of a conversation between Shmuel and Moshe, who had not the slightest suspicion that the photographer who had turned up was connected with their Arab. They feared rather that he was an undercover agent of the income-tax authorities.

I felt relieved to know that in the morning Yisrael would come and take me back to my real identity, at least for a day or two. During the hours of work that remained I indulged in all kinds of loose language against my employers and against Jews in general. Whenever Shmuel or Moshe instructed me to do something, I'd ask Jaber to tell them that "the Palestinian revolution will get you, you Zionist pimps," and other subversive stuff, which caused Jaber to look at me with wonder. He certainly had to employ all his virtuosity, such as it was, to translate my rantings and ravings in a way that wouldn't offend our employers' ears.

My last day of work at Coliseum Halls went by relatively fast. I had already gotten used to the heavy work and to the accompanying filth. The foul smell that my body exuded didn't annoy me in the least; it only bothered those who had to stand next to me. At the end of the day I asked Moshe to give me the wages I had earned up to then. "A friend of mine is going to the camp and he'll come by here tomorrow and will bring the money to my family," I explained. Moshe grunted and in an offhand manner gave me ten shekels. "You'll get the rest later, so you won't suddenly feel like disappearing on us."

That night, back in our stuffy room, I drew my companions into a political conversation. The success of this last day had given me fresh courage and Fat'hi Awad's share of my being was now greater than that of Yoram Binur. As I understood it, the three youths supported the leftist organizations such as the Popular Front for the Liberation of Palestine, which was under the leadership of George Habash. Thair and Jaber had already

15

managed to spend some time in jail in Gaza—Jaber on a charge of throwing stones at an Israeli vehicle and Thair on suspicion of having hurled a Molotov cocktail. I asked about the conditions in prison and the interrogations they had been subjected to.

"It's nothing," Thair said. "They kept a sack over my head for some hours and then beat me a little and asked me questions. I didn't admit a thing."

"And did you throw it?" I asked.

He was careful with his reply. "What does it matter? The main thing is I didn't confess."

I also told them about the hardships we were going through in Balata: curfews, searches conducted by the army in the dead of night, and friends who had been arrested without a sentence, a procedure known as administrative detention.

"We thought that Jews cause less trouble in the West Bank, but apparently matters are bad there as well," Thair said. "They should simply be wiped out."

I took advantage of the direction that the conversation had taken and began to speculate, in as abstract a fashion as possible, about the feasibility of committing an "action" in our place of work. The youths allowed me to spin out a fantasy of sabotage, even if it was only a matter of spoiling the food in storage. At the end of the conversation Jaber and Thair noted that our boss, Moshe, wasn't so bad as far as Jews went. "You have to watch out for him on money matters, he always tries to take something off the wages, but apart from that he's pretty decent," they said. But I couldn't quite fathom what decency they found in that damned exploiter.

After we'd turned off the lights and curled up under our raggedy blankets, Thair asked me if I knew a certain Hassan Abd Al Salim. I replied that I didn't know any Hassan with that last name, but I pronounced the name Hassan with a nonguttural *H*—a mistake that no Arab would ever make. Thair straightened up in his bunk, gave me a blood-chilling look, and corrected my pronunciation of the name. I pretended I hadn't heard him but my nerves were taut as a wire. The correction was a sign of the beginning of suspicion. From now on they were liable to probe me further and with such intensity that I wouldn't be able to withstand it. The knowledge that

16

Yisrael was going to arrive soon to take me out of there made things easier. Still, I didn't dare close my eyes until the regular rise and fall of my companions' breathing indicated that they were fast asleep.

The next thing I knew, someone was prodding me in the ribs with his feet. "Come on now, come on, get up!" I heard, and I leaped up from my mattress on the floor, ready to take on all comers. Yisrael stood there, smiling but holding his nose. "You stink like a real Arab," he observed in his typically enlightened manner. Hamdi, Thair, and Jaber had already gone to their day jobs at the pastry shop. Before waking me, Yisrael had managed to take a shot of me in the room.

"Take me away from here, quick," I begged him.

"What's the rush? Stay, work for another day or two," he answered cynically, still keeping me at arm's length to avoid the smell. I hastily gathered my meager belongings, and we hurried through the corridor, down to the street level, into the parked car, and off to Yisrael's house in one of the more civilized neighborhoods of Tel Aviv.

I took a hot shower and rubbed down my aching body with a stiff brush until my skin glowed a bright red. Next, I helped myself to a cup of coffee. Yisrael was pestering me; he couldn't wait to hear all about what had happened, but for the moment I ignored his pleas and stepped out into the street. The weather was extremely pleasant. After greeting the Arab street cleaner with a nod of my head, I went over to where my car was parked and found a week's worth of bird droppings on my car cover. I shook it briskly, folded it, and put it away in the trunk. As I stepped on the gas, the car leaped forward and I embarked on a cruise of the city. Viewed from the driver's seat, Tel Aviv seemed soothingly familiar. The act of driving, shifting gears, accelerating, and braking afforded me a sense of mastery, and slowly I regained my confidence and the security of knowing that I was, after all, myself.

17

TWO

Binchu

I SPENT THE SIX-DAY WAR, like all children my age, in the ground-floor shelter of my parents' house in Jerusalem. We fortified the entrance to the shelter with sandbags, and my mother stocked it with food, including tinned meat, packages of matzoh, and a great many jars of homemade jam. The siege of Jerusalem in 1948 was still fresh in my parents' memory, as it must have been for all the older generation of Jerusalemites.

I can't recall much from those days that we spent in the shelter, only a few explosions that sounded very close by, when the Jordanian artillery scored some direct hits on neighboring houses. A phone call that we received when the fighting was at its peak was especially exciting. It was from my brother, who had fought in the first battle for control of East Jerusalem; he was calling from the UN headquarters, which the Israeli forces had seized from the Jordanian Legion. (UN personnel had evacuated the luxurious building which was once the residence of the British High Commissioner.)

Defense Minister Moshe Dayan's first act when the war was

19

over was to provide the Jewish public with access to the Wailing Wall. My classmates who visited the Wall returned to tell of the strong emotions that they had felt at this sacred site. A few days later I went to see it for myself. The Old City was still tightly sealed off, and one could hear the occasional sound of gunfire. The only way for civilians to approach the site was by a circuitous route which ran partly along the walls of the Old City. Armed soldiers were stationed along the route, to guarantee the visitors' safety. I joined the procession that was raising clouds of dust as it wended its way up the dirt path that had been hastily cleared by military tractors.

At long last, I found myself facing the ultimate symbol of the Jewish nation's yearning for Zion—the Wailing Wall. The stones were impressive, huge and ancient, but I didn't feel anything akin to the excitement and enthusiasm that I witnessed in the surrounding crowd. It was certainly some wall, but it was nothing more than a wall to me. Then I remembered the tales of my classmates who'd already been there, and the reports about the many tears they had shed. I couldn't afford to return to my class without having had a similar experience, so I pinched myself over and over until the pain was sufficient to bring a few tears to my eyes. I simply concluded that at the age of thirteen I lacked the understanding to fully appreciate the significance of the occasion. The painful pinches I gave to myself were not an expression of skepticism; they were a self-inflicted punishment for the insensitivity that I attributed to myself in contrast to the widespread jubilation of the crowds.

When I was a boy, my closest friend was the hired gardener who sometimes tended my parents' garden. He was a rather crazy old man of about eighty who went by the strange name of Alter Tobenhaus. Old Tobenhaus had a wire coop in his yard where he used to keep several pairs of pigeons. On occasion, when some of the squabs had matured, he would ceremoniously invite me over and together we would visit the old Yemenite slaughterer who lived down the road. As the blood of the fledglings trickled onto the sand in the Yemenite's backyard, Tobenhaus would already be smacking his lips, as he described the wonders of the pigeon soup that his wife was going to prepare for him that evening.

The old man's pigeons intrigued me, and after some time I

struck a deal with him. Taking advantage of my mother's absence one afternoon, I brought Tobenhaus five avocado plants that she'd been nurturing and exchanged them for a pair of young pigeons, which were thus spared the butcher's knife.

Tobenhaus took me with him to visit the Old City of Jerusalem shortly after the divided city was reunified. We went to see an old friend of his, whom he'd known in the days before 1948 —that is, preceding the existence of the State of Israel. This friend was a Moslem Arab who lived on Copts Street in the Christian Quarter. To my surprise, he and Tobenhaus, who were about the same age, held their conversation in Yiddish, a language of which I don't understand a word. So I joined the friend's son, Ishak, who, as I recall, was a saddlemaker by profession, and while the two old men gossiped, he showed me a large pigeon coop he had on the second floor of his store. I ended up buying a pedigreed pair of his feathered specimens. My acquaintance with Ishak opened doors for me among other pigeon breeders in the Old City, and within a few months I was a familiar presence in several households there.

A large and sophisticated dovecote soon replaced the small wooden crate on the roof of my parents' house. The increasing number of transactions in which I was involved were financed by my babysitting earnings, but whenever I was interested in acquiring an especially rare or precious pair of birds, I wouldn't hesitate to stick my hand into the pocket of my father's jacket where his wallet lay unguarded.

Of course, being young and inexperienced, I suffered several setbacks. Once, a strange fit must have overcome me, for I promised to sell all my pigeons to Issa Shahin, an Arab restaurant owner I knew from East Jerusalem. Only moments later I regretted the deal and for several hours I wrangled with Shahin—a shrewd merchant if there ever was one—over the amount of damages I should pay him for canceling the deal. Finally we agreed that he would keep a pair of purebred Egyptian pigeons which I had recently purchased for their beautiful rich brown color.

There was also an Iraqi Jew by the name of Aryeh Zehavi, a clerk in the local post office, who was always well dressed and whose hands were covered with gold rings. Aryeh Zehavi took advantage of me. Each time I got my hands on a pair of rare pigeons he would buy them from me for peanuts, using all kinds of false arguments. On the other hand, each time he had common specimens with which I was not yet familiar he would sell them to me at an exorbitant price. In particular I remember a pair of Damascus doves that I had kept for a long period without knowing their worth. Since they took good care of their fledglings, I even used to smash their eggs in order to give them other, more precious ones (I thought) to care for. Aryeh Zehavi purchased that pair from me for a negligible sum; the next day he told me with mock excitement that an Arab breeder who visited him had told him of their great value. Known in Arabic as *mawardi* (flowery), the doves turned out to be the only pair of their kind in the entire country. The only thing I ever got from that con man was his Arab name, Fat'hi, which had been given to him by his parents when he was still in Iraq. I first appropriated that name, as a boy, when I got tired of my Arab acquaintances mispronouncing my own.

A few months before the Six-Day War broke out, I began to take riding lessons with Yehuda Alafi, the owner of a riding school. During the war, while he was doing reserve duty, I took care of his horses together with a group of youngsters who were also his pupils. When he returned from the war our relationship grew closer. Yehuda Alafi spoke fluent Arabic and it was he who really taught me the language. I used to join him when he went to the livestock fairs in the West Bank to buy and sell horses. I would study the manner in which he conducted negotiations with the Arab merchants, and when I didn't understand a certain word, I would insist that he tell me its meaning. Once Yehuda purchased a restless, strapping stallion, which he tied to my tiny Citroën and left in a parking lot while we concluded our market day with our customary plate of houmus in one of the tiny restaurants that still exist opposite the walls of the Old City. When we came out, horse and car were nowhere in sight. The horse, we discovered, had managed to drag the car a few dozen yards to the small public garden, which had more grass to offer than the parking lot.

My low grades at the snobbish high school to which my parents sent me didn't interfere with my "horse and pigeon business," as my father angrily called it. I spent most of my time going between the riding stables and my pigeons on the roof. At school it was decided that I would have to repeat the ninth grade. This harsh act merely succeeded in alienating me even further from school and from social life in general. I used to spend the long and tedious school days in anticipation of the moment when I would be able to return to tending my pigeons, or to the riding lessons which I was now giving at Yehuda Alafi's school (in exchange for which he would let me go on riding excursions for free).

The following year, when I finally made it to the tenth grade, I chose to take Arabic and Middle Eastern studies. I used to fall asleep during the Arabic classes because I already knew everything that was being taught. The teacher was strict; he scolded me and gave me a low grade.

A year before finishing high school I sold all my pigeons to an Arab friend and bought myself a Ford, which I particularly enjoyed parking alongside my teacher's car in front of the school entrance.

When I completed high school, after five years (instead of the usual four), and with the help of several private tutors, who had to take extra pains on my behalf, I succeeded in passing my matriculation exams. In August 1973, I was drafted, and arrived at a military base near Tel Aviv, where new conscripts were received and classified. Like the majority of my classmates who had completed Middle Eastern studies in high school, I was curtly informed by the recruiting officer: "You're going to Intelligence." I was disappointed, because I wanted to join a fighting unit, but I remembered from previous conversations I had held with friends that the Intelligence branch wouldn't be able to intervene if I volunteered for combat duty.

I went over to the office of the Haruv patrol, a reconnaissance unit, which at that time was responsible for the security of the Jordanian border. After being subjected to a series of tests, including an exhausting run accompanied by terrible shouts from the unit's physical fitness instructors, I was marched together with a few others to the base's storerooms. We were supplied with army uniforms, including brown boots (more prestigious than the ordinary black ones) and a "paratrooper's tunic," which is cut to emphasize the male physique.

23

After receiving our equipment we were taken to a basic training camp somewhere in the West Bank, which the Israeli army had taken over in its entirety from the Jordanian army. What a lucky group we felt we were, to be accepted by such an elite unit.

The army was nothing like what I had imagined it would be, and I spent my first night in the isolated training camp crying silently inside the sleeping bag with which I'd been supplied. On our second day we were instructed to stand in formation outside our barracks after drinking "a lot of water." We hastened to follow orders, and before long a huge fellow in khaki pants and a white T-shirt arrived. Sergeant Ekhaus, the terror of the base, reminded us how important it was to drink a lot of water before exercising to prevent dehydration and proceeded to explain the importance of developing physical stamina. He completed his lecture with a shout: "TO YOUR RIGHT, JUMP!!!" For the next hour he had us running up and down the steep slope of the mountain at whose foot the camp was located. In the following days it was enough for one of the instructors to tell us to wait outside after drinking "a lot of water" for me to feel a deadly fear that was in no way proportional to the actual physical stress that the training involved.

My encounter with the forbidding military environment was a traumatic one and the tremendous tension to which we were deliberately subjected made me a nervous wreck. The slightest deviation on our part from the tight schedule which was imposed on us resulted in additional physical exercise and the deprivation of some hours of sleep. Because I attached great importance to even the slightest threat, this policy of increasing the pressure was especially effective in my case. The nickname that the other soldiers gave me, Binchu (derived from my surname, Binur), was often supplemented with a slighting adjective—"frantic Binchu."

A month after I had so bravely volunteered for combat duty, I was ready to do anything in order to leave the isolated camp and the arduous basic training. During one of our sessions with the formidable Sergeant Ekhaus, I simply stopped running, and my buddies had to carry me for the rest of the way. They weren't gracious about it, and cursed me roundly for the extra effort I was costing them. Among those who reluctantly sup-

ported me was Yisrael Cohen, who stood out as a superior soldier and was consequently awarded the signal honor of having
to carry the heaviest machine gun in the platoon. From basic
training onward, Yisrael showed the utmost contempt for me
because of my inferior soldiering. (It was this same Yisrael, of
course, who joined me as my photographer when I embarked
on my posing project. I evened the score with him then; I saw
his fear as we entered the Jebalya refugee camp in Gaza, which
was hostile and unfamiliar territory to him.)

When we returned from the disastrous training session I
asked to be examined by the doctor, claiming that my back
hurt. To this day I'm not sure there was any real physical basis
for my complaint. What is certain is that it didn't succeed in
getting me released from that base. However, my company
commander and the officer directly in charge of me apparently
understood that my breakdown was the result of emotional
stress and they had several talks with me. Finally I was given
the dishonorable assignment of guarding the barracks while
the other recruits were out for routine exercises.

One Friday, the buses stood waiting for us in the parking lot. It
was one of those rare Fridays when we would get to go home
for the weekend. We'd had no sleep the night before; it is accepted practice that leave from basic training has to be
"earned" with an endless series of tasks, ranging from check-
ups on the maintenance and cleanliness of our barracks and
weapons to exhausting physical endurance exercises during the
night.

Now, together with the rest of the platoon, I climbed onto
the bus and settled into a seat. Suddenly, someone came running from the base headquarters. The rumor quickly spread:
"There's an alert. Leave is canceled." I hadn't been home in six
weeks and the bad news was more than I could take. I had to
fight back the tears of disappointment that welled in my eyes.
As we were busy unloading our packs, which mostly contained
dirty laundry for our mothers to wash, the bus driver turned
on the radio and a somber announcer left no doubt in our
minds: War had broken out.

That night we saw our instructors—those omnipotent creatures who could keep us on our feet and running all night long

—standing in full battle dress on the parade grounds. The company commander was carefully checking their equipment, making sure that all was in order. They went off to war, but we weren't considered fit for combat yet, so, under the supervision of a few staff members who remained behind, we were kept busy loading ammunition onto the trucks which would take it to the front. Loading ammunition later entitled me to wear the special medal that was conferred on all those who had taken part in the Yom Kippur War.

After the war the army decided to dismantle my reconnaissance unit, and some of us were transferred to the sabotage unit of the paratroopers, which was highly prestigious and considered superior to the unit we had just come from. The atmosphere was less formal and the rigid discipline of basic training was replaced by better treatment on the part of our commanders. My soldiering benefited accordingly; I got used to the military rules of the game and overcame my inordinate fears. My physical endurance improved, and I would run about ten miles a day on my own initiative. But my image in the eyes of others remained pretty much the same, and I was often still referred to as "frantic Binchu."

Once, some of us were selected for a special mission in Ramallah, an Arab city near Jerusalem which is famed for its magnificent garden restaurants. At the time, many Israelis were attracted to these excellent restaurants, and local youths had the habit of setting fire to cars which bore Israeli license plates while their owners were stuffing themselves inside. This seems to have been an organized act of resistance to the Israeli occupation, and my squadron was called upon to try to catch the instigators in action. We were given a couple of Mercedes-Benzes with Arab license plates, small Beretta pistols which weren't very accurate but had the advantage of being easily concealed, and instructions to cruise the streets of Ramallah in search of saboteurs.

I was stationed not in one of the cars but across from Naum's beautiful garden restaurant. As I sat there, on a stone fence, the mistress of the house next door came up and asked me what my business was. I replied in Arabic that I was just a student on vacation. This first attempt at posing met with only partial success. Although the suspicious matron didn't take me for a

26

member of the occupying forces, neither did she find my cover story convincing and she called the police. I was taken to the local police station, on a vagrancy charge, and the military administration had to send over an officer to get me released.

In the eyes of the soldiers who did their regular service in Ramallah, we outsiders seemed like a mysterious elite group. When we returned to our base in the evenings, the sentries at the gate would come up to our cars alive with curiosity. One of them once pointed at the luggage compartment and asked with a grin, "Bring in any Arab heads today?" At any rate, we must have been too obvious, or perhaps the car torchers simply grew tired of their game, for our glorious campaign failed to trap even a single arsonist.

My knowledge of Arabic was often exploited. In the course of our training we spent a month at a physical fitness installation situated by the Mediterranean where for a month we concentrated on areas such as unconventional warfare and hand-to-hand combat. One of our instructors was a blond, muscle-bound judo champion named Gabi Resnick. Gabi punished anyone who disturbed his lessons by giving the offender a swift kick in the ear.

One time, as we were going down to the beach for a lesson on how to leap from a speeding jeep while simultaneously opening fire, our judo champion espied two Arab fishermen spreading their nets in the shallow waters. Recognizing a golden opportunity to demonstrate his skills, as well as the potential benefits of hand-to-hand combat, Resnick turned the jeep in their direction and promised, "Wait till you see what's coming." Our commanding officer, who was present, stopped him and ordered, "Binur, go over there and send them packing." I approached the two fishermen, called them out of the water, and told them that a secret army maneuver was about to take place, that the man in charge was a bloodthirsty killer, and that they had better leave that part of the beach as fast as they could. Then I returned to the group, who were observing with interest how two Arab fishermen flee in panic when threatened by a confrontation with Israeli paratroopers. Resnick, a little put out by my intervention, asked me, "What did you tell them to make them run away so fast?"

27

"I told them this is a restricted military zone," I answered laconically.

"Well, that's also a method," said the champion sadly, disappointed that such an easy prey had been snatched from his hands. He revved up the jeep and began throwing us off, one by one, onto the sand.

The closest thing to war that I experienced while in the army was the time my unit spent up in the Golan Heights, facing the Syrians. We were taken there on Independence Day of 1974, and I remember the scene as we drove through the center of Tiberias on the way to Golan. From the bus I watched the joyful crowds thronging the streets, armed with the traditional plastic hammers which squeak whenever they hit anything, usually the head of some unsuspecting passerby. The festive carnival mood didn't rub off on me. I knew we were going to a trouble spot. On the Golan a war of attrition was in full swing; Syrian shells were raining down on Israeli positions and the situation in general was bad. Not only were we deprived of home leave for the celebrations but we were going to some lousy front and who the hell knew when our next chance for leave would be.

During our first weeks in the Golan we were assigned to lie in ambush night after night in the hopes of intercepting the Syrian commando units that used to infiltrate the border with the aim of sabotaging Israeli tanks. We were soon transferred to the brigade headquarters, located in an abandoned Arab village. The miserable village dwellings were deserted and seemed to have been left in a hurry. In some of the houses I found pots still on the primus stove, filled with rotting food and covered with spiderwebs. From one of the houses I took a book of the Koran which lay on the floor, apparently overlooked by looters who had preceded me. Only a few elderly people had failed to get away before the Israeli forces arrived and remained behind in the village. They supported themselves by bartering with the army cooks; in return for a bunch of nana leaves (a mint-flavored herb) they would get sardines and other relatively soft foodstuffs that the toothless old villagers could manage. A few months earlier I had been given paramedical training and it was in this capacity that I served

28

during our stay in the area. The medicine cabinet was under my supervision, and I took advantage of my easy access to give some elementary aid to one of the old men, whose face was almost completely eaten away by a severe skin infection that had been neglected.

On one of my excursions through the village (which reminded me more and more of the stories about Arab villages abandoned during the War of 1948), I met an old woman of about seventy who was wailing as she wandered in the alleys which were lined with military vehicles. I calmed her down a bit and found out the reason for her distress: she claimed that two soldiers had stolen her donkey, which was the only living creature left to her in the village. I was naïve enough to be shocked and—what was worse (or better)—to go along with the woman and lodge a complaint, demanding that the theft be thoroughly investigated. Needless to say, the sergeant major of the brigade, to whom I presented the case, was not impressed. I was reproved in typical military fashion ("One ass looking for another") and told to drop the matter.

With these words echoing in my mind, I did the best I could to calm the woman, which under the circumstances amounted to sending her off with two aspirins, courtesy of the Israeli Defense Forces. Trying on my own to find out what had happened to the donkey, I established ties with the noncombatant personnel: the drivers, the cooks, and those in charge of supplies and provisions, who were generally looked down upon by the combat soldiers.

Although I didn't uncover the donkey's whereabouts from them, I did hear another story which was far more horrifying than that of the theft. One of the cooks told me that when they had first arrived, long before we had, some of his colleagues captured two girls who were found wandering about in the village. They locked the girls up in one of the deserted buildings and exploited them sexually. "They let them wash from time to time with water canteens," he told me, "and they had great fun with them."

Until then I hadn't believed that members of the Israeli Defense Forces were capable of such things; now, one more small naïve belief was shattered. My experience with the woman and her donkey had taught me something about trying to defend

29

the rights of others; this time I preferred to keep what I had heard to myself.

After completing the initial training period, I decided that I wanted to train as an officer and was accepted to an officers' course. As soon as I arrived, an enterprising young officer saw me and was impressed by my appearance and by the fact that I came from one of the army's crack combat units. He decided to make sure that I would be a cadet in his platoon and lavished special attention on me during registration procedures. When those were completed, he informed me that I was to be the duty cadet in his platoon, which meant that I had to assume all the duties of the platoon commander, while under supervision, and my leadership qualities would be tested.

The responsibility that befell me caused me great confusion. Unlike many of the other cadets, I had never held command over other soldiers and totally lacked leadership experience. When I had to make an announcement to the other cadets in my platoon, my shouts echoed throughout the building, without any results worth speaking of.

Once I was entrusted with a sackful of compasses that were to be used for navigation purposes. The total estimated worth of the compasses came to hundreds and hundreds of dollars— and I lost them. I literally "lost my bearings." My superiors were considering whether to court-martial me for negligence and, ever the "frantic Binchu," I was beside myself with worry. About a week later I found the compasses in a corner under my bed, where they had apparently been all along.

From start to finish, I was a failure in the course. The officer who had banked on me was furious. He found it difficult to accept the fact that he'd made such an error of judgment, and developed instead an extreme hostility toward me, which was understandable, considering my lack of achievement as his cadet.

Toward the end of the course, I was summoned to an interview with the commander. The implications of such a summons were as clear as could be. I entered, drew myself to attention, and smartly saluted the lieutenant colonel. My long-suffering instructor then launched immediately into a litany of all his grievances. Now it was my turn to defend myself. I was asked to state whether I saw any reason why I shouldn't be expelled from the course. I responded, "It would be a shame to waste all the time I've spent as a cadet. The army will gain more on its investment if I am commissioned as an officer . . . I don't necessarily have to be stationed in the best unit." The senior commander somehow accepted my arguments and allowed me to complete the course, which I did with the lowest grade possible.

After a short vacation I was stationed as an officer at a training center about three miles out of Ramallah and a quarter of an hour's drive away from Jerusalem. At this camp the army trained recruits who weren't destined to join combat units but would become drivers, cooks, or technicians. Many came from an underprivileged social background, and weren't expected to demonstrate a high proficiency as fighting soldiers. Others were men who had previously been rejected for military service. After the Yom Kippur War, the army instituted a policy of calling into active service hundreds of civilians who for various reasons had previously been exempted from military duty. The computer surveyed the names of men who had not been drafted upon reaching the age of eighteen, and those whose earlier problems had been relatively minor were now conscripted. In the intervening years, however, some of these "light" problems had developed into hardened ones. A man who hadn't been drafted because he smoked hashish now joined up as a junkie. Another, who had been convicted of petty thievery in his youth, now showed up driving a huge American car and exuding a threatening aura of violence. Their basic training in this camp was basic indeed. Recruits arrived and left every two months, which prevented any real relationship from developing between the staff and the soldiers. Needless to say, the army didn't bother to send its very best officers to serve as instructors at this base.

I arrived in the camp a young and energetic officer used to the standards of a combat unit, and I firmly decided to apply those standards to the instruction of the recruits now under my command. I threw myself into the job body and soul. The first time one of my soldiers failed to jump to attention when I went by, I had him handcuffed and put in the cooler. Today, I can look back and recognize that the man was a junkie who had just had his daily fix. Another recruit announced in the middle of a field exercise that he was "going home," whereupon I hit him in the face, tied him to the center post of the assembly tent, and when he continued cursing and threatening me, fired a round of bullets into the sand between his legs. In another case, the men went on strike, protesting against the poor quality of the food that they were getting; I pounced on the leader of the revolt and gave him a sound beating.

It's no wonder that the seriousness with which I applied myself to my new responsibilities brought on a wave of formal complaints against me. On more than one occasion the base commander found it necessary to cover up for me when representatives of the commissioner in charge of investigating soldiers' complaints came to follow up on charges that I was abusing the recruits.

The training center was very different from the kind of army I had been accustomed to. Officers ate in a separate mess hall and lived in separate quarters, away from the instructors who weren't officers, not to mention the recruits. For the first time I was able to witness corruption among the higher ranks at close hand. After a while I began to catch on, and I transferred most of my responsibilities to my platoon sergeant, who was a cunning type and quite able to handle the job. He used to put nails in the soles of his boots and then deliberately walk past the conscripts' cots at night with a metallic-sounding goose step.

The nearness of the base to Jerusalem made my life easy. I spent as much time as I could in the comfort of my own home. With the officer's salary I was now receiving, I purchased an old BMW motorbike, which substantially shortened the travel time between the officers' barracks and my room in Jerusalem.

The military government in the West Bank has an administrative function, but of course it receives assistance from other army units whenever necessary. In such cases the soldiers who are brought in are "annexed" to the administration, and within city limits they are under orders from the military governor of that zone. During the period that I was stationed at the training center, our company was sent to nearby Ramallah on two occasions. The first time, we were ordered to patrol the city and carry out routine police duties. While we were there, I spent a week as a junior officer in charge of a few patrols and observation posts, and became familiar with the various parts of the city. The second time we were deployed in Ramallah, it was in order to subdue demonstrations and impose a curfew on the city, which had turned into a hotbed of resistance against the Israeli occupation. (Ramallah continues to play an important role in the resistance to the occupation within the current context of the Intifada, the Palestinian uprising in the West Bank and the Gaza Strip.) The administration in Ramallah decided to crack down on the local population and put an end to the unrest, which in the jargon of occupation was referred to as "disturbances of the order."

Proof of the seriousness of the administration's intentions came when we were supplied with clubs. The soldiers received simple elongated clubs, while I, as an officer, received a short club made of black mahogany with a lacquered finish. At the edge of its handle was a short leather strap which was meant to be wrapped around the hand so that a victim would have no opportunity, between one blow and the next, to make off with the legal property of the Israeli Defense Forces.

The deputy governor of Ramallah, a major of short stature but with a loud voice, happened to be a fluent speaker of Arabic. He drove around the city in a command car, announcing through a loudspeaker that "as of today the city will be under total and absolute curfew," to which he added the obvious conclusion: "Whoever violates it will be punished." We received instructions to maintain the curfew without compromise: "You will arrest any local who is caught outside his home and bring him to the administration. After the curfew comes into effect you will fire on the tires and windows of parked cars and shoot holes in the water tanks on the rooftops." The order to fire, intended to terrorize the civilian population, was restricted to officers, of course; ordinary soldiers were forbidden to shoot on their own initiative.

In the evening I was joined by the commander of our training camp, who wished to take a close look at my mode of operation. We made the rounds together, and when we reached Ramallah's central square, the senior officer stopped our jeep, drew out his brand-new submachine gun, and let fly with a spray of bullets, smashing the streetlamps to smithereens. This shot initiated a nightlong orgy of military display, in which I was a willing participant.

The curfew in Ramallah lasted several days, during which I was kept busy, assigning my men to their posts and deploying them throughout the city. I would patrol among the positions, driving around in a jeep. I kept one soldier with me, a man by the name of Malachi who came from Tel Aviv. He was about thirty-five at the time, and a real thug, a violent man with a black belt in karate.

A couple of days after we arrived in Ramallah, I was patrolling a wealthy neighborhood where the residents, who were forbidden to leave their homes, spent most of their time idly lounging in their yards or on their balconies. Outside the entrance of one of the houses stood a boy of about fifteen. Perhaps he was tired of being confined within the boundaries of the house, or maybe he was on his way to fetch something nearby. My jeep screeched to a halt. "Come over here!" I ordered. The boy's parents were sitting in the garden of their villa, but now, sensing trouble, they approached the gate. I, however, had no intention of releasing the young violator, wishing to follow my instructions to the letter. I took hold of my club and waited for the boy to come to the jeep. Instead, he went pale and looked alternately at me and at his parents, as if imploring them for help. His father argued with me through the metal bars of the gate but was afraid to step out because of the curfew. I got out of the jeep, ignored the family's cries that their son had "just stepped out for a moment," and brought my club forcefully down on his shoulders. The boy began crying hysterically. I grabbed him by the collar and plunked him down before the front fender of the jeep. "Now start running, dog," I instructed him in Arabic.

Malachi, the violent soldier whom I had assigned to my jeep, surveyed the whole scene with interest and only commented dryly, "You're real tough, sir."

Several blows and a few slaps later, I deposited the boy at the administration building. As far as I know, he was held there for several hours, and was duly registered and released. The state treasury grew richer because of my successful catch, for the boy's father was fined for his curfew violation.

After leaving the frightened boy behind at the administra-

34

tion building, I went on another round, again accompanied by Malachi. This time we ran into a truck that was passing through the silent streets. Its license plates indicated it was from Jericho. I overtook the truck and blocked its way with a sharp right turn of the wheel. The truck stopped and, like a Doberman trainer unleashing the fiercest dog in his pack, I ordered Malachi, "Go see why the fellow is violating the curfew." He administered a few awesome slaps to the surprised driver, and then loaded him onto our jeep. Before returning to the administration, I drove several meters in reverse till I reached the back of the truck and fired on its wheels.

In acting the way I did I was by no means an exception. Suspects who were brought to the police station for interrogation were made to stand and wait in the narrow gap between one of the buildings and the surrounding wall. Two heavyset policemen walked along the narrow passageway and hit them with bare fists and with wire cables. A while before we arrived in Ramallah, members of the border police, who, unlike the army, are permanently stationed in cities in the West Bank and Gaza, had clubbed a demonstrator there to death.

The feeling of unlimited power that I had in those days was also expressed in other, more humane ways. As one who had it in his power to determine the fates of others, I didn't hesitate to knock on the door of an Arab locksmith I knew and ask whether he needed anything. A woman whom I caught violating the curfew convinced me that she had to get medicine for her sick husband. I gave her a lift in my jeep, to the doctor's house and back, so that the other soldiers wouldn't harass her. Whether committing brutal violence or performing acts of kindness, the sensation is the same—it is the feeling of the power that one has over others.

My achievements earned me a recommendation to serve as judge on the military court in Ramallah. Military courts in the occupied territories consist of one head of court, who has a legal background, and two ordinary army officers who rotate from time to time. Sentences are determined by a majority vote and the officers can overturn the head of court in the event of conflicting opinions.

One case brought before us illustrates well the workings of

justice under the occupation. A farmer was accused of assisting a terrorist group, on its way to carry out an act of aggression within Israeli borders, by giving them food and water. In his first statement, which was read in the court, the accused denied the charges. In a second statement, which was also read in court, he "remembered" all the details and confessed. We all knew—judges, military prosecutor, and defense attorney—by what means the confession had been procured, but the issue was never raised for discussion. Later we retreated to the judges' office and the head of court instructed the other junior officer and me about the considerations relevant to determining the sentence. We concluded that the crime was a relatively mild one, and were aware that the accused had already spent several months in prison. "If we release him immediately it will create the impression that we are criticizing the security forces for the prolonged period of arrest," the head of court explained, "so we'll let him sit another month—that's not too terrible—and then he'll be released." We made a quick calculation of the length of time he had already spent in prison, added another month for good measure, and pronounced the fellow's sentence.

What last remnants of naïveté I still retained were lost toward the end of my service. I was among a group of infantry officers with a good knowledge of Arabic who were sent to participate in a covert operation which had just been initiated by the army. We were instructed to train southern Lebanese militiamen in the use of weapons and combat methods as part of an extended program to assist the Maronites of Lebanon. During this period, rumors were circulating freely concerning Israeli secret service agents who eliminated persons opposed to the Israeli involvement in Lebanon. In addition, our protégés, the militiamen, used to brag about their participation in massacres of the Moslem population, especially in the famous battle of Tel Al Zaatar, where the Christian militias, with Israeli assistance, defeated the Palestinian defenders of the refugee camp after a very long siege. One of the Lebanese soldiers in my charge, a youth of seventeen, sent a shiver down my spine one evening when he related to me how he had brought a Palestinian woman and some of her children down from a fifth-story balcony—not via the stairway.

Tales of torture, murder, rape, and pillage perpetrated by the Christian Phalangists against the Palestinian population were routine, and were doubtless known to the Israeli Intelligence officers who supervised the Phalangists. Years later, when the committee investigating the massacres at the Sabra and Shatila refugee camps interrogated Ariel Sharon, Rafael Eytan, and others, they claimed that they had no way of knowing that the Christian Phalangists would commit such atrocities. I could only laugh in the face of such blatant lies.

During the time that I spent in Ramallah and later on in training the Lebanese militiamen, my Arabic improved considerably, especially with respect to military jargon. After completing my three and a half years in the army, the standard term of service for an officer, I studied Arabic language and literature at the Hebrew University in Jerusalem. After one year I dropped out. I couldn't stand the courses because the professors regarded the language as merely an object of study and not as a living language. One woman I knew, who had completed her master's degree, was typical in this respect. She could decipher ancient Egyptian papyruses from two thousand years ago, but she wasn't able to order a cup of coffee in an Arab restaurant.

Like any veteran soldier, I had accumulated several pieces of military equipment in the course of my service—items which I had simply never bothered to return to the army. Among the miscellaneous paraphernalia, the black mahogany club from Ramallah took pride of place. It looked fine hanging on the wall, first in my room at the officers' barracks and later in my room in Jerusalem. One day, when I was moving out of a beautiful house in Abu Tor, the only mixed Arab-Jewish neighborhood in Jerusalem, I loaded the club into my car along with other personal belongings, and left for a moment to attend to some other business. When I returned, the club was gone, undoubtedly stolen by an Arab neighbor. A curious instance of poetic justice.

THREE

Abu Naim

THE ARAB NEIGHBORHOOD in Jaffa was once a wealthy community where people lived comfortably. But many of the inhabitants fled in the wake of the occupation by the Israeli armed forces during the War of 1948, and Jaffa's Arab population diminished considerably. The few hundred families that remained were soon joined by evacuees from other Arab population centers. The Israeli government had no interest in having a hostile Arab population scattered all over the country, and so concentrated it in several central locations, of which Jaffa was one. Today, the municipality of Tel Aviv (to which Jaffa was annexed) would like once again to relocate the local Arab population. The Arab neighborhood is located right by the sea and investors are well aware of the area's outstanding real estate potential. The inhabitants are forbidden to renovate their homes and any house that is left standing empty is bulldozed by the city. The homes that are still occupied sit amid the rubble and debris of the houses that have been torn down, a sight which adds to the impression of misery. To the west, a

39

slope that runs down to the sea has been turned by the municipality into a huge garbage dump. An unpleasant stench and a
thick cloud of bottle flies descend on the houses every evening
and serve as an additional incentive for residents to leave the
neighborhood.

When the developers have their day, the dump, which en-
croaches on the sea, will undoubtedly be covered with fancy
villas. The land will be designated exclusively for luxury housing and the Israel Land Administration, a government agency,
will lease it only to "army veterans," a seemingly neutral expression which, in Israel, clearly distinguishes between Jew
and Arab.

In the meantime, the area, which was once a thriving center
of commerce, is now mainly known as a source of crime and
illegal drugs. The only outsiders who visit here are Israeli drug
users and workers who come from the occupied territories and
lodge in one of the cheap boardinghouses.

☐ ☐ ☐

I first heard about Abu "Naim's" (not his real name) flophouse
from Makram Houri Mahoul, a journalist who grew up in Jaffa
and knows it well. Makram comes from one of the Christian
Arab families that remained in Jaffa after 1948. I met with him
before setting out on my posing project in order to have him
fill me in on what was happening in the Tel Aviv area. Like
many others, he was skeptical about my chances of success.
Before we parted, we drove past Abu Naim's place in my car
and Makram pointed it out to me. "There are a lot of stinking
joints like this one around here. I don't believe you'll be able to
get into them," he told me then. Later, when I was standing on
Yefet Street in the "slave market," I heard about the place
again. Going to Abu Naim's place seemed like a good way to
start mixing with Arab laborers in Tel Aviv in a relatively
short time.

Yisrael stopped his Autobianchi on the outskirts of the neighborhood. "Binchu, go over to that Abu Naim whatever and
check it out. If it looks risky, tell him you'll return tomorrow,
and come back to the car. I'll be watching you. If you haven't

come out of there after twenty minutes, I'll leave, and in three hours I'll come around again with the car. If I hear any noise from inside I'll enter. In any case, we'll meet tomorrow morning here, in Jaffa."

As we got out of the car, we tried to avoid the curious looks that were sent our way from an Arab coffeehouse across the street. It was the sort of place where the patrons sit out front on the sidewalk, sipping strong coffee and smoking their nargilehs.

"Goddamn! I can't believe this is Tel Aviv!" Yisrael exclaimed. "It looks like an Arab town." I grabbed a tight hold of my orange plastic shopping basket, checked to see that the keffiyeh and Arab newspaper were on top, where they would catch the eye of any passerby, and began walking through the dark and filthy streets.

It was about seven in the evening, a reasonable hour for a hired laborer to be returning from work. People were sitting in front of their houses, to escape from the stifling midsummer heat. The humidity, combined with years of neglect, had had its effect on the spacious Mediterranean mansions; they were crumbling.

Out of the corner of my eye I could see Yisrael following my movements from afar, and the knowledge that he was backing me up gave me a welcome feeling of security. That I wouldn't be spending the night on the sofa in his living room, with Teresa, his dog, lying on the floor beside me, seemed to me remote and unreal. I came to a small grocery on the corner and decided to go in to get information about the location of Abu Naim's house, which I couldn't quite remember. Shopkeepers generally know about everything that goes on in their neighborhood.

The store was a modest one and reminded me of grocery stores in Jerusalem in the sixties. The shelves contained fish preserves and houmus in small tin cans that, along with half a loaf of black bread, make up one meal for a workingman. In the small refrigerator, the top of which served as the owner's counter, there were some basic milk products. Behind the owner were more shelves with a disarray of cigarette packs, bags of candy, and canned goods.

Two customers were engaged in comparing the prices of canned tuna fish from Europe; the cheapest came from Portugal. The shopkeeper cut a loaf of bread into two equal halves for them. While debating the price of fish, one of them pinched his half of the bread to determine how fresh his supper for the day was going to be. A third customer was surveying the assorted products with a bored air while combing back a tangle of greasy hair.

"*Asalamu aleikum ya jamaa,*" I said, addressing my greeting to nobody in particular. "Perhaps you know where Abu Naim's place is?"

None of the customers paid any attention to me. The shopkeeper, a shriveled man of about sixty, came slowly forward from behind the counter, took me by the arm, and gently steered me to the entrance.

"Down there, beyond the blue gate, there's an iron door. Go in through it to the yard and make an immediate right turn to where the workers' quarters are. His sons get mad if somebody enters the house by mistake."

The shopkeeper's directions were precise and a former mansion revealed itself beyond the iron door. A large two-storied house, with balconies looking out on all sides, it had clearly once been an elegant residence. Things looked different now, however. Both sides of the paved path that led up to the house were strewn with discarded refrigerators and cooking stoves and old bedsteads. To the right was another iron gate. Going through it, I went down three steps and approached what had originally been intended as a stable or an animal pen. I entered it and found myself in a tiny entrance hall which branched out onto three large rooms. The rooms were full of beds arranged as in a military barracks, one alongside the next with hardly any space in between.

In one of the rooms, a man was sitting by himself at a small dilapidated table that had a grubby and rather cracked veneer. He was eating salad out of an aluminum bowl. From time to time he picked up a loaf of bread, tore a large piece of crust off it, soaked it in the salad juice, and stuffed it in his mouth, so that he was barely able to chew.

"*Marhaba,*" he greeted me in a soft-spoken voice.

"*Marhabtein,*" I greeted him in return. "Any spare beds?" I asked.

"The men haven't arrived yet and most of the beds are free,

but take that one." The man pointed to one of the beds. "It's next to the window and also next to me, so we can chat a bit."

After I had set my basket down on the bed, I joined the man at the table. His name, I learned, was Abed. *"T'fadal,"* he said, offering me a hunk of bread and shoving the bowl of salad toward me. We ate in silence for a while. After a few days of not speaking Arabic, I was slightly unsure of myself and preferred not to be overly talkative, so I concentrated on reading an article in the weekly newspaper *Al Biader Al Siasi* that I had brought with me. "He who stands before you," Abed broke the silence, using ornate and flowery language, "he who stands before you, sir, has frequented every sinful den imaginable. I have peddled hashish and needles too. I have stolen and I have lied and I have even, Lord help me, lived with a Jewess."

Abed was about thirty, his voice was deep, and his eyes had the dull expression of a man who has seen everything, who knows that whatever he might come across now would be nothing more than a repeat performance, a show whose plot he already knew.

"And now?" I asked him.

"Now, Allah be praised, I walk in the path of the righteous. I've seen the light. No more Jewesses and no more trouble." And Abed proceeded to tell me his story, how, like many other Moslem village youths in Israel, he had discovered the true religion. He came from the village of Ara, located within the borders of Israel. At some point in his tumultuous life he had begun meeting regularly with the village sheikh. Gradually, as a result of the sheikh's persuasiveness and his own deep despair, he began visiting the mosque and observing the Islamic laws. He told me a lot about his conversion, embellishing his words with phrases from the Koran. For my part, I intimated that my "inclination" was toward the revolutionary Palestinian left, which, at the very least, implied an attitude of indifference with regard to religion. Abed continued to explain that he worked in Tel Aviv occasionally, as a gardener, but he said, "This city is foul and I try to be here as little as I can. It's much better in the village, where it is quiet and one can go to the mosque every day."

As we were talking, an exceptionally miserable-looking group of men arrived: the street cleaners of Tel Aviv. They were men of all ages, young and old, most of them from Jebalya and a few from other places in the Gaza Strip. They contented themselves with a brief "Good evening" and went directly off to sleep in one of the rooms.

"Poor devils." Abed nodded after them. "With what they earn one can't make a living at all. They're lucky they have an arrangement here. They only pay three shekels a night." Unlike the workers from the occupied territories, Abed's overnight presence in Tel Aviv was entirely legal. If he preferred Abu Naim's unsavory lodgings to any other it was only because of the cheap price.

It was approximately nine in the evening, and Abed and I were still seated by the table, which was littered with salad leftovers, cigarette butts, and bread crumbs on top of the grime that had accumulated over the years. Abu Naim, a big fat man dressed in a gray galabia and cheap plastic sandals, shuffled into the room. He first exchanged a couple of words with Abed, who addressed him with deference, employing the honorary title of Haj, which is bestowed on Moslems who have undertaken the pilgrimage to Mecca and bears witness to their faith and devotion.

Then, after conversing with Abed, Abu Naim turned to me. "You're sleeping here tonight?"

"Yes," I replied.

"It's five shekels, and you have to pay in advance. Where do you work?"

I remembered that Abed had told me that the charge was only three shekels a night. I supposed that the discrepancy was due to the fact that I was not yet a regular customer, and I decided to hold my peace. "I don't have work yet. I only arrived from Balata today."

A hand was extended toward me with demanding insistence. Abu Naim's five sausagelike fingers were eagerly stretched out so that I could clearly make out in his upturned palm the lines which supposedly represented his various traits. I imagined that the most prominent line in Abu Othman's hand was that of avarice.

"Five shekels," he demanded. I fished a ten-shekel note out of my pocket and handed it to him. "Please, ya Haj, let it be for tomorrow as well." With unconcealed delight, he fingered it for a moment and then it disappeared somewhere among the countless folds of his galabia. "You're a good fellow, paying in advance. Well, turn out the lights so the neighbors don't get angry and call for the police. You're forbidden to be here. You're lucky I take pity on the homeless and don't leave them to sleep in the gutter." Abu Naim soared off in praise of his own virtues, and shared with us his thoughts on how the flophouse that he provided for the sake of the poor workingman caused him to incur heavy losses, trouble with the authorities, and fights with his children, but would no doubt tip the scales in his favor when his time came and his good and bad deeds were weighed in the presence of Almighty Allah.

A loud knock was heard on the iron gate outside. "Police!" was the first thought that flashed through my mind. Abu Naim, who was already on his way out, opened the gate. *"Wein aladala, ya sidi? Wein aladala wawein inti?* [Where is there justice, sir? Where is justice and where are you?]" someone called out loudly, and into the room strode a short stocky man with somewhat vulgar features and reddish hair. He was wearing blue gym shorts that exposed his hairy legs and a short-sleeved white shirt. The only button on the man's shirt that was fastened concealed a small potbelly; a gold medallion on a massive gold chain glittered against the curly mat of hair on his chest. He stopped and surveyed us with a happy smile, revealing a few extra carats of gold.

"I'm Ahmad Abu Halil, but everyone calls me Abu Al Az [the father of splendor]. They already know about my room in Shapira, so tonight I am here with you, and maybe in the coming nights as well." I extended my hand in greeting and Abu Al Az shifted his own hand from where it was (energetically scratching his private parts) in order to shake it. Then he sat down beside us and lit up a Time cigarette, the first in a long chain that would end only when sleep overtook him. It would then be renewed the next morning, even before he set his bare feet (in sore need of a pedicure) on the floor, which was covered with cigarette butts from the previous night.

Abu Al Az, who looked much older than his thirty-three years, had been living in Tel Aviv for the past twelve years. He peppered his conversation with Hebrew words, and during a brief dialogue that he held in Hebrew with Abed, I couldn't help noticing that with his accent he could just about pass as an Israeli Jew of Middle Eastern extraction. If he had presented himself as such, in the proper circumstances, I, for one, wouldn't have suspected him for a moment.

I asked him who "they" were who knew about his room in Shapira (a south Tel Aviv neighborhood) and on whose account he found it necessary to come and keep us company at Abu Othman's place. As soon as I reminded him of his room his face lit up and instead of answering my question he launched into an ecstatic description.

"By Allah, friends! What isn't there in that room in Shapira? A bed that is something—king-sized! It's a joy to rub one's dick on it. I swear, even that bastard Begin doesn't sleep on anything like it. [He was referring, of course, to Menachem Begin, the former Prime Minister of Israel, an anachronism even at the time.] And a shower! You just turn on the faucet and out comes hot water. When you shower it's blazing hot, like a young girl's pussy on fire. And after the shower," Abu Al Az continued as the eyes of Abed, the born-again Moslem, almost popped out of his head, "I sprinkle some rose water here and here and here"—Abu Al Az pointed to his groin and his armpits—"so that the Jewesses will go crazy over the smell of my balls."

I had to repeat my question. "What do you mean, who are 'they'?"

"The neighbors and the police. One night some friends were over at my place and we had a party. We drank a little and there was some noise. So the neighbors got upset. Maybe they were put out because I didn't invite them, but you know, we had some kef [hashish] and I really didn't need the whole world to be there. So they informed on me that I don't have a license. Now the police will probably come every night to look for me. So I'll sleep here for a while until they get tired of it and the whole thing blows over."

Abu Al Az was referring, I knew, to the permit which would allow him to remain within the boundaries of Israel after midnight. Residents of the occupied territories could apply to the

military government for such a license. If the applicant did not
have a record of being a "security risk," and if the Shin Bet
raised no objections, and if his Jewish employer was in favor of
it, then the license was granted. Because Abu Al Az earned his
living by buying a few crates of fish from the fishermen of Jaffa
and selling them in the Carmel open-air market in Tel Aviv, or
occasionally by working as a painter, he didn't stand a chance
of getting a permit. As was the case for thousands of others, it
was illegal for him to remain in Israel overnight. The police
and the authorities responsible for the security of Israel knew
about these infringements but didn't care to enforce the law
too strictly. Any large-scale action against the workers who
slept in Israel would antagonize Israeli employers, who formed
a pressure group to be reckoned with. And the police would
have to stage raids on hundreds of locations all over the country: in the cities and in the outskirts, in restaurants, orchards,
everywhere. The investment in time, money, and manpower
would hardly be worthwhile. As things stood, the police were
content to carry out "selective raids" just to keep the situation
under control. Sometimes these raids were executed on the individual initiative of a bored policeman looking for some action
to while away the hours of the night.

□ □ □

The transition back to my borrowed identity after a few days
of rest and the resulting tension had caused me to feel tired.
"Tomorrow I have to find work," I said, "so with your permission I'll wash up and then go to sleep." Abed gave me directions for getting to the bathroom: out into the yard and around
the back of the room to the left.

When I got to the bathroom, I stood beneath the exposed
light bulb that dangled from the ceiling and took a look around.
Cockroaches of a fantastic size that I had never seen before
swarmed all over the place. Some of them silently disappeared
into hiding, while others, seemingly aware of their superiority,
scuttled around at my feet. The room was medium-sized with
two small stalls at its far end. In one of them, the rusty end of a
pipe stuck out from the wall at about a man's height—this was
the shower. Another stall, with a wooden door weakly hanging

on to one hinge, was the toilet. It was a sight: the bowl was filled to the brim with the scummiest and most foul-smelling filth, threatening to flow over at any moment onto the cracked cement floor. Next to the bowl was a large tin can, like the kind used to hold pickled cucumbers, from which water had to be poured into the toilet in order to flush it. The revolting sight and unbearable stench indicated that it had been a long time since anyone had bothered.

My own urgent needs vanished as if they had never existed. I just washed my hands and picked up a broken shard of mirror that was lying about to look into as I took out my contact lenses. I had to make sure that no one was about to enter the room as I did so. Contact lenses aren't common among Palestinians in Israel. To be on the safe side, I had learned the Arab expression for lens, *kzaz ain* (glass eye), and in case any questions were raised I had a story handy about my poor eyesight and a doctor in Ramallah who had prescribed the lenses. That evening I simply preferred not to have anyone notice the optical gizmos in my eyes.

When I returned, Abu Al Az was already stretched out on his bed, chatting with Abed, who was waiting his turn to use the bathroom, a towel bearing the initials of the Israeli Defense Forces wrapped around his neck.

"Do you have a *mushut?*" Abed asked, turning to me.

"What?" I stalled, pretending I hadn't heard.

"*Mushut, mushut,*" Abed repeated his request.

"Damn," I thought, "what the hell is a *mushut?*"

Abed continued to stand in front of me and Abu Al Az sent me an oblique look from his bed. Thoughts raced through my mind with lightning speed: if Abed needed something and, not understanding what it was, I told him I didn't have it, and later he saw a *mushut* in my possession—then I'd be in trouble. On the other hand, I couldn't tell him I had it, because I didn't know what it was. At a loss, the best I could do was to emit an extended mumble, a sort of "hmmmm" which meant neither yes nor no, and shrug my shoulders. Then I turned away from him and walked deliberately over to my bed.

"Not everyone likes to let someone else use their *mushut,*" said Abu Al Az to Abed. "Here, take mine," and he handed him a small black comb.

"Goddamnit, me and my Arabic," I thought furiously. The years I had spent as a reporter for West Bank affairs had increased my vocabulary in such areas as politics, civil rights, and the law. But it was with the simple, mundane words that I had a slight but sometimes embarrassing gap in my knowledge of Arabic.

"I'm not one of those who care," I hastily retorted. "I simply don't have a *mushut.*"

I met Yisrael the next morning at a coffeehouse in Jaffa which was reasonably distant from the boardinghouse. As an extra safety measure, we sat in an alcove inside the coffeehouse.

"Right on, Binchu," Yisrael said while he ordered coffee and a sesame-covered *burekas* (a light pastry) filled with salty cheese. "I didn't believe you'd have the guts to sleep overnight in that place."

Thus fortified by Yisrael's acknowledgment of my daring, I set off to look for work. Yisrael followed me at a distance, just as he had the night before.

"I work mechanic in garage what fixes Peugeot cars in Nablus." I presented myself in this way in pidgin Hebrew to several garage owners on Salame Street, which connects Jaffa to south Tel Aviv; the road is lined with small workshops and garages.

The answer I kept hearing was "No need," and in fact every garage already had a number of Arab workers, stationed in various positions next to cars that were being repaired and smeared with oil and grease. I would greet my fellow workers with a nod and move on to the next potential employer. But all to no avail. I despaired and was ready to turn back and relax in Yisrael's company until the evening, when I would have to return to Abu Naim's.

But just then the owner of an electrical repair shop for cars called me over to his office. "Yosi Levi" (not his real name) was a macho character of about thirty-five with a gold chain hanging on his chest that made him seem like an Israeli version of Abu Al Az. He sat behind a table, slurping his cup of coffee and fondling the nylon netting of an expensive tennis racket, as if to say: when will the workday ever be over so I can leave my garage and go have a game of tennis?

"Can you clean floors and make coffee?" he asked.

"Yes, sir, but I am very good mechanic, do overhaul to all machines and fix them."

"You'll be here every morning from eight sharp until five in the afternoon, and you get ten shekels."

In order not to arouse even the faintest suspicion I tried to haggle over the wages, which were not enough for subsistence, let alone supporting a family. "Arabs here are a dime a dozen, and they're all looking for work. There's no reason why I should pay you more than I have to," Yosi stated conclusively, but without any trace of malice.

I began working and for a while I merely prepared coffee and swept the cement floor. There was only one other regular worker there, a dark Arab youth from Jaffa whom the owner called Daga. I never found out what inspired that name, which I never heard of either before or since.

One day, I took advantage of Yosi's absence to perform a few quick repairs that involved some welding. Daga, who'd been entrusted with the responsibility of running the garage until the owner's return, was impressed by my work and later he duly reported that "the new worker knows the job."

Within a few days Yosi put me on routine repair jobs, in addition to my cleaning and coffee-making duties. The jobs mainly involved replacing fan belts or putting in new spark plugs and alternators, which with certain types of cars means lying underneath the engine and receiving a generous helping of grease and dirt.

I had always known that a garage like Yosi Levi's could provide a fairly respectable income; now I discovered that it was a gold mine. A woman brought in an old Volvo claiming that the "engine stuttered." Within half an hour I had cleaned the points, replaced the spark plugs, and synchronized the ignition. Yosi charged the woman one hundred shekels. In half an hour I had earned my wages for ten days.

Because Yosi was good to me (even when I deliberately made some mistakes he didn't get angry), I soon began to cooperate and sided with him against the customers. My sense of identity was unclear enough during that time as to allow me to justify this stance to myself by thinking that "those Jews should be had for what they're worth." For instance, after I completed a

50

job on the car of one customer who seemed to be wealthy, Yosi called me into his office. "Fat'hi, what exactly did you do with this gentleman's car?" he asked.

"I synchronized the ignition, refitted the plugs, replaced and adjusted the fuses, and I had a real difficult time tuning them, by Allah!"

Yosi and I both knew that fuses can't be "tuned." It takes a minute or two to install them and that's all there is to it. I peered over the customer's shoulder, and exchanging a look of complicity with my boss, I noticed that he'd charged the client a considerable sum of money for the "fuse-tuning" item.

I hardly conversed with Daga. This industrious youth had grown up and lived among Jews and the differences between us were supposed to be practically insurmountable. He respected me, however, because I was older or perhaps because, as a son of the camps, I represented to him the suffering and poverty of the Palestinian people. And his respect increased when I demonstrated my professional know-how. During lunch breaks he would take tomatoes and fresh bread out of his bag and offer to share them with me. When he went to the nearby kiosk to buy himself a soft drink, which I couldn't afford on my meager salary, he'd buy a drink for me as well.

Daga had a big gray jeep. One could see that it was a machine that belonged to a mechanic, because every part of it was renovated and every inch was shining. At the end of a workday Daga would start the car and the engine purred so quietly that one knew it had recently been overhauled.

The six-cylinder jeep was the same kind that the police use, especially the Intelligence units that often used vehicles disguised as civilian cars. One day I teased Daga: "That jeep of yours is just like the jeeps of the *muhabarat* [the Shin Bet] in Balata. How did you get a jeep from them? Do you work for them?" I knew, of course, that the jeep had been bought at one of the army surplus auctions and had been overhauled by its new owner. My provocative question caused Daga's face to darken and the smile on it disappeared. "You're crazy," he countered. "I purchased this jeep." From that day on he kept his distance and tended more to emphasize his status as subordinate to Yosi but superior to me.

The customers would cozy up to Yosi and Daga, cracking

51

jokes and asking after their health, obviously a desperate attempt to leave the place with a reasonable bill. Yosi laughed along with his customers, but when the time came for settling accounts he continued to laugh on his own; the clients became rather melancholic when they saw their bill. I kept hoping someone would strike up a conversation with me as well. One day I had my chance. Replacing an alternator, I was lying beneath a handsome Peugeot with sweat dripping into my eyes and burning like acid.

"What's your name, boy?" I heard a pleasant voice ask. The Peugeot's owner had arrived early to pick up his car.

"Fat'hi, sir. Fat'hi from the Balata refugee camp."

I moved my head out from between the car engine and the concrete floor and grinned. He was a respectable-looking man, dressed in a matching gray suit and tie in spite of the hot weather. He returned a noncommittal look and warned me, "Be careful when you take it apart, boy. And take care not to mess up the car with dirt."

In the middle of one not particularly busy workday, Yosi said, "Come, Fat'hi. Bring your things along and come with me." I got into his small Subaru van and we began driving south. I didn't know where we were going, but a ride in a car was a welcome departure from routine. I trusted Yosi enough not to be worried. It was a rather intimate occasion, sitting in a car by my employer's side, unlike the ordinary work situation back at the garage.

"One day I want to come to visit your family in Balata. I know where it is, more or less, because I was there once when I was doing reserve duty in the army."

"Really, Mr. Yosi, it isn't good for you to come to us. Our young people maybe get angry and maybe they throw some stone at your head." In fact, at that time there was no serious danger involved when a Jew visited a refugee camp, provided he was not hostile in his manner (as an armed settler would be considered, for instance). But I enjoyed being deliberately provocative.

"What, is it that bad among you?" My boss was horrified.

"Yes, really, our people don't like Jews."

Yosi grew a little pale and became silent. I swelled with

pride, thinking, "Here in Tel Aviv I'm a lousy worker and he's the almighty employer. But Balata is independent territory as far as he's concerned. His superiority over me is confined to this place; over there he'd be afraid of me."

We stopped in front of the skeletal structure of a building in a nice suburb. "This is the house that I'm building. Since there isn't much work at the garage today, you'll help the electrician who's installing the wires here and when you finish you can go straight home."

"O.K.," I answered, and for the first time since I began working for him he thought to ask, "Where do you stay? Go back to Nablus every day, eh?"

I didn't describe Abu Naim's place for him. I just said, "I sleep in like a hostel. Every night five shekel."

Nissim, the electrician, received me with a broad smile. He spoke Arabic and so at long last I could stop speaking pidgin Hebrew, which was starting to get on my nerves. We worked alone, just the two of us, inside the skeleton of the villa. I chiseled grooves in the wall and he placed electric wires inside them. From time to time we took a break, during which we would have a short conversation.

"Where are you from?" Nissim asked me in Arabic.

I gave him my usual story: Nablus, Balata . . . the works.

"Oh, I have a lot of friends in Nablus," he said.

"Who?" I asked, curious to know.

"You don't expect me to remember all their names. What do I know? Arabs. Who live there."

I muttered inaudibly, picked up the iron chisel, and resumed hammering small grooves into the cast-cement walls.

The lack of minimally decent facilities at Abu Naim's, where I spent my nights, left its mark on me. I slept on a hard bed and found it impossible to shave properly. Like most of the hired laborers I met, I didn't have a change of clothes. So it was no wonder that my appearance grew increasingly disheveled. Despite this, Yosi, my boss, liked me, probably because of the nice profit the garage was making each day with the help of my cheap labor.

"Fat'hi, make me a cup of coffee," came a shout from Yosi's office, interrupting my thoughts.

I searched for Yosi's personal glass. Only Yosi drank from

that glass, and woe to anyone who dared even to touch it except when bringing him his coffee. As I prepared the coffee, I listened to the large radio that sat on the windowsill of the office next to the sink and the coffee heater. The radio normally kept us company during work hours, but right now there wasn't any music on. A news report was mentioning that it was the anniversary of the 1982 massacre in the Sabra and Shatila refugee camps in Lebanon. There had been unrest all over the West Bank that day, and a youth in Deheishe had been shot and wounded by soldiers. A slight shiver crept along my spine. I was all too familiar with the sight of soldiers advancing across a refugee camp in formation and arresting youths with a great show of brutality. I poured boiling water into two glasses, one for the boss and one for a visitor who was sitting with him. "Please, Mr. Yosi," I said, setting the steaming coffee down.

Yosi, who apparently wished to impress his guest, addressed me. "Say, what's your name, eh? Fat'hi . . . Fat'hi. Why don't you change it so it'll be easier to remember? Maybe Rafi or Danny?"

I was outraged. It wasn't enough that the man was paying me starvation wages, and that his people denied me the right to even aspire to freedom and independence. He also had the effrontery to suggest that I give up the little that remained to me, that I drop my name and assume the incongruous aspect of a Jew.

"Really, Mr. Yosi, people see that I am Arab and how can I cheat people? Also, I am not an Arab who change their name for the Jews. I am born Fat'hi and I die Fat'hi."

Yosi's guest gave me a glowering look. "This guy is a nationalist. You'd better get rid of him," he said to Yosi reproachfully, as if my refusal to change my name in order to make things easier for the Jews was a serious act of subversion and a dangerous expression of Palestinian national sentiment that could threaten him even in the heart of Israel.

Yosi considered me thoughtfully. He didn't like to lose a worker who already knew the job. "His mind's set on nuts and bolts," he replied, determining my fate favorably.

During the time I lodged at Abu Naim's, a group of youths from Rafiah, which is in the Gaza Strip, joined Abed, Abu Al

Az, and me in our room. They worked in the open-air Carmel market in Tel Aviv. There was also Halil, a bedouin Arab from the Damon area near Haifa, who worked as a cook in one of the restaurants in Tel Aviv. Every evening the Rafiah gang returned from their day's work at the market with a bagful of vegetables that they'd received from the wholesale merchant with whom they worked. Majdi, the group's leader, would send one of the younger ones, usually a sixteen-year-old named Yassin, to the nearby grocery to buy bread and a can of houmus or fish preserves. In the meantime Majdi would shower, and when he emerged he'd be dressed in gym shorts and a white undershirt that accentuated his sinewy bronze muscles. He would then sit down by the dilapidated table and devote himself to cutting up the vegetables into a fine salad.

Relations between the workers from Rafiah and Abed and Halil, the two Israeli Arabs, were amicable. The only time an argument broke out was when an ardent supporter of the PFLP arrived from the Nuseirat camp in the Gaza Strip. This man did not give his name. After the initial acquaintance, a lively debate broke out in the room with regard to the Jews. Almost all those present agreed that "Jews are trash and only understand brute force." (The generalizations and strong opinions voiced against the Jews as a group reminded me of Friday-evening conversations in the living rooms of some of my Jewish acquaintances, when "Arabs" was the topic of discussion.) The new fellow from Nuseirat was the only one who insisted that there are Jews—those who support the idea of a democratic secular state in Palestine—with whom it is possible and necessary to maintain a dialogue.

The conversation shifted to an argument over an Arab member of the Israeli Knesset, Muhammad Watad, who was a representative of the United Labor Party (a Zionist party on the political left). Abed defended Watad and told us that it was only through his efforts that the renovation of the Hassan Bek mosque in Jaffa had been authorized. The others, myself included, countered with the claim that he had only acted in his own interest to advance his political career, and not for the sake of the Palestinian people. Majdi even told us that friends of his who worked in a restaurant in Herzliya once saw Watad dining there in the company of a Jewish woman and that "without a doubt he had slept with her." This unfounded, and most likely false, rumor excited everyone, and the ensuing conversation about the corrupt conduct of the member of the Knesset died down only with the arrival of Abu Naim.

The flophouse owner surveyed the men who were sitting or lying in various positions on the ten beds that were densely arranged in the room. "Everyone here paid?" For an answer he got a silent chorus of head nods and mutterings.

Only Abu Al Az opened his mouth. "Yes, *ya tamaa* [miser]."

"So then, if each of you will put down a shekel, I'll go make tea for you. If you don't pay in advance, you won't get any. Yesterday I was given promises. I made strong tea with a lot of sugar, and then the sons of bitches didn't want to pay. I swear I lose money on this tea business, but I wouldn't feel good if you went to sleep without drinking something warm."

"Greedy bastard," I heard someone comment from the corner of the room. "The biggest crooks in Gaza don't dare take more than half a shekel for a cup of tea."

But everyone paid up. With a fresh batch of shekels in his tight fist, Abu Naim waddled into the adjacent room and then into the third one in order to collect the tea money and to make sure that no freeloaders had sneaked into his place.

As soon as he left, Abu Al Az vented his familiar theme: "*Wein aladala,* fools, where is there justice, in the name of Allah?!"

We had already learned to expect this "battle cry" to be followed with some nice, unrefined entertainment. Abu Al Az hadn't spoken much during the previous conversation, having preferred to pick his nose and stare at the ceiling, but now he was raring to go and every pair of eyes was on him, every ear cocked, in anticipation of his buffoonery.

The mischievous showman pulled a piece of crumpled paper from his pocket and threw it disdainfully onto Abed's bed. "Read what's written there and translate it for us," he demanded. Abed complied and laboriously translated: "The regional court, a receipt for a fine in the amount of four hundred shekels."

Abu Al Az snatched the paper and stuffed it back into his pocket. "You think I have to sleep in this stinking joint?" Then he launched into an eloquent description of his room in Shapira, taking advantage of the fact that many of his audience hadn't yet heard of the incomparable treasures he had in that room. It turned out that the police had caught him sleeping there, and he'd been summoned to trial. Abu Al Az stood up in the small clearing between the beds, drew himself up to his full height, which wasn't much, pounded his chest, and leveled his gaze at the back door, as if he saw some superior force standing right behind it.

"I told her, the judge, that Jewish cunt," and here he switched to Hebrew: " 'Your exalted and honorable and noble honor, you are indeed the judge here upon earth, but there is another judge' "—here he pointed dramatically above at the dust-ridden fluorescent lamp that was flickering on the ceiling —" 'the judge above us, whom we will all have to face, and if you give me a penalty that's too severe, your honor, and I'm just a poor worker who works here to earn his daily bread, how will you face Him on Judgment Day?' And so"—Abu Al Az shook with barely controlled mirth—"she only gave me a four-hundred-shekel fine. Everyone gets at least a thousand."

Halil, the bedouin cook, was gazing at Abu Al Az with total admiration. A short while ago Abu Al Az had promised to take him along on a weekend visit to Jenin, where, he said, they would "screw a woman whose husband owes me a lot of money."

Abu Al Az basked in all the attention he was receiving. "The trial was nothing. Now, if you like, I can tell you about Ahuva!" He let us plead with him for a few minutes, while he suggestively ran his finger between his lips. Workingmen in our situation are separated from the company of women during the week; on the other hand, we have daily visual contact with provocative and scantily clad Jewish women. Abu Al Az had our mouths watering and was stretching our curiosity beyond the limits of endurance; no one had any intention of letting him get away without telling his story. He must have loved hearing our entreaties, and it was clear that he obtained a vicarious release from relating his lewd tales to such a supportive audience.

"Some two weeks ago," he began, "maybe more, I can't exactly remember, I met a friend of mine. A Jew by the name of Sammy. I had just finished selling the fish at the market, I was

57

in a good mood, and all I wanted was a good fuck. 'Sammy, ya Sammy,' I asked him, 'where is there justice?' That Sammy fellow knows me and he knows that when I ask a few times about justice it's a sign that I'm horny as hell. He told me about a woman friend of his, a beautiful girl of seventeen. Seventeen! A plague on her religion. Sammy was real nice and he gave me her phone number. I called her and said"—he switched to Hebrew—" 'Ahuva darling, how are you? My name is Abraham and I want to come visit you today.' She gave me her address and invited me to visit her that very evening."

Abu Al Az described at great length how he prepared himself for the meeting and then he continued: ". . . I knocked on the door to her flat, and it was opened by a woman seventy years old who could barely walk." Here the storyteller began to shuffle between the beds, wiggling his belly and his behind. "I said to her, 'You're Ahuva? I'll be darned! You're Ahuva?' She answered, 'I am,' and I almost had a nervous breakdown."

Abu Al Az paused. Halil and Yassin, the youngest worker of the Rafiah gang, were driven to distraction. "Well, tell us. Come on. What happened in the end with that old Jewish witch?"

"She wanted to go to a bar, so I took her to a bar and we drank whiskey," Abu Al Az revealed, humming to himself. The two continued to press him, and with the greatest pleasure, as if by means of that Ahuva, whose existence seemed doubtful, he were avenging himself on all the Jewish women who were out of bounds to him, Abu Al Az described in minute detail the wild night of passionate sex that he shared with the old woman.

Frankly, I was not crazy about Abu Al Az's homespun pornography. His skills as a storyteller were undeniable, but the lack of credibility and his desire to attract notice at all costs didn't appeal to me. In keeping with my image as a "son of the camps" and a relatively educated person, I tried to maintain a certain distance from him.

This was appreciated by the others, and especially by Majdi, the leader of the men from Rafiah.

He turned to me and broke the heavy erotic spell that Abu Al Az's story had cast on the crowded room. "Well, how's work these days?" he inquired. By changing the subject and addressing me thus, he pointed up the alliance that our disapproval formed against the irrepressible Abu Al Az.

"Allah be praised, I still work at the garage on Salame Street."

"And what do you do there?" asked Majdi.

"How do you mean? I'm a car electrician and that's my job over at that Jew's place."

"Wow, so you have a *sanaa*, you have a *sanaa*," shouted Halil, who was lying in the bed next to me. His face, with its rapturous expression, still showed the lingering influence of Abu Al Az's story. Halil moved closer to me and took a friendly hold of my hand, as if he'd just discovered that for several days he'd been sharing a room with an illustrious statesman. *Sanaa* means a craft, and Halil's excitement was due to the fact that I was a professional craftsman, the only one residing at Abu Naim's at the time.

"How much does the Jew pay you?" he was curious to know. I mentioned a sum that was slightly higher than the actual one.

"You're crazy! Come with me tomorrow morning to Talal's garage. He's a Forty-eighter, an authentic Jaffaite. I know him well. Work for him and you'll make ten times more than you are now. Why mess around with the Jews?"

In Jewish society, where every mother dreams of her boy becoming a doctor, or at least a lawyer, being a car electrician or a mechanic doesn't count for much. But here at Abu Naim's, among people who are obliged to hire out their muscles to the highest bidder—even if (like Majdi, for instance) they have completed a university degree—because they don't really have any other job opportunities, to be a mechanic is regarded as the pinnacle of achievement. One is the practitioner of a specialized trade, sought after by employers, and able to earn a salary that is a few shekels higher than that of a menial worker. Since my purpose was specifically to work for a Jewish employer, I politely declined Halil's offer.

One evening, I lay on my bed reading the newspaper *Al Biader Al Siasi*. That week, Israeli soldiers guarding the Cave of Machpela in Hebron (reputedly the tomb of the Patriarch Abraham, and a major bone of contention, since both Jews and Moslems regard it as a holy site and a place of worship) had shot an Arab woman after she attacked one of them with a knife. I had already heard about the incident on the radio while at work. In the Arab newspapers the affair was presented as the "cold-blooded murder of an Arab woman in Hebron." On the back page of *Al Biader Al Siasi* there was a full spread on the woman, including a photograph of her with her husband and children. The paper called the woman a *shabida*, a title given only to Moslems who have achieved martyrdom in the name of Allah; they have secured their place in the next world.

"What's with that woman?" Majdi asked me, noticing the photograph.

"She was killed by the occupation," I answered in the proper revolutionary spirit.

Majdi snatched the paper from me and feverishly read the article. His dark, handsome face grew ashen and his bulging muscles contracted spasmodically. Suddenly, he grabbed me by my collar, lifted me clean in the air, and flattened me against the wall. I was paralyzed with fear, certain that my identity had somehow been revealed and that the hour of reckoning had come. I knew that here, in Abu Naim's Palestinian enclave, there was no one who could, or would, help me.

Majdi tightened his grip on my shirt, and white foam flecked his lips. "By Allah," he swore, his face barely an inch away from my own. "By Allah, the first Jew I meet now . . . the first Jew . . . I'll bash his head against the wall until his brains spill out. Cursed dogs! Murderers of women and children."

I made a desperate attempt to disguise the violent shaking which had overcome me. "May Allah destroy the Jews," I said weakly, and with my sleeve I wiped off the spittle which had sprayed me. Majdi, regaining possession of himself, released me and I fell back on my bed, completely drained of energy.

The next day I contacted Hassan Jibril, a journalist and friend from Shati camp in the Gaza Strip, and asked him to come up to Tel Aviv for a few days. "I need you to stay with me at a place where I'm lodging," I told him. The experience with Majdi shook me and I didn't feel safe on my own anymore. In a situation like that I wouldn't even have time to get out Feisal Al Husseini's letter.

Hassan knew of my project and had seen the letter. He was well suited to my purpose, for he was sly and cunning, and quite capable, for instance, of telling an outright lie without batting an eye. So Hassan arrived and he too took up residence in Abu Naim's rooms. He was appalled by the filth and the crowded conditions there. Although he came from the Shati refugee camp, where living conditions are far from ideal, he was as fastidious in matters of cleanliness as he was in other areas.

We were careful not to give away the fact that we knew one another, and only on the third day of his stay did we make a formal acquaintance.

"Fat'hi Awad, mechanic and electrician, from Balata."

Hassan shook my hand. "Hassan Jibril, unemployed journalist, looking for a restaurant job, from Shati."

Majdi, who was listening to us, hastened to introduce himself to Hassan. Soon they were immersed in a lively conversation.

"As a journalist, you're probably familiar with the situation in the prisons?" Majdi asked Hassan, who nodded assent. "Then you've surely heard of [here Majdi mentioned two names], who were murdered in prison."

"I have," Hassan answered. "They were killed because they cooperated with the prison authorities and were suspected of betraying their people and collaborating with the Jews."

It was clear that the subject weighed heavily on Majdi's mind and that he'd waited a long time for an opportunity to discuss it with someone "political." It touched on one of the most sensitive issues in the occupied territories. The moment political prisoners in one of the Israeli prisons suspect that someone among them is a collaborator, they dispatch him.

"People shouldn't be killed without a proper inquiry. They should be given a chance to respond to the accusation and then be warned. You see," Majdi added, unable to cover his pain, "those two were friends of mine, and when I was in prison and someone quarreled with me over personal matters, he spread the rumor that I was an agent as well. It was a total lie and I was lucky I wasn't killed."

"That's how it is in a situation like ours," Hassan coolly observed. He seemed to be enjoying the fact that Majdi thought him to be an activist and well connected enough to convey his complaint to the powers that be in one of the Palestinian organizations.

After a couple of weeks, I stopped working at Yosi Levi's shop. The experience seemed unlikely to yield any new revelations, and my relations with my boss had reached a plateau and were unlikely to develop any further. I envied him as I saw how he raked in profits as a result of my work, for which I myself received a pittance. Yosi still owed me a small sum of money, but the loss seemed insignificant when viewed against having to explain to Yosi my reasons for leaving. He would probably offer to raise my salary and I would have to refuse that as well. So I simply didn't show up. However, I stayed on at Abu Naim's for a while. Hassan, who remained there as well, would wander about Tel Aviv during the day, visiting friends from Gaza and the refugee camps who were employed as restaurant workers. In the evenings we would get together and exchange thoughts on the posing project and on the political situation in general.

As a final act, I wished to have a photograph taken of Abu Naim's place and of the lodgers. "I'm interested in writing something about the lives of workers in Tel Aviv so that the world will see how much our people are suffering," Hassan said one day to the men assembled in the room. "Tomorrow evening I want to bring an Italian photojournalist here. I know him and he's friendly to our cause. He'll just take a couple of pictures and then he'll go away." All he asked, Hassan said, was that the men remain silent, so that Abu Naim or (even worse) his notorious sons wouldn't find out about it.

By that time I had acquired some status among the workers, so I took it upon myself to question Hassan thoroughly about his intentions. I demanded to meet Hassan and the photographer at some distance from Abu Naim's before they came there.

"After I see his Italian passport and speak with him I'll come back and confirm that it's safe for everyone to be photographed. But not beforehand, on no account." Hassan agreed to my condition and it sounded reasonably safe to the other men. "This is a national mission of the first order. We'll be photographed and brother Hassan will tell the whole world of our plight." I lectured the workers in the best oratorical Arabic I could muster.

Everyone was convinced, at least to some degree, except for Abu Al Az. The professional survivor apparently sensed that something was fishy, or perhaps he simply wasn't willing to endanger his last foothold in Tel Aviv. Propaganda for the sake of the suffering Palestinians didn't interest him in the least.

"You're a bunch of lunatics!" he exclaimed. "He'll take pictures and they'll be published and then the police will close this place down and we'll be arrested. We won't be photographed, no way!" He turned to Hassan. "And tell your photojournalist not to dare come here."

Majdi, who was in favor of being photographed, answered, "If you, ya Abu Al Az, don't want to be photographed, then there's no problem. Just stay away and you won't be included. I've already sat in prison and I don't care."

Abu Al Az felt he was being cornered, so he issued a threat. "If that photographer comes anywhere near here, I'll call Abu Naim and his sons and they'll bust his camera as well as his face." Majdi and I advanced on him in such a manner to make him try a new tack. "Maybe the whole story of a photographer is bullshit. Maybe it's the *mubabarat* [Shin Bet] who want to involve us in a provocation. It isn't worth it to mess around with this business."

This was a definite insult directed at Hassan. The public allegation that he might be an agent working for the secret services called for an emphatic and swift response. Otherwise, the rumor would spread, far beyond the walls of Abu Naim's miserable boardinghouse, and would cause irreparable damage to Hassan's honor and reputation. Hassan was aware of this and he pushed Majdi and me aside in order to confront the accuser directly. "My name is Hassan Jibril, you hear? Jibril." He repeated the name, alluding to Ahmad Jibril, one of the leaders of the PFLP.

The effect of the name on Abu Al Az was dramatic and instantaneous, like that of a snakebite. Although he was physically capable of demolishing Hassan in a matter of seconds, he went pale as a ghost. "I didn't mean to offend your honor." He was trembling. "I respect any Jibril, whether he's from Gaza or whether he's from Syria."

63

The next day Yisrael arrived, but the other lodgers apparently got cold feet at the last moment and were late in returning from work. Hassan and I ended up being the only ones photographed, stretched out on our filthy mattresses. This was the last event which I either witnessed or participated in at Abu Naim's.

FOUR

Second Thoughts

EVEN THOUGH Abu Naim's flophouse was certainly an unattractive place, I had become used to it. My status among the other lodgers was established—I had the most comfortable bed, for instance—and I knew that Abu Naim himself regarded me as a regular when he began charging me three shekels a night rather than five, which he had asked for in the beginning. One might almost say that I felt at home where I was, and this was precisely what led me to discontinue my stay there. Being at ease was a sure sign that nothing new was about to happen, and it seemed to me that I ought to try something else.

It was always hard to leave a familiar situation and enter a new experience. I moved into Yisrael's studio and relaxed for a couple of days. Then, when I had gathered sufficient energy, I set out to look for another job, willing to take on anything, provided it was located in Tel Aviv itself, where the residents are all Jewish, as opposed to Jaffa, where the population is mixed.

I went from store to store and offered myself for hire. *"Fi shurul?* [Is there work?]," I asked, and most of the shopkeepers knew how to reply in Arabic: "*Ma fish* [There isn't any]."

I walked the entire length of Dizengoff Street, the main street in Tel Aviv, until I reached its northern end, where the center of the city's nightlife is located. It was noon and hardly anyone was around, except for some Arab workers who were busy hosing down the sidewalks and setting up tables in front of the restaurants. Outside a restaurant that hadn't opened yet, a group of Arabs were sitting on the tables, talking among themselves and smoking cigarettes. I greeted them and asked whether their employer needed another hand. No, they said, this restaurant already had enough kitchen help. But one of the men jumped from the table on which he was sitting and beckoned. "Follow me. There's a place here where someone left this week and maybe they haven't found a replacement yet." I obediently went after him. On the way he introduced himself and I gathered that he came from one of the villages in the north of Israel. His clothing, his confident demeanor, and his way of walking, all showed that he was well acquainted with the area, knew exactly where he was going and how to speak with the local business owners.

We passed a hedge on which lay a brown flannel shirt that had probably fallen off one of the clotheslines that were strung up on the balconies above. Without slowing his pace, the fellow who was with me gathered up the shirt as one would pick a fruit. With another energetic gesture he thrust it in my arms and said, "Put it in your basket."

"But really, it belongs to someone. I don't want any trouble," I protested. The shirt was a little stiff and gave off the clean aroma of laundry detergent.

"Put it in your basket and don't think too much about it. The way you look you need that shirt much more than the people who lost it."

We had already advanced quite a bit as we conducted our little argument; I didn't see any point in returning to put the shirt back where it had been found. I looked quickly around, as if I wanted to make sure that the shirt's owner wasn't chasing after me, and tucked it away in the depths of my basket.

We arrived at a small pub. A sign proclaimed its name: Hatuki (Parrot). There was a live parrot there, kept in a large cage by the entrance, where he busily gnawed at sunflower seeds. Behind the bar sat a woman of about thirty. She had a dark complexion and a youthful appearance. Her black hair was pleated into many thin braids that were woven, African style, with tiny colored beads.

My escort indicated that I should stay behind a moment and went straight up to her. "*Ahalan*, Ofra, I heard that Afif left this week. Well, I've found an excellent fellow for you—Ali. He's been a good friend of mine for a long time. He's got lots of work experience and you can trust him with everything. You're lucky he's looking for work just now and it's worth your while to take him." My benefactor continued talking with Ofra about this and that, about how business was going, and about Afif, her former employee, who had found a job with better pay. Throughout the conversation he interpolated remarks that he had made up on the spot, about my good qualities and our long period of friendship and so on.

"O.K. What did you say your name is? Ali? Come back here at four this afternoon and you'll start working," Ofra instructed me. As we parted I warmly shook my new friend's hand. "Allah bless you, thank you from the bottom of my heart." Considering that he had just met me for the first time ten minutes earlier, I couldn't fail to be impressed by his show of solidarity.

Back in Yisrael's house, over a cup of coffee, I began to entertain doubts about my new place of employment. I had already acquired enough experience working for Jewish employers. Most of the things that could happen to an Arab worker had already happened to me; what hadn't didn't seem sufficiently interesting to justify another prolonged period of boring work, cooking and cleaning in some low-class restaurant in Tel Aviv. In view of this, I told Yisrael that I thought I'd go back to Jerusalem for a short rest. Perhaps during the interval one of us would get a good idea for the next posing "event," which should be something new and interesting.

Yisrael wasn't the least bit sympathetic toward my defeatist line of reasoning. "C'mon, Binchu, did you think you were going to pose as some kind of a millionaire or something?" I hadn't the strength to argue, so I made up my mind to go ahead with the new job, for as long as I could take it.

Work hours at the Parrot were from 4 P.M. to 4 A.M. The pay was approximately one and a half shekels an hour. Every three days Ofra paid me in cash and, as usual, there was no mention of any benefits whatsoever, not even those which an employer is bound by law to provide. I worked in a tiny kitchen which was about two meters by three. Because I had to live up to my recommendation I needed to learn quickly on the job. One new skill which I gained was how to prepare *shuarma* on a spit, which would then rotate slowly throughout the evening, roasting in the upright grill that was on display at the back of the bar. I would lay out pieces of turkey dripping with blood on the cutting board in the kitchen, along with a whole sheep's tail, which had a whitish color and in which the defunct animal's anus could still be clearly discerned. Between every two slices of turkey I would skewer a hunk of fat from the tail, which would lend the cheap meat the flavor of mutton. For the sake of this illusion the customers were used to paying good money.

The pub was a small place with regular customers. All in all, a family atmosphere prevailed: it was much more relaxed than at the Coliseum Halls, for instance. In addition to Ofra, the slim Yemenite, there was her sister, a pretty young woman of about twenty-five, and a friend of theirs who used to help out sometimes, an enormous, well-endowed woman. Finally, there was a young waitress by the name of Osnat. Needless to say, I wasn't really a part of the family. I was a servant. They all ordered me around: "I see our Arab is a little idle, so let him take out the glasses and wash them over again." If there was any free time I would be told to clean the kitchen or sweep the pavement in front of the restaurant. I liked sweeping the sidewalk, as it provided me with a chance to breathe some fresh air and see people. Once, when Osnat had some friends visiting, I overheard one of them ask about "her" Arab worker. I also clearly heard her answer: "This Arab, I swear, with just a little improvement he could be a Jew."

During the late hours, police patrols would occasionally come by the pub and ask Ofra to show them her license; sometimes they would fine her for keeping the place open past the required closing time. While speaking with Ofra, one of them might fix his gaze on me, like a hunter spotting his quarry. When I told Ofra I was afraid of being harassed by the police, she answered, "You don't have anything to worry about. Most of the cops in the area are friendly with me and if you're arrested I'll be able to get you out."

But to be on the safe side Ofra asked me to bring her my ID certificate so she could take down my personal data. She claimed that the police required this procedure with regard to all Arab employees. I was apprehensive when I handed my Jordanian ID to her the next day. But she merely glanced at the document from the Hashemite Kingdom and returned it to me; not the faintest glimmer of suspicion showed on her face. All she asked was that I translate the relevant information so she could write it down. When she asked me where I was staying, I told her that I shared a rented flat with friends who worked in other restaurants, which was untrue at the time, but which I imagined was more in keeping with her expectations and didn't necessitate a lengthy explanation.

There were nights when I was afraid to go back to Yisrael's studio on foot. I didn't want to be detained by a police patrol at four in the morning. So I persuaded Ofra to drop me off in the vicinity of the studio when work was over. "If I am arrested I don't come to work tomorrow and you even be called to the police station for checking, and it will be waste your time." This line of argument was effective; Ofra agreed to drop me off near Yisrael's studio after work.

There was one night at Hatuki that brought home most strongly all the feelings of frustration and humiliation that I had experienced as an Arab worker. Ofra's sister, Michal, had a boyfriend, a handsome man with an athletic build, who used to come to the pub during work hours in order to help out or just to sit over a drink in his girlfriend's company.

It was about two in the morning and most of the customers had already gone. I was in the kitchen washing dishes and returning leftovers to the refrigerator so they could be recycled the following day, when Michal and her boyfriend, laughing excitedly, pushed their way into the kitchen—which hardly had enough room for one man alone to move around in. They squeezed themselves into a small corner between me and the refrigerator and proceeded to kiss each other passionately.

69

I lowered my eyes and concentrated on washing the dirty dishes in the sink, carefully going over each plate, so I wouldn't embarrass them with my presence. The breathing got heavier as they got bolder, and for a fleeting moment I thought I might as well enjoy the little scene that had come my way. I ventured a peek at them out of the corner of my eye.

Then a sort of trembling suddenly came over me. I realized that they had not meant to put on a peep show for my enjoyment. Those two were not the least bit concerned with what I saw or felt even when they were practically fucking under my nose. For them I simply didn't exist. I was invisible, a nonentity! It's difficult to describe the feeling of extreme humiliation which I experienced. Looking back, I think it was the most degrading moment I had during my entire posing adventure.

I stuck with my hated position at Hatuki more out of inertia than by virtue of any strength of will. In the meantime I had an opportunity to move in with a group of Arabs, residents of the Israeli town of Um Al Fahem. Since they were citizens of Israel, they weren't illegally living in the city, and the flat was rented for them by the restaurant at which they all worked. An acquaintance of mine, Mahmud, who knew about my project, was staying there and suggested that I stay with them for a while.

When I arrived he was waiting for me alone in the flat. He showed me around. In the kitchen I found clothes hanging to dry. Near the sink were a few cups and a kettle. It didn't seem like real meals were ever cooked there. The living room contained an old black-and-white television and a table and, since it also doubled as a bedroom, beds which served as sofas during the day. A poster on one of the walls featured a brand-new BMW motorcycle. Motorbikes have always symbolized freedom and independence to me. Even misery is relative, I thought, as I looked at the poster; at Abu Naim's flophouse the walls had been absolutely bare.

About an hour after I arrived the other residents of the apartment came in: Abu Kasem, Haled, Hussein, and Faress. Mahmud introduced me to them: "This is Ali from Balata. He's a friend of relatives of mine and will stay with us for a few days."

70

My presence was accepted as natural and I was invited to join them for their meal.

They had brought a bag with them bearing the name of the restaurant where they worked and containing some pita bread and various salads. When we ran out of pita, and were still hungry, Abu Kasem, the eldest of the group, took a few shekels out of his pocket and turned to the youngest, a tall, good-looking youth. "Hussein," he requested, "go to the bakery and get some more pita." Hussein checked his shirt pocket to confirm that his ID card was in place, and asked Abu Kasem whether there were any police detectives about. Abu Kasem assured him that the coast was clear and Hussein left.

It was around seven in the evening, an hour when innocent pedestrians aren't ordinarily arrested in the streets, and I professed astonishment at their caution. "What? You Forty-eighters also have trouble with the police? You have an Israeli ID, don't you?"

"What do you know? In the West Bank you call us 'Jews,' but for the cops here we're one hundred percent Arabs, and it's bad news when they get their hands on us," replied Abu Kasem. Then he added, in a tone of a scientist stating a universal law: "The policeman is the greatest enemy of the Arab workman in Tel Aviv." A cockroach went by and Abu Kasem brushed it away indifferently. The entire place was infested with cockroaches. The lodgers seemed to have given up fighting the creatures and simply ignored them.

Abu Kasem was a small, wiry man of about fifty. Having worked for the same restaurant chain for ten years, he was now a "grill man," a job that was considered fairly high up in the hierarchy. Previously he had been a watchman for one of the kibbutzim near his town. Finding work in Um Al Fahem itself was out of the question. "Our land has all been appropriated by the Jews, so there's nothing to cultivate. There aren't any factories either and no other jobs, so we depend completely on the Jews for work."

As we were talking, Abu Kasem brought out a bottle of cheap Israeli vodka, took a long swig, and passed it on. I looked at him reprovingly as befits a devout Moslem.

"That's how it is. I work long hours standing at the grill. The owner doesn't allow us to eat meat, only fish or poultry.

When there's a lot of work the owner treats me well, and when there isn't much to do he simply ignores me. I get to see my family once a week. So I drink. It's the easiest way. Today I've already finished a bottle, and this"—he pointed at the label on the vodka bottle—"is already my second round for the day." Hussein, who had returned with the pita, joined in the conversation. He wanted to prove that the Arabs from the occupied territories are not the only ones who suffer. "At the restaurant they were looking for someone educated to sit by the cash register. I brought in my cousin, who is studying computers at Tel Aviv University. When they saw he was an Arab they said they didn't need anyone anymore, and a few days later they brought in a Jewish guy who hardly finished elementary school."

The television set was on and the news broadcast had begun. A report of a terrorist attack on a Jewish synagogue in Istanbul was accompanied by harrowing images of the victims being taken away for burial. I felt like starting a discussion in order to observe the reactions of my companions, but the phone rang just then and interrupted the conversation. Abu Kasem picked up the receiver and called Hussein over to accept the call. "It's Hadas," he said. After a few seconds, Hussein grew visibly angry. His face turned yellow and he pounded violently on the table in front of him. "What do you want from me? What do you suppose I think about it?!" he shouted, and slammed down the receiver. A few minutes later he calmed down sufficiently to tell us what the argument had been about. "That was my Jewish girlfriend. She saw the news and called to ask me what I thought about the [Palestinian] organizations attacking a synagogue in Istanbul and killing the Jewish worshippers. I'm fed up with having to justify myself every time something like that happens. They demand constantly that you prove you aren't a terrorist and want you to apologize for everything that happens in the world."

After a few days I left the apartment. As usual, I gave no advance notice. At the same time I also quit my job at the Parrot. The next morning, when I was out for a stroll on King George Street not far from Yisrael's place, I heard a voice call out behind me: "*Ahalan wasahalan*, ya Fat'hi!" I cursed the day I was born, I cursed the world and all the Jews and Arabs in it.

Had I really gotten so involved in my project that I couldn't avoid posing for a day or two?

Turning around, I found myself face to face with Yassin, the youth I had met at Abu Naim's place. He stood there in his shabby clothes and gave me a broad grin. "*Marhaba*, Yassin," I responded, pressing my cheek to his and smacking my lips loudly in the empty air in the traditional manner of greeting an old acquaintance. I thought to myself that I needed him now like a hole in the head. "Ya Allah, ya Fat'hi," the youth wondered, "you must have found a real good job. The way you're dressed so fine." I hastened to confirm the explanation that Yassin had unwittingly provided me with: "Yes, *ya habibi*, I'm now working in a car repair shop in Herzliya, praise Allah. I have a good salary and one day off every week, which happens to be today." I was concerned that Yisrael or somebody else I knew might pass us in the street, so I steered Yassin into a nearby café.

"Everyone's asking about you and wants to see you. They say because you have a *sanaa* you found a good job, so you don't have to stay at Abu Naim's anymore." Yassin looked about him with wide-eyed curiosity. "You know, ya Fat'hi, since I've been working here I haven't been in a place like this. This is my first time."

Using my pidgin Hebrew, I ordered two cups of coffee. Yassin filled his with an incredible quantity of sugar, stirred it with great care as if cherishing a special treat, and sipped it with visible pleasure. I was overcome by a warm feeling for this pleasant youth, who was, by necessity, mature beyond his years. From what he told me it seemed that he'd recently been fired. Majdi had lent him a little money so that he could go out and look for another job.

"I've got something for you," I said. "Kitchen work in a restaurant, but it's a small place and pretty comfortable." We finished our coffee and stepped out into the street. I asked Yassin to give my regards to Majdi (which I meant in all sincerity) and to Abu Al Az (out of a sense of duty), and told him how to take the no. 5 bus to Hatuki. I had good reason to believe that they needed someone there to do kitchen work.

I continued on my way and when I reached Dizengoff Street I entered another café, where I poured three glasses of brandy down my throat, one right after the other. My encounter with Yassin had turned out well. We had shared a light moment and maybe I'd even helped him out. But I was bothered by the feeling that I couldn't go down a street anymore without some- one recognizing me as Fat'hi. I was tired of my posing act. Yes, I could mislead any Jewish employer with regard to my nation- ality and be accepted for work, but in the end all that would happen was that a certain number of events would repeat themselves over and over again. In addition, I had already be- gun to forget who I really was. It was important for me to go about as a Jew again for a few days; maybe I'd be able somehow to counteract the increasing domination of my Palestinian identity over my own personality.

When I got back to Yisrael's place I informed him that I was taking a break for a few days. Yisrael had some serious matters of his own to contend with at the time, so he didn't apply the full force of his pressure to convincing me that I should stay.

That day, at noon, I once again removed the cover from my Citroën, shook off the dust and dry bird droppings, and sped off to Jerusalem. The main purpose of my return home, though not consciously formulated, was to try to relieve my tensions in the company of a woman, something which had been sorely lacking since the project had begun. As an Arab imposter it hadn't been possible to form any sort of relationships with women. Nor, I discovered, was it possible even during my brief return to myself. Instead I drowned my sorrows in the few bottles of brandy, vodka, and arak which I had at home. For three days I didn't leave my bed except to go to the bathroom or to replenish my supply of drinks. The bottles piled up around me, together with cigarette butts, old newspapers, and other rubbish, creating a carpet of emptiness and despair.

In the "slave market" on Yefet Street, Jaffa, waiting to be picked up for work.

All photographs by Yisrael Cohen

Working as a laborer in the Coliseum Halls, Tel Aviv. In the foreground is Shmuel, the owner's father.

At the Parrot restaurant on Dizengoff Street in Tel Aviv, where I worked from 4 P.M. to 4 A.M.

After being taken aside, searched, and roughed up by border police during a Gush Emunim demonstration in Jerusalem. Note that the policeman has confiscated my keffiyeh.

At an Arab stall in a Gaza street where items found by Gaza laborers in Israeli garbage cans are offered for sale.

In Fat'hi Raban's house, Jabalya refugee camp. Months later, on a street in East Jerusalem, I bought the painting pictured here for six shekels (four dollars).

With Fat'hi Raban's children, Jabalya.

With guests at a marriage ceremony of a friend in the Shati refugee camp, Gaza Strip.

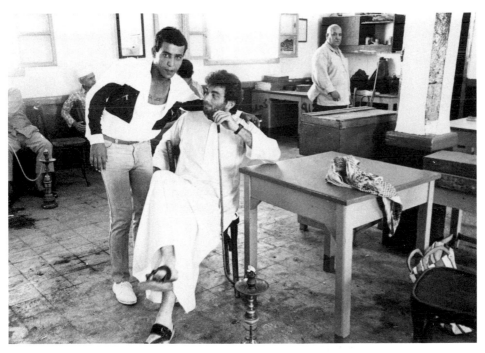

In a coffeehouse, city of Gaza. I'm smoking a nargileh, the traditional Arab water pipe.

The cattle market in Nablus. I went there with a man from the Jelazun camp who supplements his income by selling sheep.

The coffeehouse in Jelazun refugee camp. The young man is one of the group who told me about the Palestinians' *sumud* (survival strategy).

The wedding in Deheishe. Next to me, with glasses, is my dear friend, Hamdi Faraj, the groom.

With bedouins near the town of Hebron.

Routine ID check, Hebron.

Selling grapes in the Beit Hakerem neighborhood, West Jerusalem.
"I remember the time when we lived in peace together, like brothers,"
said an old Jewish woman who bought two kilos of grapes from me.

FIVE

Miri

AFTER THREE DAYS of wallowing in my depression, I received a phone call from Yisrael, who brought me sharply back to life with his no-nonsense attitude. We agreed that it was time to try a fresh approach, since I was burnt out in terms of posing as a hired worker. So this time, when I went back to Tel Aviv, I stashed my work clothes in my orange plastic basket and left them behind. Instead of the worn jacket and old pair of trousers, I enjoyed putting on the fanciest rags I had in my possession, which I had purchased in New York City and kept for special occasions. I hoped that wearing stylish clothes would make me seem a little out of place, provincial even, in the informal Israeli surroundings. Now all that remained to disguise me as a Palestinian Arab were the newspaper *Al Biader Al Siasi,* and the Farid cigarettes that I carried with me, and the keffiyeh which I nonchalantly flung around my neck.

Out to have a good time, Yisrael and I hit the Shoftim pub, one of the more popular night spots in Tel Aviv. As always, it was impossible to find empty seats there and we stood on the

75

sidewalk, waiting for a table. "Yisrael, what's new?" a woman called from one of the tables, and we went over to where she was sitting. Miri was about thirty years of age, with olive skin and a full body. She and Yisrael exchanged a few words, from which I gathered that they'd known each other for a while, though apparently they hadn't seen each other in quite some time.

Miri invited us to join her table and introduced the thin blond man who sat opposite her as Hans from Holland. Yisrael, in turn, introduced me as Fat'hi from Nablus. Miri found it difficult to conceal her surprise. "Where do you know him from?" she asked.

"We met when I was in London, and later on, back here, we continued to keep in touch."

The answer seemed to satisfy her, and to my surprise she started a conversation with me in quite good Arabic, with more than a hint of an Egyptian accent. Her parents, she explained, had come to Israel from Egypt, "and when they didn't want me to understand something they would speak in Arabic, but I managed to pick some of it up."

After a couple of beers Yisrael and I got up to leave, but before we did Miri wrote down her phone number on a paper napkin and handed it to Yisrael. "Come visit," she said to him, "and bring Fat'hi with you." Her almond eyes met mine for a brief moment, leaving me with no doubt that she liked me.

On our way home from the pub, Yisrael and I speculated about this chance meeting with an old acquaintance from his university days. It was clearly an excellent opportunity for me to form a relationship with a Jewish Israeli woman who believed I was an Arab. Yisrael summed up the situation as he saw it: "She liked you. It's worth getting in touch with her soon." The next day I asked him to phone Miri, and she invited us over to her place that same evening.

Miri lived in a small ground-floor apartment on a quiet street in the north of Tel Aviv. She had completed a degree in literature and she took odd jobs for a living. In English peppered with Arabic, I told her about the Balata refugee camp, where I supposedly came from. "Right now I'm on vacation. I'm staying at Yisrael's place and we go out looking for a good time. You have things here that can't be had in the camp, and anyway it's a chance to clear one's head from the trouble that your nice military administration gives us."

Miri listened to all this quite calmly, with an expression of evident sympathy. "I'm acquainted with the situation. When I was in the army I served, among other places, in the military administration in Gaza." This sounded interesting, but at such an early stage of our acquaintance I decided that it would be best to withhold my reaction.

Our conversation gradually grew more relaxed. In the meantime Yisrael loyally assisted me by keeping Hans preoccupied, for the Dutchman was following the developments between his girlfriend and me with obvious hostility. Yisrael kept him at bay with a rather dull conversation on the differences between Israel and Holland, the political situation, and so forth. When the evening came to an end, Miri accompanied us to the door, where she turned and addressed me in no uncertain terms. "Fat'hi, I'll get in touch with you in a couple of days. My friend is leaving and I'll be glad to see you again."

Miri's straightforwardness, and the natural and simple way she regarded my "problematic" origins, seemed to me then (and still does) to be a rare and special quality, and I grew very fond of her. In addition, I found that I couldn't easily shake off the impression that her attractive figure had made on me. Although I'd already become used to lying to just about everyone, I realized that this was going to be different. The lie that was in the making left me with some doubts. It was not that I had never sought out romantic ties on the basis of motives that were less than totally pure, such as the desire to find a partner for a one-night stand. In that case, though, such a desire was presumably shared by the partner. But I had never taken advantage of a woman in a cold and calculating fashion.

Yisrael suffered no such qualms. "If you don't like it, as far as I'm concerned tomorrow you can go off to some stinking restaurant or work in construction. This experience of having an affair with an Israeli girl is essential. A lot of Arab laborers, as well as Israeli Arabs among the university students, have affairs like that. Besides, I don't ever remember your being such an innocent angel."

☐ ☐ ☐

I restlessly whiled away the days as I waited for Miri's boy-friend to leave. I went out a lot and hung out in bars and cafés. My visits to various night spots in Tel Aviv reminded me of my earlier experience as an Arab imposter, when I was working on the newspaper assignment and was supposed to provide a first-person report on what it felt like to be a young Arab male in Jerusalem.

As part of that assignment, I went to a singles club in the center of Jerusalem one Saturday night. The men who stood in line ahead of me had no problems when they bought their tickets and entered, but when I came up to the cashier he asked me for a membership card.

"I didn't know I needed one," I answered.

"Then give me an ID."

I nonchalantly handed him a document written in Arabic that I had prepared for just such an occasion. The cashier asked me to wait and called the manager, who took the document and examined it carefully.

"Where are you from?" he inquired.

"I'm from the West Bank."

"And how did you hear of this club?"

"I'm studying Hebrew and during a lesson we read the newspaper and in it I noticed your advertisement."

The manager tried one last time to discourage me. "Are you sure you're a bachelor?"

"Sure. Look, I'm a modern man and I don't want two wives."

At this point he capitulated and instructed the cashier to accept my entrance fee. Then the manager personally escorted me to an unoccupied table. The other customers, all single men and women presumably, looked on with mild curiosity at the minor fuss that was raised around me, and the manager explained, to whoever was interested, that "tonight we have with us a great from Jordan." Apparently a guest from Jordan had a higher status in his eyes than a mere resident of the West Bank.

Everyone was seated at tables arranged around a small stage on which an entertainer was doing his best to warm up the atmosphere and get people to the dance floor. He sang accom-

78

panied by recorded music and generally gave the impression of
being a bank clerk trying to supplement his income.

I lit a Farid cigarette and surveyed the scene. Most of the
women seemed to be working women at that sensitive age
(twenty-eight to thirty-five) when they are in a hurry to find
themselves a worthy match, so that they shouldn't, God forbid,
be stuck without a husband. I asked a few of them to dance, but
all I got in response were raised eyebrows and refusals.

At the end of my unsuccessful search for a dance partner, I
returned to my table. A little earlier my accomplice, a colleague
of mine at the newspaper, had arrived. Rachel Mehager had
already managed to shake off some hopeful dance partners and
now she sat down near my table. I struck up an innocent conversation with her and then I asked her to join me on the dance
floor. As we danced I drew Rachel toward the windows. The
club was situated on the top floor of one of the tallest buildings
in Jerusalem and the city could be viewed in all its glory.

"Beautiful, wallah beautiful Jerusalem," I said to her in English, in a loud voice, for the benefit of the other dancers
nearby, "and you know, it was all Arab, Palestinian, until you
took it away from us."

But my minor provocation failed to arouse much interest.
The couples dancing next to us were too caught up in the excitement of their activity to pay attention to such insignificant
matters. When the lights dimmed and soft music was played,
Rachel took advantage of the more intimate atmosphere to
whisper in my ear that while I had been making the rounds
trying to find a dance partner, the woman who was sitting at
the table next to mine wanted to check the contents of the
cigarette pack I had left on the table, in case there was a bomb
in it. "One of the staff went over and examined it and told her
that there were only cigarettes in the pack."

The dancing went on and in a loud voice I said to Rachel, "I
have a nice house in the village of Silwan near Jerusalem. Why
don't we go out there and have a drink?" The couple who were
dancing closest to us turned their heads and looked at us with
curiosity. Rachel "agreed," and as we left, the entire kitchen
staff, who were all Arabs, stood in a row near the exit and
stared at us shamelessly. My show of confidence was, from
their point of view, a demonstration of the impossible.

Another club I went to with Rachel was a little less tolerant. A woman whom I approached and invited to dance went directly to the manager and demanded to know why he let "that Arab" in the place. The manager apologized and promised that it wouldn't happen again.

During that period Rachel and I also spent some time visiting cafés in the center of the city. We would walk together and embrace. One day Rachel's mother received an anonymous phone call informing her that her daughter had been seen walking about in the company of some Arab thug and she, the mother, was warned that she'd better do something about it.

□ □ □

Finally I received the long-awaited phone call from Miri. She invited me over, quite enthusiastically, I thought. When I arrived, however, there was another guest there, a thin bearded fellow by the name of Yossi. Miri, completely at ease, as if guests from refugee camps were an everyday matter in her house, introduced us to one another. "This is Fat'hi Awad from Nablus, and this is Yossi from Tel Aviv." The fellow winced and settled farther back into the couch he was sitting on, as Miri went into the kitchen to prepare coffee. For several minutes there was complete silence in the room. Yossi and I conducted a mutual scrutiny that seemed to me like some ancient ritual in which two men in the company of a single woman try to assess their respective chances of winning her favors.

A biker's helmet that lay at Yossi's feet provided a pretext for breaking the probing silence. "Do you have a motorbike or a Vespa?" I asked in English.

"A bike."

"What kind?"

"Triumph."

"They're hard to repair, aren't they? No matter how much you fix them they'll always leak oil. Does yours leak oil?"

The ensuing silence, given the tense atmosphere, seemed interminable. When at last Yossi broke it, he totally disregarded my question, and said, "You know, this is the first time I've sat at a table with an Arab talking with him like this."

The directness of his confession took me by surprise. I felt like blurting out, in flawless Hebrew, "You think you're sitting with an Arab, you dumb Tel Avivi," but instead I said, "Ah, yes. There's not much chance for Arabs and Jews to meet."

Miri came back carrying a tray with three cups of aromatic black coffee and a small plate of cookies. She chose to seat herself closer to where I was sitting than to Yossi, and my victory seemed an accomplished fact. To all outward appearances, Yossi accepted his defeat with gentlemanly good grace and the conversation loosened up. Yossi told me that he had participated in the Lebanon War as a member of a combat unit, whose role he didn't elaborate on. I knew better than to press him for details; there are things one simply doesn't tell an Arab.

He asked me about life in the occupied territories. His questions made it clear that, like most Israelis, he didn't know a thing about what goes on there. I told him a lot about the massive land appropriations, the arrests and the frequent roadblocks that had become a routine part of life in the West Bank and the Gaza Strip. And I told him about the difficulty of living for twenty years under military rule, which, though not the most severe imaginable, was still enough to make life unbearable for us. "My strongest principle, as a member of a people that doesn't have its freedom, is the *sumud*, to stick to what there is and try to carry on life as normally as one can, in order to get through this difficult period."

"But how can you want a state of your own when you don't have any recognized leaders?"

"The leaders that we have or had in the occupied territories your administration expels or arrests. Besides, we have a leader whose authority most of us accept, myself included."

"And who is that?" he asked.

"Abu Amar [Yasir Arafat], of course. You call him a terrorist, but for us he's an admired leader and is even considered to be too moderate. We gave him the nickname the Old Man, just as you did with your Ben-Gurion."

"And where exactly do you want to establish this state of yours?"

"In the West Bank and the Gaza Strip. A lot of us believe that one day we'll be able to establish one secular democratic state that will include all of what you call Israel and we call Palestine." I was reciting the ideology of the mainstream in the PLO for his benefit.

"And after you get your state in the West Bank and the Gaza Strip, you'll try to take over all of Israel. That's what you really want, isn't it?"

"I don't deny that there are many who would like to have it that way, to return to their homes in Haifa and Jaffa, for instance. I'd also like it. But for most of us it's already clear that this isn't possible. Returning to pre-1948 Palestine will remain some sort of dim aspiration, and that's different from an actual struggle. Among you there are those who want to annex all of Jordan and parts of Syria and Lebanon, and that desire doesn't automatically turn you into active terrorists."

Yossi listened with great interest to what I had to say, but when I had detailed my political objective—the desire for independence—he spouted a string of clichés that were direct quotes from certain Israeli politicians. The clichés sounded as if they had taken a direct route from his ears to his mouth, without passing through the critical faculties that reside in his brain. "I've fought against you Arabs enough to know that you can't be trusted. The moment we turn our back on you you'll stick a knife in it. The Palestinian state could turn out to be a disaster for us and then we'll have to go to war again in order to reoccupy your territory, and it will all amount to an unnecessary waste of human lives."

I was astonished. The things Yossi was saying were often expressed by Israelis among themselves, but the direct manner in which he was flinging them in the face of an Arab who was sitting across from him was brutally rude and tactless. As a Jew, I felt very much like giving him a lesson in the art of cultured debate; as an Arab, I was incapable of continuing the conversation. He sensed my hostility (which our hostess did nothing to relieve), and after a few minutes he got up and left.

I invited Miri to go out for a drink, and we went to the Café Piltz by the seaside. Our conversation was standard for any budding romance. Miri told me all about herself, about her studies in literature at the university, about the poetry she wrote, and about her relationship with the Dutch fellow. "The evening you came over to my place with Yisrael, Hans could see that I found you attractive and after you left he staged an awful scene. He said that he hadn't even left and here I was making a pass at another guy, and an Arab to boot. In the end he even slapped me."

Miri and I conversed alternately in Arabic and in English. Because the Egyptian accent is different from the Palestinian, she didn't always understand me, and when I'd explain something in English to her we would continue to speak in that language for a while. English was a double burden for me, since it wasn't my mother tongue and I pronounced it with the typical mistakes and the accent of a native Arab speaker.

I asked Miri about her military service. "Yes, of course I served in the army. Every Israeli girl serves in the army." But she didn't go into details. As an Arab, the fact of her army service ought to have been very difficult for me to accept. Arab friends of mine who are familiar with my views regarding the future of the occupied territories and Jewish-Arab relationships in the area often ask me whether I have served in the army.

Miri interrogated me in return. "Say, Fat'hi, are you politically involved? Were you ever a member of one of those organizations of yours?" I answered that all I was interested in was good living. "With us, those who engage in politics get into trouble, and I'm not interested in that. I work, eat, and sleep," I said, laughing. "I'm exactly what the Israelis like us to be."

Miri gave me a long look. "Believe me, Fat'hi, compared with other Israelis I have a pretty good idea of what goes on in the occupied territories. I'm not political, but I hope some solution will be found that will allow the Arabs who live there to have a dignified existence. More than they have now under our military administration. You know"—she paused as if deliberating whether to disclose an important state secret—"in the army I was an excellent soldier and I received a letter of commendation from the commander in chief of the women's corps."

On the way back to Miri's we were already embracing. As soon as we arrived at her place, Miri went off to take a shower. When she came back wrapped in a towel, her long black hair damp and glistening, I was ready for her, supremely confident, waiting in her bed. We were both excited. In response to the first touch of my lips her body quivered with the anticipation of a nervous racehorse waiting for the gate to open, and I felt strongly attracted to her, because of her particular qualities and also because some months had gone by without my having been in a woman's company. Yet when Miri addressed me as Fat'hi, and I answered her "ya Mira," I felt as if what was taking place in that room in northern Tel Aviv was happening to an anonymous fellow from a refugee camp somewhere in the West Bank who had no connection with me.

The days passed with pleasant regularity, and we went about our routine with the fresh enthusiasm of a couple in the first phase of their romance. Every morning I would go to a store or a nearby bakery to buy groceries while Miri prepared breakfast. While shopping I sometimes took advantage of the opportunity to use a public pay phone and contacted Yisrael. He was enjoying his respite from me, though he listened with interest to the details of my unusual romance as it unfolded. At the end of each phone conversation he would encourage me in his not so subtle way: "Good, Binchu, good. So it looks like you've really got it going with her, eh?"

Miri wasn't working at the time, so we often went for walks together during the day, and when she had errands to do I would accompany her. She was interested in finding a job at Tel Aviv University and I went with her to the campus, where I'd spend my time reading the "Help Wanted" notices that were posted on a bulletin board in one of the offices.

On one such occasion Miri introduced me to a good friend of hers. She characteristically presented me as an Arab in a straightforward way, but to my dismay her friend turned out to be a student of Arabic and Arabic literature. In the course of the short conversation that ensued she almost succeeded, without her knowing it, in cornering me with her extensive knowledge of Arab authors. After I had somehow managed to survive the obligatory round of polite chitchat, the friend turned to Miri and said in Hebrew (which, of course, I wasn't supposed to understand), "This Arab you've got is very nice."

The entire posing affair was beginning to exert a strong grip on me. By a certain stage in the affair, all my thoughts and even my dreams, as far as I can remember, were in Arabic.

As for Miri, sometimes I had the feeling that she was getting a bit upset over our developing relationship. From her point of

84

view it threatened to go beyond the safe boundaries within which she could be confident of maintaining control over the flow of events. More than once, when she was cooking in the kitchen or was in the bathroom, I heard her muttering to herself in Hebrew, "Damn it, what am I going to do with this guy?" or "This will get me into real trouble yet."

One morning I heard someone knocking on the front door. Miri and I were still in bed. "There's someone at the door. Would you go see who it is?" she said, half asleep, but then, as if suddenly remembering something, she woke up. "It's my landlord. I just hope he doesn't see you in the apartment." As far as I was concerned, there wasn't any reason why I shouldn't meet the landlord, but when I said as much to Miri, she replied, "Are you mad? If he sees an Arab in my bed I'll be thrown out of this apartment today." She hastily got dressed, pulled the blanket over my head, and shut both doors to the bedroom.

I recalled another incident from my first posing experience, for the article in the Jerusalem newspaper. My accomplice, Rachel, and I tried to rent an apartment, presenting ourselves as a mixed Arab-Jewish couple. We selected several newspaper ads offering apartments for rent and, because we knew that a phone conversation in Arabic with a Jewish landlord wouldn't be a good start, Rachel made the phone calls.

The first apartment we went to see was in a Jerusalem neighborhood called Kiryat Yovel. The landlady, a pleasant woman of Iraqi origin, immediately noticed the newspaper I was carrying under my arm, and she addressed me in fluent Arabic: "Where do you work?"

"I write for the *Al Fajr* newspaper," I told her. Rachel too had a false identity, and introduced herself as a student at the Hebrew University.

"You know," I said, "this area was once the site of the Arab village of Beit Mazmil. I had relatives who lived here. There was everything"—I described a wide arc with my hand in the general direction of the window—"fig trees, olive trees, grapevines, flocks of sheep and goats . . ." I waxed enthusiastic.

My statements failed to provoke the landlady; she merely

took us on a tour of the house and pleasantly showed us the rooms, the closets, and other items of interest to potential tenants. We indicated that the two-room apartment was just what we were looking for. Then Rachel said, "I hope the neighbors won't create problems because of my boyfriend. In other places they refused to rent apartments to us." A distinct expression of disgust appeared on the landlady's face. "With me there are no such things. Jew or Arab, they're all human beings. In Iraq we lived among Arabs and, believe me, things were good for us there."

While Rachel and the landlady discussed the apartment and life in Iraq, I was playing with a gadget in the bathroom. A small radio set had been built into the toilet-paper holder, apparently to provide a pleasant stay for whoever was using the toilet. I turned the knobs until I reached a station that was broadcasting Arabic music. "I swear, my uncle in Amman has the same thing, but his is red," I told the landlady. She smiled and happily drew me into a conversation about life in the kingdom of Jordan. Fortunately, she had never been there.

When the time came to bring negotiations to a conclusion, I informed the woman that we liked the apartment very much, and took a bundle of Jordanian and Israeli bills out of my pocket, expressing my willingness to sign a contract on the spot or to put down a deposit as security. She refused to commit herself. "My husband might already have rented the place this morning and hasn't had a chance to tell me. Call tomorrow and I'll give you a final answer."

Rachel called the next morning. The woman apologized and told her that in fact her husband had already rented the apartment. She wished us well in our future endeavors and asked Rachel to "give my regards to your boyfriend, who seems to be a nice young man." A few hours after that conversation we asked another colleague of ours to call and inquire about the apartment. The landlady gave her all the relevant information, stating that the apartment was still available.

□ □ □

Now, concealed under the blanket in Miri's bed, I waited for her to return from her session with the landlord. I sensed that

86

our relationship had taken on a threatening dimension for her and I decided to provoke her deliberately. "You know, ya Mira," I said to her when she returned, "in a situation like ours, each Palestinian has to do something for the common cause."

She blanched. "What do you mean exactly, Fat'hi?"

"You know, everyone has to act. Although I'm enjoying myself and having a good time in Tel Aviv, the time will come when I'll have to enlist in some organization."

Miri grew pensive. Although we belonged to enemy camps we had been fairly content in each other's company up until then, since neither of us had expressed any degree of political involvement. We had created a kind of warm, comfortable nest that separated us from our environment. Now I had ventured a statement which made it clear that there was no escape from political involvement, that despite the fact that I, Fat'hi, enjoyed the simple pleasures of life, pleasures that had it in their power to unite enemies, I was still what the Israelis were used to referring to as a "potential terrorist."

"And what will you do if you join one of those organizations of yours? Will you hurl a grenade at a bus full of children?" she asked.

"I hope I won't have to do such things. Because I've studied a little, I'll probably have a job that's more connected to teaching ideology and training our youth, who need to be instructed in the tactics of struggle and prepared for carrying out missions. They also have to be taught the methods of interrogation that are used by your security forces and learn what to expect in prison."

"You know, Fat'hi, I know about those things too, but from the other end of it. Tell me, have you ever been in prison? Do you know what it's like at all?"

I swore to Miri that I had never been imprisoned. "My intention in entering political involvement concerns the future and not the past." It was clear that she was trying to hint at something and I tried to find out what it was. "What do you mean, you know about such things from the other end? Don't tell me you work for the Shin Bet or something like that." I was genuinely scared.

"No, don't worry, but during part of my military service I

was stationed with the security forces in Gaza, where interrogations were held."

We lay side by side in bed. I pulled the blanket up to cover Miri's shoulders. In one hand I held a cigarette, and with the other I caressed her body. I asked her what exactly she had done in Gaza. "Your women don't serve as interrogators, do they?" Miri hesitated for a moment. I inhaled the smoke of my cigarette in silence.

"Despite the fact that my Arabic isn't particularly good, I was listed by the army computer as a speaker of Arabic. Because of that I was transferred to serve as a secretary with the military administration in Gaza and after a short period I was given my next assignment—to be present at the interrogations of women who'd been arrested on suspicion of terrorist activity."

From what I had heard from Palestinian women who had been interrogated and released I knew of an internal directive making the presence of a woman mandatory during every interrogation of an Arab woman. This was intended to prevent the woman under interrogation from being alone in a room with only men and to forestall the possibility that she would later complain of being sexually abused. In contrast to reports by Palestinian male suspects that they underwent violent and humiliating interrogations, I had never heard of a woman being abused during interrogation, except for one case, when a woman from Gaza who was held in detention in Jerusalem aborted a fetus, apparently as the result of violence on the part of the interrogators.

But as Fat'hi I pretended not to know about the directive, and asked, "How do they interrogate the women there? Do they beat them severely?"

"No, apart from a slap here and there, there aren't any beatings. But they know their job and where to apply the pressure. There are a lot of shouts and threats. The parents are brought in to cry a little in front of the suspect and they'll ask her to confess and 'be done with it.' In the case of one young woman they found a photograph of her posing in a bathing suit, so they threatened that if she didn't confess they'd make sure that all of Gaza would see those pictures. You know how it is among your kind, the people there would say that she's a whore."

88

I asked her if she had also been present when men were interrogated. No, she told me, the men were interrogated in isolated and soundproofed rooms which no one who was not a member of the interrogation unit could enter, not even the Chief of Staff. "But," she continued, "the prisoners who were waiting to be interrogated were made to stand outside, for many hours, in order to 'prepare' them for the interrogation. Sometimes they were ordered to stand on their feet all night and hold their arms up, and the soldiers who guarded them would hit anyone who got tired. I couldn't watch it."

Miri told me about a prisoner, apparently an important one, who had been forced to carry a heavy armchair instead of just standing and waiting for his turn to be interrogated. "All night he ran from one wall of the prison yard to the other with the armchair in his arms. When I passed by he had already been doing this for several hours. His feet were swollen, his body was burning. It seemed as though any moment his veins were going to burst from the strain. Like all of the prison staff, the soldier who was watching over him knew me. He said, 'Miri, do me a favor, I have to go take a piss, so keep an eye on this prisoner for a moment. The instructions are that he mustn't stop running.' The moment the soldier left I made a sign to the Arab that he could set down the armchair and I approached him. It was like standing next to a furnace. I didn't have water and there wasn't time for me to bring him any, so I spat on my hand and wiped his forehead. That was all I could do and if they'd have caught me I would have been in real trouble."

I had no reason to doubt what she was telling me. Just a short while before, an acquaintance of mine, a religious man with right-wing views who lived in one of the West Bank settlements, told me how shocked he was at what he saw during a recent tour of reserve duty as an officer in Gaza. One night, after making some arrests, the security men covered a prisoner's eyes and instructed him to run at top speed in several directions. "After he'd gotten used to running blindfolded for short distances and had lost his sense of direction, they made him run straight into a wall."

Hearing Miri's stories about the methods of interrogation employed by the Shin Bet, I felt a little like Mata Hari must have felt when she extracted information from the statesmen whom she entertained in her bed. It was mainly a sensation of power, knowing that I was able to use the intimacy of the occasion for purposes which were unknown to my partner. "And how were they as human beings, these interrogators?" I questioned further.

"Like you and me. There were nice ones among them and less nice ones. But you should be aware, Fat'hi, that these men know everything, everything. You have no idea how dangerous they can be, not just for the Arabs but for us as well, for Israelis. When you say that you intend to be active you should know that they are capable of finishing you off before you can feel a thing."

"For us, all those interrogators are dogs," I said.

"This affair I'm having with you now could cause me a lot of trouble," Miri continued, speaking more or less to herself. Then she propped herself up on her elbows and leveled her gaze at me. "Swear to me by all that is dear to you, by your mother, that if they arrest you and interrogate you, you won't say a word about your relationship with me. Whatever happens —being beaten, remaining handcuffed for two days running, or with a sack over your head—you won't mention me. It could ruin me. You hear, Fat'hi? It could ruin me and my family. You don't know yet what they're capable of."

I was surprised by the depth and force of Miri's fear. It's obvious that the Shin Bet isn't a benevolent force, but in Israel the Jewish population generally has no fear of it. Ordinary Jewish citizens simply aren't conscious of its existence.

The following Friday, Miri was supposed to leave for the weekend to visit her parents. She had arranged for an acquaintance, an air force pilot who had to return to his base that same day, to come and pick her up. "He's offering me a lift, but hopes for more," she told me with a conspiratorial smile. We were drinking coffee together as she waited for her admirer to show up. "You can stay here until Sunday," she said, and offered me the key to her apartment. I politely refused. The show I was putting on for Miri's sake was as tiring as my other poses, even if it was more pleasant. I was afraid that one day, or rather one night, I would say something out loud in my sleep that Miri would overhear and the whole thing would blow up.

90

"You know, Fat'hi, I had a dream about you last night," Miri interrupted my chain of thought. "I dreamt that you were coming to visit me with a mask covering your face." This was one of the rare instances during the entire period of my posing when I was totally taken by surprise. I quickly thought of the various occasions on which she could have discovered the truth about my identity. Maybe a girlfriend of hers had popped out of nowhere and had recognized me, or perhaps Yisrael had decided to add a dimension of his own to the project and had revealed the truth to her. "What do you mean, a mask, ya Mira?"

"I don't know. Some sort of dream like . . . strange . . ." I was relieved to learn that Miri hadn't discovered the truth. As for the meaning of dreams, everyone may draw his or her own conclusions.

A few minutes later there was a knock on the door. I rose to open it, but Miri gently pushed me back into my chair and went over to the entrance. I watched, and through the crack that opened I saw a light khaki uniform, sporting one "falafel," indicating the rank of major. "Hi, Ronnie, good morning. Please wait for me outside and I'll be with you in a couple of minutes. . . . No, you can't come in right now. There's someone here." Miri went into the bedroom and quickly packed some personal things.

"Why don't you let him come in?" I asked.

"That's just what I need, for an air force pilot who's infatuated with me to meet my Palestinian lover."

"Wonderful, ya Mira," I said, "If there's any place where a Palestinian is worth more than an illustrious Israeli air force pilot, then it's here in your home."

I decided at this point that the best thing to do was to simply disappear. Our romantic relationship had begun to be a strain on Miri, and I was also getting anxious. It wasn't particularly pleasant to deceive someone as I was doing with Miri, but it was no use crying over spilt milk. At the time I wasn't capable of offering her much in the way of an explanation and to this day I don't believe that an explanation would have helped any.

Yisrael told me that in his opinion I should at least have phoned Miri. Others who learned about the affair, even months after the event, told me that I had behaved dishonorably, like a cad, a low-down heel, a coward, etc. I thought, and still think today, that disappearing was the only way to end the affair; any attempt at words would have been a wasted effort.

So I didn't tell Miri anything. I just left the key to the apartment in the mailbox, and when she phoned Yisrael on Sunday to inquire into the whereabouts of Fat'hi, he answered, as I had requested, "Fat'hi had urgent family matters to attend to and he returned to Balata. He asked me to give you his warm regards."

Several months after the posing project, I was interviewed on a popular talk show on Israeli TV. During the preliminary interview I had with Rivka Michaeli, who hosted the show, I told her the story of Miri and me, in broad outline, without going into details. "What, you didn't even bother to get in touch with her? You're a real scoundrel! During the show I'll ask you about this affair and at least you'll have a chance to apologize on the air."

Immediately after the show, Miri called me up. "I found your number in the phone book. I still can't quite believe it." She had watched the show in her parents' house, in her mother's company. "I screamed. I went berserk. I told my mother that the woman you were talking about was me, and she told me to stop bothering her with such nonsense."

SIX

Secret Number

I HAD OFTEN HEARD Palestinian residents of the occupied territories complain about the rough treatment they receive when they go through Ben-Gurion International Airport. The humiliation of this experience seems to be felt in particular by the well-to-do and the intellectuals, who rarely have occasion to deal with the Israeli security forces. The laborer who is treated roughly at some remote roadblock may be equally proud and sensitive, but he has grown used to confronting the Israeli authorities on a daily basis and will generally respond with indifference rather than indignation when insulted by a soldier or a policeman.

In his book *The Third Way*, Raja Shehada, a well-known lawyer from Ramallah, describes a routine incident with an ironic awareness, and conveys a sharp sense of the grief caused by this unfortunate state of affairs.

Shehada was approaching the airport in his car when he was stopped and subjected to a thorough search, in a rather arbitrary and rude manner. Among other things, he was forced to

spill out a bag of dirt that he had bought for some plants in his
garden, and it was only with difficulty that he persuaded the
soldier in charge to allow him to pour it out on the road and
not inside the trunk of the car. The incident culminated in an
order to dismantle the spare tire of his car. "But I am not a
mechanic and I didn't know how," Shehada writes. "The soldier uttered threatening remarks and looked dangerous. . . . I
opened the driver's manual to the page where it said 'How to
Change a Tire' and began reading the instructions."

Ever since the murderous attack carried out by three members of the Japanese Red Army inside the air terminal on May
30, 1972, in which twenty-six passengers were killed and eighty
wounded, the airport has been under strict surveillance. Fully
armed soldiers guard the roads leading to the airport twenty-
four hours a day. Vehicles bearing Arab license plates are
stopped and the identification papers of the passengers are me-
ticulously checked. At the terminal, plainclothesmen stand on
every corner, wearing loose-fitting suits which conceal their
guns. Arabs who travel abroad are thoroughly searched, and
when they return to Israel most of them are subjected to questioning which can last several hours. It is difficult to argue
against the necessity of such security measures and precau-
tions, but the ways in which they are implemented sometimes
deviate from generally accepted norms.

One incident that I know of illustrates how such "necessary"
procedures are often exploited and directed toward different
ends than those for which they were originally intended. The
case concerned a known collaborator who in part owed his
considerable fortune to his close ties with the occupation authorities. On one occasion, returning from a business trip to
Europe, he expected to receive his customary privileged treatment. To his surprise and dismay, however, he was held for
several hours while the airport security personnel investigated
him. Finally, he was ordered to undress and his body was
searched, as though he was suspected of being a drug smuggler.
For the powers that be, this was apparently a way of letting
him know that he had fallen from their good graces. The man
had tears in his eyes as he told me the story. Like many others,
he didn't object in principle to a tight security watch over the

airfield; he was only upset by the way in which it was conducted.

□ □ □

I wanted to get a taste of what it was like to visit Israel's major gateway to the world in the guise of a Palestinian Arab, so I decided to pay Ben-Gurion Airport a visit. When I asked Hassan to join me, he was reluctant to do so and agreed only after I promised not to reveal the connection between us in the event that I was arrested or interrogated. We would pretend we were there separately, and we each chose the name of a different fictitious acquaintance who was supposedly arriving from Europe and whom we were going to meet.

I donned my proletarian outfit, using a rope instead of a belt to tighten the baggy pair of pants. Once again, I checked my basket and made sure that it contained the regular Farid cigarettes and a copy of an Arabic newspaper. Since this was going to be a deliberate provocation and stood a good chance of ending in a confrontation with the security authorities, I asked Yisrael to follow us in his little Autobianchi and to remain in the vicinity in case things got too complicated.

In order to evoke the treatment that would be given to someone coming from the occupied territories, I wanted to arrive at the airport in a taxi bearing a Gaza license plate. So Hassan and I went to the Arab taxi station on Yefet Street and approached one of the drivers from Gaza. The driver wasn't too keen on the trip. He could foresee trouble and claimed to be in a hurry to return to Gaza, but when I offered him fifty percent more than the standard rate, his opposition wavered and he finally agreed.

We got onto the freeway and within fifteen minutes we had left Tel Aviv behind and reached the exit leading to the airport. A couple of minutes later we were at the roadblock which Raja Shehada described in his book. A soldier raised his arm, signaling us to stop, and instructed the driver to park the taxi on a little traffic isle cordoned off in the middle of the road. He came over and checked the driver's papers and then surveyed Hassan and me. My appearance was far less respectable, which may be why he singled me out, instructing me to get out of the car and go to the prefabricated shed that stood on the side of the road. While this was taking place, a steady stream of Israeli cars continued to pass us on their way to the airport.

A sergeant sitting by the entrance to the prefab seemed to be in charge. He asked me, in Arabic, if I had any luggage.

"No, just my basket with some personal belongings."

"Go get it!" he ordered.

When I reached the car the driver scowled at me and looked like a doomsday prophet whose blackest predictions had come true. I winked at Hassan and returned to the sergeant with my basket, which he took and set down at the foot of his chair.

"Stand straight while I search your things," he barked as he rummaged through the basket and turned out its contents. After he had examined each of the various items, he turned to me again. "So what are you here for?" he asked.

"A friend of mine is arriving from Frankfurt today and I've come to meet him."

"At what time?"

"*Wallah*, I don't know exactly, but sometime before noon. They told me I could check the list of arrivals at the airport to find out exactly."

The sergeant had no patience for the details of my story. He muttered something to himself and cut me short. "*Hawiya!*" he demanded. I took out my tattered blue Israeli ID and handed it to him, sticking to my principle of being truthful with the police or the military where formalities were concerned. The sergeant scanned the document over and over again, then alternated his gaze between the document and me. "This is it," I thought. "The game is over." I'd been identified as a Jew and I was sure that after questioning me for a few minutes he would send me away.

Instead, the sergeant got up from his seat, walked right past me, and approached the taxi. Later, Hassan told me that the sergeant had asked the driver if I was a Jew or an Arab. "The driver said, 'An Arab, can't you see?' " Hassan was then asked the same question. He was scared, and not knowing how much I had revealed, preferred to tell what he knew to be the truth, that I was a Jew. The contradictory answers seemed to confuse the soldier. He came back to me. "Tell me, where did you steal that document?" he asked. "You aren't a Jew."

"That's my ID. I didn't steal it."

He wasn't satisfied with my answer. "All right, then, wait on the side. You'll soon tell us exactly where you got this from," he said, waving my ID in the air.

The sergeant began reading the information from the ID into his walkie-talkie. I waited obediently, and was comforted by the sight of a car that had broken down across the way. The driver had opened the hood and was tinkering with the engine. It was Yisrael.

When he finished communicating his report, the sergeant came over to me. "So tell me, are you a Jew or an Arab?"

"You saw my ID, didn't you?"

"Wait a second, if you're a Jew, then why are we talking in Arabic? Don't you know Hebrew?"

"I do, but you spoke to me in Arabic, so I answered you in the same language."

I switched to Hebrew, but retained a thick Palestinian accent. Within two minutes a white Ford Escort bearing a police license plate reached the roadblock and dramatically screeched to a stop, effectively barring the way of the taxi from Gaza, which was still standing on the traffic isle. A fairly high-ranking police officer stepped out of the car and told me to enter the prefab. When we were inside, the officer turned to me and asked the same question once again: was I a Jew or an Arab? Once again I repeated my answer. "Damn," said the officer, "I've never seen anything like this in my life! A Jew who looks like an Arab and travels in an Arab taxi. I'm going to call someone higher up to deal with this."

Now it was the officer's turn to mumble something into the walkie-talkie. This time a man in civilian clothes arrived, a tall fellow in his early thirties. He came over to where I was standing, by the wall, looked at me closely for a few seconds without saying a word, and went back to confer with the officer. I was told to wait outside the shed while they discussed my case. I was relieved to see Yisrael, still "busy" with his car. Later on he told me that I had seemed pale and scared, even from a distance. Then I was told to go back into the shed. The tall man accosted me and asked, "You claim you're a Jew?"

"That's what's written on my ID."

"So why do you speak Hebrew with such a strong Arabic accent? Speak normally."

"Look, I've been living among my Arab friends for a long time now, and I've gotten used to it. But I'm sure I'll get back my Jewish accent if you let me live here among you for a couple of weeks or so."

The man eyed me with distaste. "Anything but that. Personally, I'm for having you get out of here as fast as possible . . . after we find out exactly what your story is, of course. And by the way, what do you mean about living among Arabs for a long time? What are you doing with them? How do you make a living?"

"I live with friends in Gaza. That's where I'm comfortable," I replied innocently.

"And work? What do you do for a living?" he pressed.

"Whatever there is," I answered truthfully. "Sometimes I work in restaurants, washing dishes, you know. Sometimes as a car mechanic. The main thing is to make some money."

"In Gaza?"

"No. There's no work there. In Tel Aviv."

"And where do you stay in Tel Aviv?"

"Sometimes with friends from Gaza and sometimes in a hotel."

"A hotel?"

"Yes. For Arabs. Some guy in Jaffa rents us beds."

"Ah, I see. Tell me something else, my dear Jew. Have you served in the army?"

I saw no point in lying. They could get most of the information anyway, just by checking my ID number with their computer.

"Yes, I have."

"Where?" I told him the name of my former unit. "That sounds good. Who was your commander?"

"Uri Shoshan."

"What did he look like?"

"*Wallah*, he had a mustache and was kind of tall. Like an Arab."

"Like an Arab, eh?" My interrogator sounded seriously wounded by the comparison.

During the interrogation, the shed, which ordinarily housed

only the sentries on duty, began to bustle with activity. All sorts of policemen and other security personnel arrived on the scene. Some of them offered advice to the team that was dealing with me on how to solve the unusual problem they were faced with, and others merely looked at me as one looks at a strange new breed of animal. My chief interrogator stepped away for a consultation with his colleagues and then came forward again with a new approach.

"Tell me," he asked, "do you work for a government agency or anything like that?" All those present in the room waited expectantly for my answer. In Israel, anything relating to security is held in high regard, and the men who take part in security operations enjoy the esteem and the implicit trust of the population at large. My interrogators must have come to the conclusion that I was engaged in the prestigious duties of an undercover agent. One young soldier looked especially remorseful. Just a moment earlier, as I was standing outside, he had viciously jabbed his rifle butt into my stomach as he cursed all the "Jew maniacs who join forces with the enemy."

Now I'd suddenly become a kind of hero, and my confidence began to perk up somewhat. "I'm not with any government agency. If dressing like an Arab and speaking Arabic and traveling in an Arab taxi is a crime, then arrest me; if it isn't, then I'll thank you to stop messing with me," I said.

"Yes, yes. Everything will be all right. We haven't mistreated you so far, have we? But you must understand that a case like yours isn't a normal occurrence, and we have an obligation to investigate each case. Surely, as an Israeli, you can understand?"

"O.K., so get your investigation over with and let me go," I answered.

"This is getting us nowhere," said the officer. "Let's call Motke," and for a third time the walkie-talkie went into action. Within a few minutes Motke arrived, a man of about forty with the physique of a professional bodybuilder. From the awed silence which greeted his entrance, I understood that he had a special status. He was truly frightening, and I couldn't help thinking that I wouldn't want to be left alone with him in an isolated interrogation cell. If matters ever reached that point, Motke wouldn't even have to touch me—just his fearsome face and overwhelming self-confidence would do the trick. All he would have to do is ask and I would volunteer any information I had. I would reveal the most intimate details of my life, just so he wouldn't lay his hands on me. I had the feeling that others before me had already laid bare their hearts to him.

Motke huddled for a moment with the tall officer who'd been questioning me earlier, and then he approached me in the corner of the room. He brought his face very close to mine. His muscular arm settled across my shoulders in a mock show of threatening familiarity. "I'm giving you your last chance," he declared. I could feel his breath on my face. "Give me your LY or your LK number!"

"Number? What number?"

"Don't play dumb. You know who I am and what I'm talking about. Why cause any trouble if it isn't necessary?"

"I realize that you're talking about something to do with security, mister, something I'm not supposed to know about, but I don't have a secret number or anything like it. I . . . what can I say? I like to live the way I do and that's all there is to it."

My refusal to give the number, apparently an identification number given to undercover agents, only increased the admiration I had earned from the other men in the room, who were following our exchange with great interest. They believed that I was on such a secret assignment that in order to hide any trace that might lead to a connection between myself and the "government agency," I wasn't even assigned a number.

After half an hour of grilling they finally decided to do something with me. I was instructed to get into the officer's car. Motke followed with Hassan, and last in the convoy was the taxi driver from Gaza. We parked next to the airport police station. Motke took me up to one of the rooms and asked me to wait outside while he went in with my ID. Half an hour later he came out, with a terrifying expression. "Well," I thought, "my next stop will be a detention cell and there I'm going to have to tell Motke why I showed up at the roadblock."

He handed me my document with a look that clearly revealed his opinion of characters like me, and he instructed me to get into the taxi and leave the airport at once. I saw no point in insisting on meeting the friend who was supposed to be arriving from Frankfurt.

I spent the ride back to Tel Aviv trying to explain to the driver, who was completely confused, what had happened and what I was actually doing. He wasn't easily convinced. At first he seemed scared; he too must have thought that I was some kind of secret agent and felt that I had used him for my own shadowy purposes. Hassan insisted that I tell the driver the truth, since he feared that his own reputation in Gaza, where such news travels fast, would suffer as a result of his association with me. I showed the driver my Israeli ID and went out of my way to placate him. By the time we reached Yefet Street he was completely won over. In fact, he saw the whole project as an act of solidarity with the Palestinians, and as a personal expression of gratitude he invited me to visit his home in Gaza in the near future, and also gave me a standing invitation to make free use of his taxi whenever I needed it.

SEVEN

Off Limits

IN THE FALL of 1986 full-page announcements appeared in the Hebrew press inviting the public to participate in a giant demonstration that was scheduled to take place in Jerusalem on Tuesday evening, October 7. The demonstration was to be in support of the members of the "Jewish Underground," demanding that they be pardoned and released from prison, where they were serving sentences of varying lengths.

The story behind the demonstration was the following. On June 18, 1980, bombs went off in the cars of two mayors in the West Bank, Bassam Shak'a of Nablus and Karim Halaf of Ramallah. Shak'a lost both his legs and Karim Halaf had one foot amputated. An army demolition expert arrived to check the car of a third mayor, Ibrahim Al Tawil of Al Bireh. When the soldier opened the gate to the mayor's garage, a booby trap exploded in his face and cost him his eyesight.

The three mayors who were targeted were all members of the National Steering Committee, an organization of West

Bank civic leaders who opposed the Israeli occupation and operated under the aegis of the PLO.

Three years later, another act of violence was perpetrated
against the Palestinian population in the West Bank. A Peugeot
van entered the premises of the Islamic College in Hebron, and
its passengers, wearing keffiyehs to disguise their identity,
opened fire and hurled hand grenades at unsuspecting students
who were there at the time. Three people were killed and
thirty-three wounded.

In May 1984, twenty-eight people were arrested by the Shin
Bet. They were all Jewish settlers in the occupied territories
who were suspected of belonging to what had become known
as the Jewish Underground (the Underground for short). Some
were on their way to plant bombs in Arab commuter buses
when they were arrested. During their interrogation, members
of the group admitted to the booby-trapping of the cars of the
mayors, to the Islamic College murders, and to another crazy
plan, which fortunately they never had a chance to carry out:
to demolish the two mosques on the Holy Mount in Jerusalem
in order to make room for rebuilding the Third Temple.

Three out of the twenty-eight men were convicted of murder
and given life sentences; two others received prison terms of
seven years; the remainder received relatively light sentences
and have already been released.

What was particularly distressing about the case was that the
members of this Underground, who had murdered innocent
people and had conspired to fan the flames of religious fanati-
cism throughout the Middle East, were not ostracized by the
society from which they had sprung. On the contrary, to this
day they are embraced by the extreme right as loyal sons who
may have gone astray, but for a noble cause. They did what
others had perhaps thought to be necessary but hadn't dared to
do themselves. The activists of Gush Emunim (the political
movement that advocates expanding the borders of the Jewish
state to encompass all of "Greater Israel," which includes the
West Bank) embarked on a concentrated effort to obtain the
release of the Underground prisoners, including those who had
been convicted of murder. Petitions were circulated in support
of "our beloved sons," and a substantial part of the general
public signed. Heavy pressure was (and still is) brought to bear

upon the President of Israel to pardon the condemned men. The demonstration which was announced in the newspapers was one of the largest ever staged by the Israeli right wing.

The demonstration took place in the square opposite Heikhal Shlomo, the main synagogue in Jerusalem, less than a mile away from the Arab section of the city. A steady stream of people entered the area, which was cordoned off by the police. Most of the men were bearded and wore knitted skullcaps, a style which Israelis instantly identify with a form of religious nationalism tinged with a messianic streak. Some of the men were also armed, in typical Gush Emunim fashion. At the far end of the clearing, a large platform had been raised, decked out with dozens of blue-and-white flags. Many of the demonstrators were also waving smaller replicas of the Israeli flag.

The event was a show of strength for Israel's radical right wing, and my presence there, in my Arab outfit, was an extreme form of provocation. True, the presence of an Arab at such a demonstration was conceivable in terms of ordinary life in Jerusalem; for one thing, the editor of an Arabic newspaper could have sent a reporter to cover the event. Nevertheless, I had a profound feeling of having transgressed some boundary. I was trespassing in an area that was off limits.

I pushed my way through the crowd of demonstrators, signs, and flags and began listening to the speeches about the "beloved sons who were not guilty of any wrongdoing." The prevailing sentiment was that to spray a college campus with bullets and to freely fling hand grenades at students did not constitute a criminal offense so long as the victims were Arabs. Nor was it considered a crime to plant bombs in the cars of public servants, or to demolish buses loaded with peaceful civilians, if those being blown to pieces were Arabs.

I was listening to Rabbi Moshe Levinger, one of the leaders of the West Bank settlers, who went on and on in this vein, when suddenly a hand grabbed hold of my arm, a little above the elbow, and viciously yanked me backward. Turning, I found myself confronting a very red, bearded face which was contorted with hatred. The face rapidly fired questions at me in

English: "Who are you? What are you doing here? Where are you from?" Before I could answer, more angry faces joined the first one and I was surrounded by excited, overwrought, flag-clutching demonstrators. They had temporarily set aside the demand to pardon their imprisoned heroes, and dutifully turned to the immediate task on hand, the investigation of a newly exposed security risk—me.

"This is a public place and it is my right to be here," I protested feebly.

Under the circumstances, I could hardly have chosen a less effective argument. Some members of the crowd seemed convinced that this time they had a real, bona fide terrorist on their hands. Curses, kicks, and blows rained down on me. Curious newcomers, inquiring what it was all about, received this illuminating explanation: "There's an Arab here!" A voice in the mob cried out, "Get out of here! You have nothing to do with us!" I undoubtedly would have complied with this helpful suggestion if only I could have freed myself from the tight grip in which I was being held. And so the hysterical shouting went on: "We've caught an Arab, call the police! Quick!"

A path opened up in the crowd as people moved aside to let a border policeman through. He came up to me with an expression of stern authority on his face, and without wasting words led me away. As we left the cordoned-off area of the demonstration, we were joined by two of my captor's colleagues, young border policemen like himself. Together we crossed the street, headed toward Heikhal Shlomo, and went past it to the back where there was a very dark and narrow alley. Yisrael, who had stayed close behind us up to that point, couldn't follow us there without becoming conspicuous. There wasn't a living soul in that alley at that moment except me and my guardians; for some reason, the streetlights were out as well. These cops have a devilish knack for finding—right near the greatest commotion—the kind of dark and isolated corner which is perfectly suited to their purposes.

"Stand up straight!" I was ordered, and a direct punch in the stomach immediately followed. It was more a statement of who was boss here than an act of gratuitous violence. However, it was powerful enough to make me double up in pain, in violation of the instruction I'd just been given. A second policeman countered the effect of the blow by shoving a crooked finger under my chin, like a hook, and abruptly pulling me back to an upright position, which was a sort of grotesque parody of a soldier standing at attention. They announced their next decision: "All right! Now we'll take out everything he's got in his stinking pockets." All they found was a keffiyeh, a bunch of keys, and a wallet. Faced with these harmless objects, they made a great fuss over the keffiyeh, spreading it out and examining it from all sides. At this point I began to be afraid; maybe carrying a red keffiyeh in my jacket pocket constituted some sort of misdemeanor that I hadn't heard of. They returned the keys and the wallet to me, but one of them tightly wound the keffiyeh around his hand, as if underscoring the point that I wasn't going to get it back soon. "Now take out your ID." I was released with another blow, this time to the back of my neck. I hastily drew my Israeli ID from my wallet and fearfully handed it over. I knew that this humiliating experience could continue for hours. The policeman examining my document whistled in surprise. "We've caught a big fish here! He's got a false ID. I'm taking him over to the patrol car, and you"—he turned to his subordinates—"keep very close watch from behind so he doesn't escape." The two policemen obediently positioned themselves behind me while the one in charge escorted me, steering me by the arm. "Come on, you bastard. We're taking you to our superior now; then you're going for a ride to detention, and on the way we'll take care of you in such a way that you'll never forget it as long as you live."

The blows that were urging me to move along abruptly ceased the moment we reached the well-lit street. I was taken to a jeep of the border police that was parked across from the demonstration. A giant of an officer, well over six feet tall, accepted my ID and keffiyeh with as much satisfaction as if he'd just been presented with a firearm taken from a captured terrorist. Then he instructed me to wait a short distance from the jeep while he spoke into his walkie-talkie. He reported that an extremely suspicious ID had been found on the person of an Arab who was just apprehended at the Gush Emunim demonstration, where he had been loitering with no apparent purpose. Then, as he waited for the results of the inquiry that was being conducted on the other end, he turned back to me. "So how did you get that document and what are you doing here? You'd better tell me everything now because later it'll be much less pleasant for you."

I resisted at first, but very quickly realized that he'd be getting the information on my ID within a few minutes anyway and that he would then have two alternatives: he could either release me or detain me until my story was thoroughly double-checked. My body still ached from the blows I had received only a few minutes earlier and I had no desire to ride even one meter in the jeep with his men. I quickly came up with an alibi. "Look," I explained, "I'm studying to play the part of an Arab in a movie, and I even have a still photographer here with me. You can ask him." I pointed at Yisrael, who was standing nearby among some other photographers who were covering the event.

The officer turned to Yisrael. "Is it true what this Arab is saying? Do you know him?"

Yisrael shook his head in denial. "Look, I'm just taking pictures. I don't know who he is or what he wants from me."

The officer eyed me like a man relishing a well-prepared delicacy. "So you're lying. We'll settle accounts with you very shortly." A few minutes later, however, the opportunity for the action he had been looking forward to was snatched out of his hands. Over the walkie-talkie came instructions concerning my ID. It seemed that the police computer already had a file on me, no doubt as a result of my previous encounter with the authorities at the airport. The officer wasn't able to hide his frustration as he gave me the welcome news. "I'm giving you three minutes to get out of here, and don't you dare enter the area of the demonstration or you'll be arrested."

This time I had no intention of compromising. "I have a right to be present at the demonstration," I insisted.

"All right," the officer conceded, "but without that red keffiyeh. If I see you with the keffiyeh, I'm arresting you on the spot." Of course, there was no legal basis for this demand either. His job, as a policeman, was to protect me even if I went in there with half a dozen keffiyehs, but I had no strength left for further arguments.

I took the keffiyeh, which up to that point had had the effect of a red cloth waved before a bull, hid it beneath a bush, and then returned to where the action was. The demonstration was about to end. The flags were raised up high and the crowd began to sing "Hatikva"; they must have felt that invoking the Israeli national anthem was an appropriate gesture in support of Jewish terrorists.

Of course, the moment I reentered the fenced-off area, another good citizen caught hold of me. He huffed and he puffed and in a heavy New York accent he asked, "Where are you from?" I got mad and answered him, also in English, that if he wasn't a policeman he had better let me go, since I had no intention of going along with his game. He began tugging at me and shouting, "Get out of here or I'll call the police!" It seemed as if the presence of an Arab at their demonstration simply frightened the people of Gush Emunim.

I lost my patience and roughly shoved my persecutor away. He ran off to get the police, and I could just imagine him pestering the irate officer who had been forced earlier to let me go. With total illogic, I fantasized that the policeman would arrest my assailant in my stead. As all this was taking place, people all around me continued bravely singing "Hatikva." They stood motionless as they sang, but I couldn't remain still and moved restlessly about. Even though I was an Israeli Jew, their *tikva* (hope) was certainly not mine.

◻ ◻ ◻

In the eyes of the adherents of Gush Emunim, people like me are traitors to the Zionist cause. To me, the Jewish settlers in the West Bank and the Gaza Strip represent a danger that may lead me to seek my future elsewhere, in order to remain true to my own understanding of how to live a decent life. The situation is potentially a disastrous one, for the right wing is unlikely to accept a decision to return the occupied territories. They are absolutely sincere in what they are doing; they believe in the historical right of the Jewish people to what they call Eretz Yisrael, or the Land of Israel. By this they mean Greater Israel, which includes the West Bank, as opposed to the State of Israel within its pre-1967 borders. They view the Jewish settlements on the West Bank as an existential necessity. Should a democratically elected government of Israel, supported by a majority of the population, agree at some point to relinquish the settlements and retreat from the whole or a part of the occupied territories, there are quite a number of fanatic nationalists who would resist such a move with armed force.

During the course of some twenty years in a hostile environment, the settlements of Gush Emunim have amassed a formidable arsenal. Every Jewish household in the occupied territories has a handgun at the very least, and this minimum is far exceeded in most cases. In Kiryat Arba, for instance, the leadership has openly stated that the local Jewish residents are stockpiling firearms and other weapons so they will be able to defend themselves against a "Jordanian army" or against "Palestinian militias." Despite promises that "no Jewish citizen will ever raise arms against a Jewish soldier," prominent leaders on the right have vowed that they will not allow the return of the Sinai to serve as a precedent. When the Camp David accords were implemented and the Sinai Peninsula was returned to Egypt, the Jewish settlements in the Sinai, including the town of Yamit, were evacuated, but only after a traumatic showdown between the Israeli army and the Gush Emunim settlers, which left a strong impression on Israel's collective consciousness.

The West Bank is charged with religious-nationalist sentiments to a far greater degree than the Sinai. For many Jews the holy sites, such as the Cave of Machpela in Hebron and the Tomb of Rachel in Bethlehem, constitute the heart of present-day Jewish existence. In the event of a decision to compromise on territory in return for a peace agreement, the extremists on the right intend to act in accordance with "the everlasting will of the Jewish people, irrespective of any particular time or place." This formulation can easily be construed as an argument against the legitimacy of a democratically achieved decision. As a result, this fanatical fringe, which is a messianic outgrowth of the nationalist fervor that swept over Israel in the aftermath of the 1967 war, could bring the State of Israel to the brink of civil war.

Kiryat Arba, the Jewish neighborhood which lies adjacent to the city of Hebron, is regarded as a stronghold of the hard-core radicals of Gush Emunim. It was built largely on vineyards which were confiscated from the family of Muhammad Ali Jaabari, the late mayor of Hebron. One of the approximately four thousand Jews who reside in Kiryat Arba today is a grandchild of Ali Jaabari, who converted to Judaism, served in the Israeli army (in the Intelligence branch, no less), and married another convert with the aim of establishing one more Jewish family in the West Bank. The young man is a known supporter and member of Meir Kahane's abhorrent Kach party, which advocates a mass deportation of Arabs from the occupied territories. It is worth noting that Kiryat Arba is the only place in Israel where the Kach party is represented on the local council.

Kiryat Arba was established in the wake of the 1967 war. When the Israeli Defense Forces captured Hebron, the Arabs feared that they would be harshly dealt with. They recalled the 1929 pogroms in which approximately ten percent of the seven hundred Jewish inhabitants of their city were murdered. In the end, revenge came not in the form of a massacre but rather in the form of a huge influx of Jews who established a relatively dense presence in Hebron.

Gush Emunim was a new and active force in those days, and the renewal of the Jewish settlement in Hebron was high on its agenda. On Passover 1968, a group of religious Jews appeared in the city along with their families. They rented rooms in the Park Hotel and expressed their desire to conduct the traditional Seder there. At their head stood Rabbi Moshe Levinger, then a young and charismatic religious fanatic who was destined to become one of the leaders of Gush Emunim.

Fahed Al Kawasme, whose family owned the hotel, didn't realize that by renting out rooms to the seemingly harmless band of religious devotees, he was helping to initiate an era of mutual hatred, terror, and animosity between Jews and Arabs in the conservative Islamic city.

After Passover the group refused to leave Hebron. In the Israeli Knesset a powerful lobby formed, backing the group's demand to exercise its "historical rights" and settle there. The military government, bowing to the pressure, avoided removing the intruders by force, which would have meant risking direct confrontation, and transferred them instead to a military barracks within the city. Later, some land was appropriated near Hebron, a protective fence was erected around it, and

111

Kiryat Arba was built. To this day it is a symbol of renewed Jewish settlement in the city and in the entire West Bank. The Palestinian Arabs, from their point of view, regard Kiryat Arba as a prime symbol of Israel imperialism.

□   □   □

After attending the Gush Emunim demonstration in Jerusalem, I decided to pay another visit to Kiryat Arba, which I had often visited in the course of my journalistic activities.

The Jewish settlements in the West Bank are connected to a network of "circumventing roads" that allow an Israeli Jew to reach the settlements without having to go near any Arab towns or villages. As an Israeli journalist once put it, "It is possible to drive around the West Bank for an entire day without seeing a single Arab." On the road from Jerusalem, there is a left turn less than one mile out of Hebron, opposite a district of workshops where glassblowers ply their ancient craft, using techniques that have remained unchanged for centuries. A road sign at the turn spells out the destination: "Kiryat Arba." Unlike the other roads in the vicinity of Hebron, which are in a state of disrepair, this one is smooth and cars speed along it without any trouble.

Kiryat Arba was constructed hastily and at a minimum cost, and it shows. Tall apartment buildings, crowded together, loom in the distance, looking out of place against the rest of the landscape. The neighborhood is enclosed by a fence. Adjacent to the fence stand Arab homes, single-story houses with yards, which fit into their environment more harmoniously than the fortresslike Jewish towers which rise defensively above their surroundings.

When I arrived at the entrance gate to Kiryat Arba, I found two bored reserve soldiers stationed there. I was in my Palestinian guise. In Kiryat Arba, as elsewhere in Israel, Arab laborers worked in construction and in the few local factories and were therefore a common sight. So the soldiers allowed me to enter without bothering to check my identification.

During that period the local council had adopted a resolution to fire all its Arab employees, who up till that time had worked

112

mainly as street cleaners and municipal gardeners. It was a racist resolution with no legal basis, yet as far as I know it was executed without any difficulty. This enlightened ordinance meant that most Arab workers seldom had occasion to stray from one straight and narrow path: the main street that led directly from the entrance gate to the small industrial area. I deliberately chose to walk along the inner streets of the residential quarter. This earned me some murderous looks from the local inhabitants. As if to add to my discomfort, the streets were lined with posters of Meir Kahane.

I have often heard Jewish settlers claim that they respect their Arab neighbors and stress the good relations they ostensibly enjoy with their workers or with the shopkeeper around the corner. They boast that they, who live in close proximity to the Arabs, are the only ones who really understand the "Arab mentality," unlike advocates of the left-wing peace camp, who, they argue, live in Tel Aviv and have never spoken to an Arab in their lives. I believe that such claims are hypocritical and dishonest. The settlers' relationships with the Arab worker or grocer may be reasonably civil, but practically all the residents whom I encountered in the streets at that late morning hour had guns barely concealed beneath their clothes. It hardly seems a model of peaceful coexistence and neighborly friendship.

I wandered around aimlessly for a while, and after having a cup of coffee at a café, I returned to Jerusalem. There wasn't much for a self-respecting Palestinian to look for in Kiryat Arba.

□ □ □

Most of the residents of Kiryat Arba work in Jerusalem and commute to the city every day. Many of them who aren't politically committed were tempted to purchase apartments in Kiryat Arba because of the low price and other incentives that the government housing agency offers to settlers. Public spending in Kiryat Arba is disproportionate in other respects as well. There are more public buildings there than in other communities of a comparable size, and a greater percentage of the residents draw salaries from state-funded institutions than is the case elsewhere. Although Israeli politicians repeatedly deny it, the fact is that considerable sums of government money continue to be spent on establishing, and maintaining, Jewish settlements in the West Bank, at the expense of other national objectives.

Before the 1967 war the number one priority, in terms of government investment, was the "development towns." These were provincial towns that were expressly built for the purpose of housing the many new immigrants who arrived in Israel during the first years of its existence as an independent state. Surely it is a paradox that the inhabitants of these development towns are mostly in favor of a policy that calls for the annexation of the occupied territories and for continuing the state assistance given to the Jewish settlements.

To the list of failures of the Israeli left, I would add this: that they haven't exploited the issue of economic priorities in order to mobilize support among the disadvantaged sectors of the population, at a time when the right, with its clear-cut nationalist message, has succeeded in attracting a high percentage of voters precisely from those quarters.

This line of thinking led me to go have a look at Beit Shemesh, which is located some twenty miles west of Jerusalem. Beit Shemesh is a typical development town; hastily established and settled with new immigrants in the 1950s, it is beset with grave economic and social problems.

The first thing I did on my arrival was to go to the local snooker, as Israelis call their version of the penny arcade. It was conveniently situated in the center of town, in a large cellar adjacent to the storerooms of the local supermarket. There were around ten youths leaning over pinball machines and other contraptions which for some reason I've never been able to figure out.

Yisrael, who as usual was following me from a distance, entered and sat down at a table at the far end of the hall, where he immersed himself in a game. I strode right up to the counter and purchased five shekels' worth of tokens. I was rather at a loss, however, because I didn't quite know what to do with them, and must have given the impression of being totally helpless.

114

Some of the local youths, who'd been following me with their eyes since the moment I had entered, volunteered, in Moroccan Arabic, to initiate me into the mysteries of the arcade. The number of tokens I had purchased was apparently extraordinary by Beit Shemesh standards, and soon everyone present was standing around me, eagerly counseling me on how to press a button in order to send a silver ball flying most effectively toward a series of colorful, noisy targets.

I wasn't very surprised to learn, while exchanging a few words with the youths, that they were all unemployed. "You Arabs work cheap and it's more worth our while to receive unemployment than to work," they told me. As they were offering their advice on how to play the games, I heard a few expressions such as "This Arab's gonna strip us clean" and so forth. But I took this to be no more than light, almost affectionate banter. The only outward expression of hostility that I was aware of was a juicy curse in Arabic which I couldn't help overhearing as I left the snooker. All in all, I had found the atmosphere to be quite relaxed and friendly.

The main square of Beit Shemesh can be described with one word—provincial. I sat down at a table in an outdoor café, unfolded my Arabic newspaper, and observed the few people who were loitering about in the middle of the day. I ordered a cup of coffee and was promptly served by the waiter, who then retired indoors to continue his chat with a few men who were sitting by the counter. Yisrael arrived and seated himself at some distance from my table, where he struck up a lively conversation with a young soldier.

After a while, the waiter returned and sat down facing me. I hadn't invited him to join me and I felt that it was a little strange. I thought that perhaps he wanted to have a talk with me, but he just stared for a while, then got up and returned to his friends. Some snatches of their conversation reached my ears. Apparently they were speaking of military matters, for I could hear them mentioning the names of some weapons. A woman came out of the café and I thought she looked at me with a smile. Someone else came out after her, meandered over to the phone booth across the street to make a call, and then went back inside the café. I felt at ease. Nothing was happening, just as nothing had happened when I walked through the

115

streets of Kiryat Arba. At that moment it seemed as though Israel was a free country after all, even for a Palestinian Arab. After going through the newspaper for the hundredth time, I rose and turned to leave.

The car was parked a little way off from the center of town and when I got there I waited for Yisrael to join me. Suddenly, for no reason that I could think of, I was overcome by a burning desire to get away. Yisrael soon arrived, walking so fast he was almost running. "Let's move, Binchu! Get in quick and let's go before they see us!" I was curious to know the reason for his panic, and the moment we got outside the town limits, I switched on my tiny tape recorder. Yisrael summarized what he had seen. "You're lucky we got out of there. Another few minutes and it would have been the end of you."

"What are you talking about? They were quite nice, actually."

"What? You didn't notice?" I didn't understand what he was talking about. He explained: "In the snooker, after you left, they cursed you and all the rest of the Arabs. They followed you to the café. The boys who were in there said that you had a lot of gall to sit there waving a picture of Yasir Arafat on the front page of your newspaper, just one day after grenades were thrown at soldiers near the Wailing Wall and Arafat admitted that his organization was responsible for the attack. They said you should be taught a lesson. Remember the fellow who went over to the pay phone?"

"I remember."

"He was calling Kahane's people. They were going to beat the shit out of you. Remember that waiter who sat opposite you and stared? He was checking you out. They thought that maybe you'd come to commit some act of sabotage. And the fellow with the stick?"

"Who?"

"Just as you were leaving, there was a guy who passed you."

"Oh yeah, now I remember!"

"Didn't you feel him bring his stick down right next to your foot?"

I hadn't noticed. Although I had appeared calm throughout my uneventful stay in Beit Shemesh, the truth was quite the opposite. In fact, I had been so tense that I had shut out any manifestations of hostility that had threatened me. At some level, of course, I must have known about the potential risk, but I reacted by withdrawing from reality to such an extent that it couldn't get through to me at all.

EIGHT

Kibbutz

MY POCKET DIARY states that on Sunday, October 19, 1986, I was doing my best to be accepted as a volunteer by a kibbutz. For years the kibbutzim have accepted volunteers from Europe and the United States. The volunteers stay for any length of time and are employed in a variety of jobs, according to the requirements of the kibbutz. In return they receive room and board and a small allowance, and every few weeks they are taken on trips to various sites in Israel. The volunteer program is conducted as a tourist and public relations project, and it works well for both sides. The young travelers can remain in Israel for a relatively long period of time, and they become more thoroughly acquainted with the unique lifestyle of the kibbutzim than an ordinary tourist would, and at very little cost. The kibbutzim, in turn, gain a supplementary labor force, generally unskilled, which can perform seasonal agricultural work that is often urgent, and at very little cost to them as well.

So far, my experience as a Palestinian among Israeli Jews had been limited to contact with those who routinely exploit Arab laborers or else those who are charged with the responsibility of looking after the security of Israeli society and therefore regard every Palestinian with suspicion. It seemed to me that to include a chapter on the kibbutzim, and their attitude toward the Palestinian population, would help to give a more balanced view on the society in which I grew up. The kibbutzim are probably the best representatives of the moderate left in Israel, with its liberal ideology which stresses equal rights for all members of the human race and its high regard for the dignity of labor. I expected that I would still be treated as an Arab rather than as an individual, but imagined that in this case my supposed Palestinian identity would work in my favor. However, I quickly learned that fear, suspicion, and prejudice against Arabs existed no less among the kibbutzniks than among other Israeli Jews.

The kibbutz movements have opened offices in Tel Aviv to handle the large volume of requests from potential volunteers. The offices are supplied by the various kibbutzim with information about their conditions and what kind of help they need; volunteers are directed accordingly.

In order to make a preliminary inquiry about volunteering for a kibbutz I decided to approach the office of the United Kibbutz Movement, which is located in a rickety old house by the sea. I took Yisrael along with me as an "Israeli friend" who would vouch for the purity of my motives, in case any suspicions were aroused by the sudden descent of the volunteering spirit on an unknown Palestinian.

There were a number of fair-haired young people in the reception room. They had propped their backpacks against the wall and were absorbed in the glossy brochures with color photographs of cows and combine harvesters and other information that the kibbutz movement deems beneficial for potential volunteers. Yisrael's attention was immediately caught by a long-legged blonde, whom he regarded with undisguised interest; then he turned and gave me a grudging smile as if he'd hit upon the essence of the life I was about to experience and was jealous. I ignored him and proceeded to leaf attentively through some brochures until I got tired of them, and finally just sat, one leg crossed over the other, dangling in the air, waiting for my turn to be interviewed. As the others came out of the office, they seemed to be in an enthusiastic mood, returning to their friends who were still waiting and telling them excitedly about the kibbutz to which they'd been referred.

To the casual onlooker, my appearance (dark unshaven face; striped jacket over a white shirt) may have seemed odd among all the young drifters in their torn shorts and colorful T-shirts. But no one in the reception room reacted noticeably to my presence; they apparently viewed me as just another exotic character in a foreign land. From listening to their conversations I learned that no one had come for a prearranged appointment. They had all just arrived spontaneously that morning and by noon they were on their way to their respective kibbutzim, where they would be graciously received. A tall young man who was last on line when I arrived came out of the office and indicated that I should enter.

Two women sat behind desks in two different corners of the room going over lists, most likely detailing the placement of the volunteers who had been processed that day. "Have a seat, please," one of them said in English, without raising her eyes. I sat down, and Yisrael, who had come in with me, drew up a chair for himself and settled into it. My gaze rested on the secretary's face and I saw that she was staring at mine, her eyes wide open and blinking rapidly. She looked at me and then at her colleague, who had likewise put down her paperwork and was staring at me. My appearance, as well as the newspaper and cigarettes which I had placed on the table before me, left no doubt in their minds that I was a true Palestinian. Any further questions on the matter were unnecessary. The receptionist continued looking at me, then at Yisrael, then at the other woman, and back to me again. If, at that very moment, I had gotten up, taken a broom in my hand, and begun to sweep the office, she would have accepted my being there more naturally than she could accept me facing her like that, sitting in a chair which up until a moment ago had been warmed by an aristocratic European behind.

"I want to volunteer to a kibbutz, ya madam," I finally said, breaking the silence in English laced with a thick Palestinian accent.

"What???"

"Yes, I want to volunteer," I repeated, and went on to explain that I wished to become better acquainted with the Israeli way of life, and that since the kibbutzim were a model socialist society which upheld the ideals of peace and equality ("I heard that they even demonstrate for a Palestinian state"), I was very interested in getting a closer view of it. "Who knows?" I asked. "Maybe one day I will establish a kibbutz for our people in Nablus."

The woman in front of me addressed the other clerk despairingly, in Hebrew. "See this guy? He wants to volunteer. What shall I do?" Much to her dismay, the other woman merely spread out her hands palms up, as if to say, "It's your problem, you deal with it."

Suddenly the secretary turned back to me, her face lit up, as she had an inspiration that she thought would help her get rid of the unwelcome customer. "I'm very sorry, we only deal with volunteers from abroad, not with Israelis."

"Good, good. Then this is exactly the office which I need." I got up rather clumsily and pumped the limp hand which she extended. "My name is Ali Hussein, from the Balata refugee camp near Nablus. According to your laws, Nablus, West Bank, is foreign territory. So I am exactly in the right place."

I sat down again and stretched out in my chair. It was one of the few times that posing as an Arab afforded me a feeling of superiority and a position of strength that allowed me to view the situation with plenty of irony. But I could see that there was no point in even dreaming that a kibbutz would be arranged for me on the spot as it was with the other volunteers.

"Give me your name and phone number and we'll get back to you with regard to your request." The message was clear—it was "don't call us, we'll call you." I insisted that she give me the name of someone in charge whom I could contact by phone and she wrote down a name and the office phone number on a slip of paper. Then she went through the motions of taking down my data. I stated the name and address that were on my Jordanian ID but the Arabic sounds didn't register and finally, in desperation, the woman handed me a notebook and asked me to write it down. "Write it down here." I feigned total unconcern as I scribbled in English: "Ali Hussein, Block 27/15, Balata camp, Nablus."

Over the next few days I tried, several times a day, to contact the official whose name I had been given. I called so often that the switchboard operator learned to recognize my voice, but my man never seemed to be in.

I was afraid that the scheme of volunteering as a Palestinian for work on a kibbutz would fall through, so I was forced to consider a compromise and devise an alternative approach, involving an old acquaintance of mine, Daoud Kuttab, the editor of the English-language weekly *Al Fajr*.

□ □ □

My good relations with the editorial board of *Al Fajr* had started by chance. About a year before I began my posing project a friend approached me with a bundle of tattered photographs that were yellowing with age. "I found them in a garbage can on Harakevet Street in Bak'a. There are a lot of other papers there. Maybe you'll find them interesting?" Bak'a is a neighborhood in Jerusalem that had been built and populated by wealthy Arab families. After 1948 the buildings were occupied by Jews. I went over there immediately. The garbage can that my friend had described was brimming with old papers and files, in English and in Arabic, and a few dozen family photographs. Some of the papers had been blown by the wind along the railroad tracks that ran parallel to the street. I crammed everything I could get my hands on into the sidecar of my motorbike. My dog, Katanchik, sat on top of the pile and his weight was sufficient to keep it from all blowing away.

When I sifted through the material at home I realized that I had the entire history of a well-to-do Arab family spread out before me. The Jewish tenants of the house had apparently been cleaning out the storeroom and the old records of the Farah family, onetime owners of the house, were thrown out. A brief inquiry on the phone, with the aid of the staff of *Al Fajr*, revealed that one member of the family, a man responsible for agricultural development projects in the West Bank, lived in East Jerusalem. I brought the papers to his house and with great excitement we went over the old photographs of his family, friends, and in-laws. Daoud Kuttab, who had assisted me in locating the man, wrote up the story in his paper. In retrospect,

I realize that I was rewarded for my simple gesture of common decency with connections and an openness that would ordinarily be obtained by a journalist working with a suspicious and hostile community only after many years of continuous activity. So it wasn't easy, of course, for Daoud to refuse my unusual request.

☐ ☐ ☐

Daoud gave me a letter which stated, "Ali Hussein is employed by us. His assignment is to write an article about life on a kibbutz. We thank you in advance for any assistance that will be given to him." Daoud hesitated at first to provide me with the letter, claiming that "it could get us into serious trouble with the authorities." But eventually he grew enthusiastic over the idea and asked me to really write something for his paper. I thanked Daoud for the letter but politely declined his request to write the article.

With the letter in my pocket, I called Shlomo Leshem, spokesman for the United Kibbutz Movement. "I'm a correspondent for the weekly *Al Fajr,*" I told him, "and would like to write something about life on an Israeli kibbutz. Maybe you can arrange for some kibbutz to receive me?" Leshem, an experienced spokesman, provided me with a long list of kibbutzim all over the country. I spoke with several of the kibbutzim and the responses ranged from "Leave us alone. We're afraid of journalists, they always screw us" (Aharon Sadeh from Kibbutz Palmahim), to a genuine willingness to accept me.

I was about to contact Kibbutz Ortal in the Golan Heights, where the kibbutz secretary had agreed to host a Palestinian journalist. But before going ahead, I decided to check with my friend Amit from Rosh Pina. I knew he had ties with various kibbutzim in the north and wanted to see whether he could get me into one without my having to pose as a journalist. I preferred to be a regular participant in kibbutz life rather than marked as an observer from the sidelines. I could practically see the mischievous twinkle in Amit's eyes as he said, "Wow, that would really be something! I know just who to ask— friends of mine from N——. They're a middle-aged couple, but they're all right and I think they'll help." Amit assured me that his friends from the kibbutz could keep a secret, but expressed his doubts that I would be able to successfully maintain my pose in a kibbutz. "They see you there day in and day out, twenty-four hours a day. Are you sure you can fool them?" After posing for three months I was confident both of my skills as an imposter and of the gullibility of almost everyone. "I'll be careful not to be identified. You just try to get me in as fast as possible," I answered rather impatiently.

Amit explained my plan to his friends, Irit and Avraham Ron (not their real names), who were keen on the idea, and the three of them brought the matter before Dalia, the kibbutz secretary. Dalia was indecisive and kept postponing her answer. In the meantime I moved in with Amit in Rosh Pina so that I would be ready to make my move as soon as we got a green light. But after stalling for as long as she reasonably could, Dalia announced that "accepting an Arab volunteer was conditional on the approval of the general assembly."

The general assembly is a central feature of kibbutz democracy. Every important decision that affects life on the kibbutz must be brought before all the members. After a discussion in which every member has the right to express her or his opinion, the issue at hand is decided by a majority vote. Decisions might include: the initiation of a new industrial enterprise; setting priorities in the allocation of resources (so much for construction, so much for agriculture, etc.); or granting a year's leave to a kibbutz member desiring to try out life in the city or to study or travel.

I really wasn't interested in waiting for the general assembly's verdict, for it meant further delay and increased the possibility that my candidacy would be rejected. At that stage, so Amit later told me, Irit and Avraham intervened in my favor. They leaned on Dalia, arguing passionately for the liberal approach that was officially endorsed by the kibbutz ideology. At last the secretary capitulated and agreed to accept me according to the same procedure that was followed for any other volunteers. (Her decision later earned her scathing criticism on the part of those members who were adamantly opposed to my presence in their kibbutz.)

As a final condition, Dalia insisted on interviewing me in

person before committing herself. So one evening Amit and I paid her a visit.

"*Asalamu aleiki*, Miss Dalia, my name is Ali Hussein," I introduced myself. "I am happy to be in your kibbutz and thank you for accepting me."

After discussing various technical details about the status of a volunteer on the kibbutz, Dalia finally said, "You know, not everyone will like it . . . the fact that you're here, that is."

"Look," I answered, "if there's any trouble, I'll simply leave."

My answer apparently satisfied Dalia and we shook hands, agreeing that I would return the next day, Thursday, November 6, in order to begin my term as a volunteer. We also agreed that Irit and Avraham would be my foster parents in the kibbutz, since they had already made my acquaintance and had expressed their willingness to have me. Assigning a foster family to newcomers is a common practice in kibbutzim. Its purpose is to help them adjust and feel at home.

To the right of the road entering the kibbutz, just beyond the iron gate, stands the cow shed. When a car speeds by—for instance, a red Citroën bringing a new volunteer to the kibbutz— the cows stop feeding for a moment and follow the vehicle with an expectant gaze as it goes by. Then they resume chewing their cud complacent as before, their heads wedged between the fence rails. The Citroën, meantime, continues on its way until the road ends in a small plaza. Situated around this circle are the communal dining hall, the administration building, and well-tended lawns. The lawns are divided by narrow concrete paths that spread out in all directions, radiating from the center like the spokes of a wheel and leading to the homes of the kibbutz members. Beyond the living quarters are the industrial buildings, and the poultry and livestock areas are even farther from the center, bordering on the wire fence that surrounds the kibbutz.

The fence, the entrance gate, and the silence that dwelled in the very center of the kibbutz where I now stood (all the members being at work at that hour) imparted a feeling of isolation, as if I had entered a separate kingdom that was detached from the surrounding land.

126

Dalia was already waiting for me in her office. She introduced me to a young man by the name of Eran, who was the liaison appointed by the kibbutz to take care of all matters relating to the volunteers. I followed Eran to the clothes warehouse, where I received a couple of blue work suits that were patched in several places and seemed as if they'd been in use for many years. We continued from there, Eran pushing his bicycle and I walking beside him. I noticed that he walked with a pronounced limp. He wasn't very communicative and consistently avoided looking directly at me. Thus, in tense silence, we reached an old shack that had obviously housed the kibbutz pioneers a long time ago and now served to house the volunteers.

Eran broke the silence. "I hope you don't mind sharing a room with someone. You see, we have a large group now and not enough room." He had the defeated look of a man who is constantly being rebuked. "It's fine. I like company," I reassured him. As we parted I gave him a firm handshake and tapped my chest, out of habit, with my right hand while still holding his. Eran swallowed hard, jumped onto his bicycle, and pedaled at top speed to the dining room without once turning back.

The bare walls of the room testified that it had been occupied by temporary residents for a long time. The window looked out on the lush green lawn. One of the beds in the room was in a state of disarray and the few personal belongings of my roommate, who was absent at the moment, were scattered next to it. On a small table in the center of the room sat an electric kettle, four tins of black coffee, and a plastic bag with plain biscuits in it. I took out my pad and, writing in Arabic, recorded a few impressions. Then I stretched out on the bed with a big grin and the feeling that I had just gained a victory.

I was startled out of my sleep by someone who was shaking me by the shoulders and speaking English with a thick German accent. A blond-bearded face, adorned with a broad smile, was leaning over me. "By God, I can't believe it! How lucky I am that the Arab volunteer has been put in my room. Really great luck. Pleased to meet you." He extended his hand in greeting.

"My name is Josef Feurstein, from Munich. Already a few days ago I heard that an Arab volunteer is supposed to arrive. All the kibbutz is talking about it. It's really lucky that they put you here. My friends call me Yup."

"Pleased to meet you, Yup," I answered in my best Anglostinian.

Yup went over to prepare us both a cup of coffee. Then we proceeded to establish our acquaintance. There was no doubt about his pro-Israeli position. He was one of those young Germans who are remorseful about the Holocaust and its consequences and who come to Israel in order to atone for the past, insofar as atonement is possible. His sympathy for Israel was accompanied by a corresponding negative opinion of the Arabs. When he asked me the standard question: "Tell me, Ali, why do you choose the path of terror and murder innocent people?" I explained, with as much patience as I could muster, that the words "Arab" and "terrorist" are not synonymous. At the same time, I found myself inadvertently giving him a lesson on the realities of the West Bank. His utter lack of knowledge about what went on in the administered territories was revealed when he asked whether "the refugee camps in the West Bank are surrounded by barbed-wire fences and watchtowers." (This has never been the case. The residents of refugee camps are free to come and go exactly like the rest of the population in the occupied territories, except that curfews, arrests, and house searches are more frequent there.) It was around seven when we finished talking and went over to the dining hall.

The dining hall was located in a large two-story building in the center of the kibbutz. At the building's entrance stood dozens of bicycles, the most convenient mode of transportation within the confines of the kibbutz. Members who had come directly from work in the cow shed or the orchard, left their muddy work boots near the door. As I stood waiting for a sink to become free, so I could wash my hands, the kibbutzniks who went by eyed me with curiosity. I ignored them and went up to the second floor together with Yup.

Entering the dining hall was without a doubt one of the more unsettling events that I experienced during the entire posing project. Three hundred pairs of eyes were simultaneously raised from plates filled with potatoes and schnitzel in order to stare at me. Conversation stopped and a hush descended on the large hall. There were all sorts of faces there: bespectacled, mustachioed, dark and pale, young and old, but the stares all conveyed the same sensation—a tremendous curiosity mingled with fear. It was the fear of a stranger who had somehow penetrated their barriers and was threatening their warm and protected existence. When I stood in line at the counter and piled food onto my plate I felt their eyes boring holes into my back. I followed Yup to a table where some of the volunteers were sitting together and we joined them. I carefully folded my keffiyeh to the dimensions of a small handkerchief and struggled to wipe the nervous grin off my face.

The following morning, at breakfast, the probing stares had scarcely diminished. After the meal a husky fellow with a mustache came up to me and said, "I'm Shlomo, the work coordinator. For the next few days you'll work in construction." I looked uncertainly at the big pistol that stuck out prominently from the belt of his work trousers. Later I asked one of the members if everyone on the kibbutz walked around carrying a gun in his belt, and was told that only the work coordinator was armed, "in case terrorists get in here and try to do something."

Construction work was performed by an outside contractor named Nissim. I quickly learned to appreciate his skills as a master craftsman, and I would often use the title Hawaja (Mister) when I addressed him, as an expression of friendly respect. As on previous occasions, my working skills served as the best means of overcoming the suspicion and even hostility with which he regarded me at first, and we became a kind of team, with him in charge and me as the diligent helper. The only new thing about working on a kibbutz was that in the dining hall Nissim would invite me to sit next to him, and occasionally he'd peel a cucumber for me or pass the salt. After meals I would always prepare him a cup of strong black coffee.

Nissim and I were renovating the kibbutz nursery school, which entailed breaking down walls, modernizing the wiring and the plumbing system, and replacing the floor tiles. One day, when we were in the middle of work, the nursery-school teacher arrived with a boisterous flock of children. They had

129

come to see the palace that was being prepared for them. The children ran all over the place among the buckets of concrete and stacks of floor tiles that were scattered on the sand floor. They looked up the ladder to where I was standing. "What's your name?" they asked. "My name is Ali." I smiled at them. One of the children tugged at his teacher's sleeve and dragged her over to the ladder. "Look, look how Ali is fixing things for us on the roof." The teacher made a fine effort to give me a friendly smile, asking, "Well, and where are you from, Ali?"

"I'm from the Balata camp, near Nablus."

"And where do you live?"

"Here, on this kibbutz."

"What do you mean, here on this kibbutz?" She was taken aback. I repeated myself. Nissim, who'd been listening to our conversation, quickly stepped up and gently took her aside for a brief explanation of the situation.

On another occasion the woman who was in charge of coordinating all the building and construction activity on the kibbutz came to inspect our work. "And how is he?" she asked, pointing at me.

"Excellent," Nissim answered. "I've never had a volunteer who works the way he does. As soon as I saw what he's capable of doing I sent all the other volunteers away."

"Well, what do you expect?" she replied contemptuously. "He's an Arab."

The main social event in the routine life of the kibbutz, at least for the young people, was the discotheque dancing held on Thursday nights. The discotheque was located underground, in the central bomb shelter, which had been given to the kibbutz youth for their use. They had installed a decent stereo system, dim lighting, and a bar where beer was available. The first time I went there Yup introduced me to some of the volunteers whom I hadn't met before. Apart from Yup himself, they all belonged to a group which had come from Denmark. One young Dane with flushed cheeks offered to share his beer with me and I politely refused. I was determined to adhere to all the restrictions that a Moslem who came from a traditional society would follow. For this reason I wouldn't dance and so I stood by the wall and attempted to strike up a conversation with some of the female volunteers. Talking to them spared me from having to hide my knowledge of Hebrew. The first and most important thing they had to tell me was about a trip they had been on, a few weeks prior to their arrival at the kibbutz. They had visited the Old City of Jerusalem and some Arab youths had tried to flirt with them. According to the Danish girls, their admirers hadn't restrained their hands from getting a feel of their foreign charms. "Why are you like that? That isn't the way to flirt with a girl," they exclaimed. I spent the remainder of the evening in a desperately defensive and irritating position, trying to explain that not every Arab who fancies a tourist girl will make such a direct pass.

Some of the volunteers exhibited a wariness of me, and a few days later I discovered why. When they had first arrived, a certain kibbutz member, who was a native speaker of Danish and therefore in charge of the group, had given them a cautionary talk, warning them of the dangers they should look out for during their stay in Israel. One of those dangers, she told them, was the Arabs. They mustn't befriend Arabs, and under no circumstances should a hitchhiker accept a ride in a car driven by an Arab, because it was tantamount to risking murder or rape. That same kibbutz member, my informant told me, was one of the most ardent opponents of my being accepted as a volunteer, and had gone so far as to threaten that she would prevent other groups of volunteers from coming if I was accepted.

There was one person on the kibbutz who actively sought my company. I'd noticed a small, slightly balding man, who looked as if he suffered from a perpetual cold, sending timid looks in my direction. After a few days he got up the nerve to greet me from afar. A few more days went by and the man finally approached me in the dining hall, glancing around as he did so in order to gauge the response to his abnormal act. He introduced himself, saying, "My name is Mike and I would very much like to talk to you." He was extremely hesitant and his conversation with me seemed to demand a great deal of courage on his part.

Mike was thirtyish, a bachelor, and had come to the kibbutz from England. He was at the time a candidate for membership in the kibbutz. (Someone who wants to join a kibbutz is first required to live and work there for a year, during which time members can become acquainted with the candidate and get an impression of his suitability and skills. After the trial year they decide, in the general assembly, whether or not to accept the candidate as a member.) He didn't have a regular work assignment but performed various jobs according to the needs of the kibbutz. The social side of his life was rather grim; although he had a foster family that was supposed to help him integrate into the kibbutz, he remained something of an outsider.

Mike seemed to be very appreciative of the fact that I had come to the kibbutz despite, as he put it, "the prejudice against us that exists among you and the trouble you might get into with your extremists." I often had the feeling that I was vicariously fulfilling a secret fantasy of his to perform an adventurous deed that would break the monotony of working in the avocado orchard, eating in the dining hall, and watching the Friday movies—to go and volunteer for a Palestinian kibbutz, for instance.

One evening Mike approached me with a suggestion that sounded crazy even to me. "Ali, what do you think of lecturing to the members about the feelings of an Arab in the occupied territories and about the special problems that you have there?" I almost burst out laughing, but I somehow managed to contain myself before giving my assent. That evening I borrowed Yup's racing bicycle and rode to Amit's home in Rosh Pina in order to give him the news. Then I returned to the kibbutz and immediately began planning my forthcoming lecture, which was to be given in English. After a couple of days of euphoria and a feeling that I was about to achieve the pinnacle of my posing project, Mike informed me that the coordinator for cultural affairs was emphatically opposed to the idea. Guest lecturers are frequently invited to kibbutzim. (After the story of my posing was publicized I was asked to lecture in a number of them.) But apparently the woman in charge of the cultural welfare of the kibbutz and those who supported her were afraid of allowing a direct confrontation that might go beyond the bland bounds of a standard lecture on current affairs. In order to make up for the lecture's being canceled Mike wanted to invite me over to his foster family for coffee and cake, but that also fell through. "They're opposed to your staying here and refuse

132

to have you in their home for a cup of coffee," he told me, crestfallen and with a note of bitterness.

Mike was a good source of information about the general attitude that prevailed in the kibbutz with regard to my stay there. According to him, there were many members who argued that an Arab volunteer shouldn't have been accepted without first being cleared by the authorities in charge of security. The argument that such a permit wasn't required for other volunteers didn't convince them in the least. But those who were pleased with my presence didn't dare say so in public for fear of creating a conflict with the others.

I had another informant in addition to Mike. Once every few days I used to go over to Avraham and Irit's house. Avraham was usually off at his job, which was outside the kibbutz, and Irit would make me some coffee. Then she would tell me all the gossip about what was going on in the kibbutz. The hours I spent there were very precious ones. It was the only opportunity I had to let off steam and be more or less myself. Irit told me about an argument over my job placement. There had been an attempt to give me assignments that were considered more "prestigious" in kibbutz terms, such as at the repair shop or the factory, where solar heaters were manufactured. But the men in charge of those places refused to employ an Arab. The repair shop included a modern facility where automatic transmissions were rebuilt. It was a very successful enterprise that brought in enough income to assist other, less profitable ventures. The men who worked there behaved accordingly. In the dining hall they would stick together; like a cohort of aristocrats in stained work clothes, they had their own table, which nobody else was allowed to join.

Irit confirmed what Mike had told me: "There are people who say that we should check with the Shin Bet to find out if you are a PLO spy. They say it's a scandal that you were accepted here without a decision of the general assembly." One of the theories was that I was taking advantage of my stay there to study all the exits and entrances to the kibbutz so that when the time came I'd be able to assist terrorists who were planning to stage an attack there. This was a most absurd claim. When the need arose, a whole crowd of hired Arab laborers would be brought to the kibbutz from the nearby villages or from the

West Bank. They were employed in construction, the same type of work that I was engaged in. These workers enjoyed total freedom of movement and no one ever thought of doing without their inexpensive services out of fear of espionage or anything else.

On one occasion Irit warned me that some of the more militant members were toying with the idea of seizing me one night and giving me a sound beating, so that I would renounce, once and for all, the notion of staying on the kibbutz. That evening, as I was leaving, Irit asked me with motherly concern to look after myself, "because some of those people are capable of hurting you." I returned to my own room in the volunteers' quarters with a heavy heart. Even Yup's friendly chatter and a visit from two smiling Danish girls didn't cheer me up. It was becoming clearer and clearer that the majority of the kibbutz members considered me an unwelcome intruder. Outwardly, however, everyone maintained an attitude that ranged from polite formality to subdued friendliness. No member ever came up to me and told me to my face that it would be better if I got the hell out of there; all their objections were raised in the privacy of their rooms.

Such indirectness on the part of Israelis who belong to what is called the moderate left reminded me of a political "event" I had taken part in during the period when I was still waiting to hear from a kibbutz that would accept me as a volunteer. A group of Israeli left-wing activists, together with some Palestinian associates, staged a demonstration to protest the fact that the "green line," the international border that separated Israel from Jordan until 1967, seemed to have vanished from Israeli political consciousness. The location they chose for the demonstration was in the vicinity of Latrun, about twenty miles from Jerusalem.

I arrived at the scene in my Arab guise and joined a few dozen demonstrators who were walking along the dirt path that led to the spot where the border had been prior to 1967. There, on a bare exposed hilltop, we congregrated. Among those present were several people I knew from Jerusalem. I did

134

my best to be inconspicuous, and my simple tactics of evasion paid off—no one noticed that Yoram Binur was around. Nor did my presence there as Fat'hi arouse any special interest.

An Israeli artist unraveled a few dozen yards of green plastic canvas and symbolically stretched it across the desolate landscape to reaffirm the existence of a border that had long ago ceased to serve any practical function. The participants raised placards that were seen by no one but themselves, and after sitting in the warm sun for a friendly chat and drinking from the canteens that they had brought along for the ten-minute hike, they headed downhill again and returned to their cars. From their point of view, the demonstrators had contributed their two cents' worth and had provided a topic of conversation for the next week or two. Most of them, I'm willing to bet, hadn't seen the inside of a refugee camp in years. All those who were present at that isolated spot shared the same convictions, most of them belonged to the same educated class, and many of them were personal acquaintances. So the "happening" had been a pleasant and agreeable experience, rather like sitting in an air-conditioned lecture hall. There was an aura of naïve confidence, a feeling all around that "if we're here, then things can't be so bad."

The solidarity of the left-wing demonstrators didn't extend so far as to include Fat'hi Awad. Nobody approached me to ask who I was, where I was from, how I had heard of the demonstration, or just to have a conversation with me. I believe they avoided me mainly because of the uneasiness and discomfort that many Israeli leftists feel when confronted with Palestinian Arabs. A guilty conscience manifests itself as a form of estrangement and alienation, which is what happened in Latrun that day, and is also what happened on the kibbutz. With me as Ali in their midst, the kibbutz members were given a golden opportunity to live up to their liberal ideals within the confines of their own homes, but instead some got scared while the rest vigorously opposed the "experiment."

Writing about what happened in the kibbutz isn't easy. It's difficult for me to criticize these people, whom I prefer to the zealots who believe they have a monopoly on patriotism. I am able to understand their apprehension and discomfort when confronted by someone who threatens their peace of mind. Yet the fact that they avoided raising the issue in a straightforward manner really troubled me.

□ □ □

I was busy at work one day when Eran, the member in charge of the volunteers, showed up and asked me to come see him during my lunch break. "And don't forget to bring your ID card with you," he added somewhat brusquely.

I experienced a familiar but unexpected wave of anxiety as I put my Jordanian certificate into the upper left pocket of my shirt. I could already imagine myself being asked, politely but firmly, to take the back seat of a Ford Escort or Opel sedan, which are the cars most often used by the Shin Bet in Israel. The curtains over the windows would be drawn, of course, and I would be driven to some obscure installation to be interrogated. And I could imagine the sack, the *shabah* as it is called, being draped over my head, exuding a faint smell of urine.

However, no car was waiting for me next to the administration building. Eran, who was in his little office, took my ID and turned it over and over again, unable to understand what the Jordanian Ministry of the Interior had inscribed on it. He closely examined the photograph of Ali Hussein that was on the ID and threw a quick glance at me. I held my breath but nothing happened. Next I read to him the document number, which he dutifully wrote down. Eran then made several photocopies of the document. "What are the copies for?" I anxiously asked him. "We do this with the documents of all volunteers. It's the normal procedure . . . for insurance purposes," he lied through his teeth. I shrugged, left the office, and went back to work.

That evening I wrote in Arabic, on a small slip of paper, "Here live Ali Hussein and Yussuf Feurstein." After I read it to Yup, and also obligingly wrote his name in Arabic in his diary, I fastened the note to the door of our room with a thumbtack. I wanted anyone who might be looking for me, for better or worse, to have an easy time finding me.

Soon after, I found out that a photocopy of my ID was in fact handed over to the Shin Bet. The person who told me about it said, "They returned the copy with the comment that there wasn't any security file against the owner of the document and that he wasn't considered to be involved in any form of hostilities." Either the Shin Bet knew what I was up to and decided not to interfere or else whoever reviewed the Jordanian ID was not up to date and didn't know that Ali Hussein had in reality been shot and returned to his Maker. In any case, I was never again bothered with formalities of that kind.

By the time Mike asked, "Where did you pick up such good Hebrew?" I already knew that I was becoming careless. The game didn't interest me any longer. I did not care to explain to Mike and others why, like the vast majority of the population in the occupied territories, I supported the PLO. Nor did I find any satisfaction in endlessly demonstrating the simple fact that Palestinians are human beings, who not only are concerned with the Israeli occupation but entertain other feelings and desires as well. One shouldn't have to go to such great lengths, I thought, in order to prove such an obvious point.

Surprisingly, the dramatic improvement of my Hebrew didn't arouse any suspicions. When I first arrived at the kibbutz I spoke only a few words of Hebrew and limited my conversation to the subject of Arab-Israeli relations and the predicament of the Palestinian people in the occupied territories. Within a few days I doubled, and then exponentially multiplied, my Hebrew vocabulary. After three weeks on the kibbutz I noticed that I was speaking Hebrew almost fluently. I was barely sticking to the typical guttural sounds that are characteristic of all speakers of Arabic, or to the confusion of p with b. I also succumbed to a longing for the written Hebrew word. All the volunteers, myself included, received the English-language *Jerusalem Post*. Several scandals had hit the front-page headlines around that time and most prominent among these was the mysterious kidnapping of Mordechai Vanunu, "the atom spy." I began peering over the shoulders of the people at my table in the dining hall in order to catch a glimpse of their newspapers. I finally broke down and approached Eran: "Be a sport, ya Eran. Fix it so I can get the *Yediot Aharonot* in the mail."

"What do you need it for? It's in Hebrew, isn't it?"

"Well, umm . . . I actually decided to start studying Hebrew. A kind of crash course. And if I have a newspaper I can speed up my progress."

My request was duly taken care of.

At the same time that I started reading the Hebrew newspaper, I began to make bolder social overtures. I went to the discotheque again and decided that I was tired of standing alone, leaning against the wall as if I had taken a vow of celibacy. Wanting to join the fun, I invited a pretty young kibbutznik to dance with me. After two weeks on a kibbutz, even the most devout Moslem would have done the same, I am sure. But while the poor girl was ashamed to refuse my invitation, she was equally afraid of being seen in public dancing with an Arab. So we hopped up and down facing one another from a safe distance. Her face wore such a tortured expression that one might have thought she was being interrogated mercilessly in some godforsaken prison cell. I consider it to her credit that she later came and apologized to me for the embarrassing experience. I was captivated by her shy smile, despite her extreme coldness.

A young man who had noticed the strange dance came up to me. He was slightly drunk. He held a beer in one hand while with the other he thumped me on the back, exclaiming, "Right on, Ali. Don't pay any attention to these jerks. Dance and enjoy yourself as much as you can. I want you to know that there's a whole gang of us who are rooting for you. We know that you took a risk when you came here, and we admire you for it."

When I returned to my room later that evening, I found the same young man sitting at ease on my bed, drinking a cup of coffee he had helped himself to. Tamir was a lad of seventeen, with a lean muscular build. The beginnings of a beard sprouted in tufts between the pimples on his face. He told me that he devoted his spare time to the upkeep of the kibbutz stables.

"I have an uncle in Zarka who breeds horses and who taught me all about it," I replied.

The next day we worked together in the stable. Tamir gave me a curved prong with which horseshoes are scraped clean and watched how I tended the hind legs of one of the mares.

"Wonderful, Ali. I can see that that uncle of yours in Jordan really taught you." I seemed to have passed the test. When I

138

noticed the kibbutz boys using cooking oil to lubricate old saddles, I fetched a can of engine oil. While not ideal, it is definitely better than cooking oil, which causes the leather to deteriorate. Tamir acknowledged my contribution with a sort of gracious clearing of the throat, like a monarch accepting a gift from one of his loyal subjects, and immediately handed it to a redheaded youngster who was brushing a saddle clean. With an authoritative kick in the pants he sent the kid off to try out the new stuff, promising him that he would soon be coming to check his work. "Watch out if the saddles aren't oiled properly," he warned. I couldn't help but see Tamir, who hadn't yet been drafted, as a successful officer in an elite army unit.

I was invited to a birthday party for Amos, one of Tamir's friends. As I approached the house, which wasn't far from my own, I could hear the music coming from within. It was quiet music—Dire Straits. I paused for a moment before going in; for some reason which I couldn't quite figure out, the house seemed familiar. As I stood at the bottom of the three steps leading to the front door, all of a sudden I remembered. Two days earlier, Nissim, my boss, had asked me to climb onto the roof of that same building in order to clear away the piles of pine needles that had accumulated there over the years, and to tar the gaps that had formed between the roof tiles. The knowledge that I had repaired the house which I was now entering as a guest gave me a strange feeling.

"*Ahalan wesahalan* Ali." Tamir was trying out his broken Arabic on me. "*Marhaba, ya shabab,*" I answered with a smile, feeling as if we were all actors in a strange play. I sat down on one of the mattresses that were spread on the floor. The host had one arm draped nonchalantly around the shoulders of one of the Danish girls. Looking around, I noticed another girl, a small dark Israeli whom I hadn't seen before. One of the youths was speaking to her in whispers. On the upturned crate that served as a table were a pitcher of orange juice and a bottle of cheap Israeli vodka. This evening I didn't refrain from drinking, and as I swilled the vodka I couldn't help thinking how much my behavior had changed during the three weeks I had been on the kibbutz. I had gone from refusing to dance or drink all the way to pursuing a fairly active social life in the company of anyone who was willing to accept me.

139

As the conversation got off the ground, it turned, quite naturally, to a discussion about me. Tamir and Amos made frequent references to "those disgusting jerks who don't want you here." They mentioned the names of those who were most strongly opposed to my presence on the kibbutz, and they had a nasty comment about each. For me, on the other hand, they had only praise. "Really, Ali, we think that you're one hell of a guy, you're something special." I thanked them for their support and asked them to pass the vodka. As the evening progressed I began using Hebrew quite freely. I felt like telling everyone that my name wasn't really Ali but Yoram, just so they would leave me alone with their nonsense about Palestinians and the occupation and all the rest of it.

The goodwill which Tamir and his friends showered upon me so generously was a reflection of why I prefer young people in general—because of their capacity to accept things as they are, without evoking all sorts of doubts, fears, anxieties, and prejudices. They are direct and to the point. No doubt, too, that their loudly advertised sympathy for me was a manifestation of their rebellious attitude toward the establishment and toward the restrictive society in which they were living.

The free and easy sexual behavior at the party made me increasingly aware of my own feeling of deprivation. As I related some details of my "biography" (the refugee camp where I grew up; Bir Zeit University, where I'd studied economics; my work as a garage mechanic in East Jerusalem), I was fantasizing about holding one of the girls in my arms off in some quiet corner. Later, when we were quite drunk, Amos took out a white sheet and we each wrote something on it as a memento. I took the felt marker and inscribed a popular Arabic saying: *"Nik nik wala tastanik wala taalam erak ala kasal."* Amos was thrilled when I translated it for him: "Screw, screw, don't hesitate, so your cock won't grow lazy."

Around this time, with the help of Irit's intervention, I was transferred from construction work to an activity that most of the volunteers were employed in: picking avocados. For quite some time I'd been telling anyone who was willing to listen that I had a lot of experience as a mechanic, but all attempts to

have me employed in the factory or in the repair shop continued to meet with staunch opposition from those in charge. The
truth was that I had grown fond of the construction job, which
employed only Nissim and me. Our relations were very much
improved. He told me about his family, about the problems he
had with the kibbutz, and about his philosophy of life in general. The work hours were easy as well, and I didn't have to
wake up early or make any extraordinary effort. Work in the
avocado grove, on the other hand, began at four in the morning, when we would be thoroughly soaked by the dew as we
squeezed ourselves in among the branches in order to get at the
fruit. The advantage of the job was that it brought me into
closer contact with the kibbutz members and with the other
volunteers. The latter were almost exclusively employed in
picking avocados and in working at the dining hall.

One evening I found Tamir in my room, drinking a cup of
coffee, which he habitually helped himself to with typical kibbutznik chutzpah. "Has anyone spoken to you yet, Ali?" he
asked in a worried voice.

"About what?"

"Last night the volunteers' quarters were broken into and
some foreign currency and passports were stolen. People are
saying you're the one who did it. The police are supposed to be
coming here to investigate the matter." A routine police
checkup could mean the inglorious end of my sojourn in the
kibbutz. The false accusation stemmed, of course, from the fact
of my being foreign and different. "Damn all small, restricted
societies!" I thought. I was sick and tired of the kibbutz. Every
morning I went off to work in the avocado grove, followed by
the daily sequence of dining hall, room, conversations with
Yup or other volunteers, supper, and bed. I was tired of seeing
the same people every day. And now, to top it off, I was a
criminal by common consent.

I decided that I should leave the kibbutz and conclude that
phase of my posing. That evening I told Dalia, the kibbutz
secretary, "I phoned home and was told that my father is very
sick. So I have to go for a few days in order to look after him.
I'll be leaving tomorrow morning." Dalia was sorry to hear
that I had to leave—she had grown to appreciate my diligent
and conscientious work—but she promised that she would con-

vey the information to the work coordinator. Next I informed Irit that I had had enough of picking avocados to last me a lifetime. I packed my belongings and explained my situation to Yup, who tried his best to get me to invite him to my home in Balata. Tamir, who heard that I was leaving, almost crushed my hand when he came to say goodbye, and expressed his hope that we would meet again.

In the morning, as I was waiting for Amit to come pick me up, I learned that during the night someone had broken into the kibbutz store and had stolen a few items and some money. The circumstantial evidence was clearly not in my favor. My story about a sick father could easily be construed as an excuse for my hasty departure, which, of course, it was. But I had no intention of staying on in the kibbutz just to establish my innocence.

The electronic gate of the kibbutz remained open after we passed through it, as if to say that now that the Palestinian threat had been removed there was no further need to defend the place. I took off the keffiyeh that was tightly wrapped around my neck and shoved it deep into my basket, which I chucked into the back seat of the car. Amit concentrated on driving, while I helped myself to a pack of Noblesse cigarettes which I found in his jacket. I've been smoking these cigarettes for years, and it was with unrestrained pleasure that I lit up and inhaled the smoke. My mind was blank. Well, not exactly. I was thinking about an attractive woman I'd met a couple of weeks earlier at the pub in Rosh Pina and wondering if there was any chance I'd be able to meet her that evening.

For several weeks after leaving the kibbutz, I spent most of my time back home in Jerusalem, lying around in an inebriated state. I was doing a poor job of relaxing; my recent experiences kept coming back to me, disrupting my peace of mind. One day I received a newspaper from Amit. It was a regional publication, and Amit had marked one of the articles in it. I assumed it was one of those pieces about the occupation that some of my friends insist on sending me, so I set it aside. Then I received a phone call from Amit that spurred me to take a second look at the newspaper. The title of the article was "Arab Volunteer Stirs Protest in Galilee Kibbutz." It took me several minutes to realize that it was about me; when I finally did, I read it over and over again. The article read as follows:

"A West Bank Arab, 39-year-old Ali H., was recently accepted as a volunteer in one of the region's kibbutzim. Ali's presence has been causing an uproar and many members oppose his stay on the kibbutz for security-related and other reasons. Members are complaining that such a sensitive issue was not presented to the general assembly for discussion.

"Ali, a car mechanic, reached the kibbutz on the recommendation of Jewish friends from the village of Rosh Pina whom he had met in leftist circles. His request was brought before the kibbutz secretariat, which responded affirmatively, after consulting the coordinator in charge of volunteers and a family that agreed to provide him with a foster home after working hours.

"The secretariat believes that nothing out of the ordinary has taken place despite the ensuing controversy. In every case where a volunteer arrives independently of the Kibbutz Movement, the matter is brought to the secretary's attention, to approve the matter. In this instance some members believed that the general assembly's approval should have been sought as well.

"The volunteers' coordinator said that as far as criteria for accepting volunteers went, there had been no evidence that Ali was involved with drugs or alcohol abuse.

"Ali recently went to visit his family and has not yet returned to the kibbutz. He announced that his father was sick, but there were those who saw a connection between the fact that he hasn't come back and the latest events in the West Bank, which must have put the young man in a delicate position with regard to his relations with Israelis."

NINE

Jebalya

MY POSING PROJECT was originally intended to be carried out among Israelis, whose reactions and attitudes toward the Palestinians working in their midst were my main concern. After my experience at the Coliseum Halls, however, I became interested in investigating the background of the day laborers who perform all the dirty and unpleasant jobs in Israel's cities. They come mostly from the lower classes or from refugee camps, whose residents are the poorest among all those living in the occupied territories. I decided that Jebalya was where I'd make my first attempt at posing as an Arab in Arab surroundings, precisely because it is an extreme example of living conditions under Israeli military rule.

Jebalya is one the largest refugee camps in the area which Israel occupied in June 1967. It was hastily erected by the United Nations Relief and Works Agency (UNRWA) on a site located to the southwest of the city of Gaza, in order to provide temporary shelter for the tens of thousands of refugees who fled to the Gaza Strip in the aftermath of the War of 1948. (In

Israel this war is known as the War of Independence; the Arabs term it the Catastrophe of 1948.) They came from Arab towns and villages in the southern part of the new Jewish state, such as Majdal (Ashkelon), Sdud (Ashdod), and Yibneh (Yavneh). As time went by, Gaza grew in size and the refugee camp developed alongside it—a shantytown on the outskirts of the city where seventy-five thousand inhabitants still live in cramped and squalid conditions. This "temporary" camp has been standing for forty years. It was here, on December 8, 1987, that the first riots started, which quickly spread all over the West Bank and the Gaza Strip, forming the beginning of the current full-scale uprising, known as the Intifada.

I approached my journalist friend Hassan Jibril and asked him to assist me in entering Jebalya under my assumed identity of a West Bank Palestinian. We made an appointment to meet at his home in Shati. From there he was to take me to Jebalya, and he would introduce me to the contacts he had recruited in the meantime.

About an hour's drive along the coastal road south of Tel Aviv, one meets the tail end of a long line of vehicles moving at a very slow pace. Half an hour later, the Erez barrier comes into sight. A watchtower looms in the center, its sides padded with a protective layer of sandbags, a machine gun mounted on top. Large concrete blocks prevent approaching cars from speeding up. These deterrents mark the dividing line between the democratic State of Israel and the occupied Gaza Strip, administered by Israel's military representatives. In order to contain the entire installation, the road has been broadened at this point. One can imagine that from the perspective of someone who is flying by in a helicopter—a Prime Minister, let us say, or a Minister of Defense—the road looks somewhat like a boa constrictor which has just swallowed a rabbit, a thin hose that swells at a certain point and then returns to its ordinary thickness. About fifty thousand workers travel through this swelling from Gaza to enter the borders of Israel every day. The border police stop only those who are considered particularly suspect, since it is impossible to check on everyone.

A disheveled reserve soldier, tired of seeing the hundreds and thousands of cars going by day after day, wearily waved my taxi through. Yisrael accompanied me. (We had decided that he'd join me for my first day in the refugee camp, and I planned to introduce him as Daniel, an Italian photojournalist interested in documenting some scenes of the Israeli occupation.) The taxi continued on its way until we reached Gaza.

Because it was more than a year since I had last visited Shati, I had forgotten the exact route to the camp, so we stopped for a drink at a coffeehouse in the city of Gaza, where we could ask for directions. It was a large place, and empty except for one young man who was seated not far from us and who honored us with an impudent stare. The view from the coffeehouse took in both the military administration building and the Gaza jailhouse, which together formed one compound, surrounded by a barbed-wire fence. After we finished our cups of sweet tea I went over to the counter to pay our bill. To my surprise, the manager refused to accept any money and hinted that the young man in the corner had already paid for us. I protested politely and walked over to thank our benefactor, who had apparently made note of the fact that we were strangers in the area. I took the opportunity to inquire how we could reach Shati, but instead of giving helpful directions the young man began to question me about who we were going to meet there. Of course, I had no intention of revealing Hassan's identity, so I gave him a false name. After a brief conversation it turned out that the fellow was convinced that the purpose of our visit to Gaza was to purchase drugs, most likely hashish. He did his best to intercept the deal that he believed we were going to make in Shati and tried to persuade us to be his customers. Finally he escorted us to the taxi, all the while rolling a sizable portion of hashish between his fingers, right out in the street where anyone could see it. He made me promise on my honor that in the future if we ever needed hashish we would purchase it only from him.

The insistence with which this brazen character interrogated me about the purpose of our visit wasn't surprising. Neither was his boldness in openly displaying a quantity of hashish. It is very rare for the military authorities not to know about criminal activities within their jurisdiction. In addition, drug dealers do not enjoy a very high status in the Arab underworld, as Islamic law forbids the use of drugs. So those who wish to turn a nice profit by dealing in drugs often serve as informers, and

147

in return the authorities are willing to look the other way. The special interest that the young crook showed in us no doubt derived from his practice of conveying information to some agent about his encounters with people who were on their way to Shati.

We picked Hassan up at his home in Shati, returned to Palestine Circle in the center of Gaza, and from there went to Jebalya. There are still some remnants of asphalt on the road to Jebalya, dating from way back when. But the thinly spread surface has mostly disappeared under the sand.

Sand similarly covers all the streets and paths inside Jebalya, threatening to swallow any vehicle that isn't equipped with front-wheel drive. To reach our destination we had to leave the main street of the camp and then drive through a sandy lot where several car skeletons were scattered about. Chickens and countless children immediately surrounded the car, which we abandoned as soon as it began to sink. Proceeding on foot, we wended our way through an intricate maze of alleys.

From the houses sewage pours directly into open canals that run through the camp like ugly, foul-smelling scars. The streets are so narrow that one man barely clears their width; on both sides his shoulders will brush against walls that are covered with sheet metal and corrugated iron. Laundry hanging in the streets makes them seem even narrower. I also noticed something that struck me as rather curious. On practically every clothesline, carefully laundered plastic bags hung among the worn-out raggedy clothes. It was not until later that I learned that the bags are used by men to carry their lunch with them when they go to work inside Israel.

Hassan introduced us to Fat'hi Raban, my contact in Jebalya, the only person in the camp who knew who I really was and why I was there. I also knew a few things about Fat'hi. He was an artist who, about five years earlier, was arrested and sentenced to prison because of the "incendiary"—that is, nationalistic—nature of his paintings. Israeli artists and members of the left rallied to protest his imprisonment and staged demonstrations in Tel Aviv and in front of his home in the refugee camp. Fat'hi and I were to become much better acquainted during the course of my stay in Jebalya. Although he knew that I was in

148

fact called Yoram, he got a kick out of the fact that my alias was the same name as his, and he would address me as Fat'hi even when we were quite alone and safely out of the range of prying ears.

Hassan, Fat'hi Raban, and I held a brief consultation, after which Fat'hi took us to the house where I was going to stay for the next couple of weeks. Streets in the refugee camps have no names. Each block has a number and every house in the block has a number. An address is composed of both numbers separated by a slash—for instance, 28/6. There aren't any postmen either, and all mail is delivered to the local shopkeepers, if it arrives at all. Often the mail is distributed by a local policeman.

As we walked through the streets of Jebalya with Fat'hi, I was able to observe how intimate a place a refugee camp can be. Practically every person we encountered, many of them sitting idly in the entrance to their homes, greeted Fat'hi as we went by. At the same time they looked inquiringly at Yisrael and me.

Yisrael (alias Danny, the Italian photographer) advanced through the narrow alleys as if he were walking barefoot on burning coals. A veteran reserve soldier who was acquainted with such places only through the windows of a military reconnaissance vehicle, he surveyed the surroundings warily, in anticipation of trouble.

It was an unsettling experience for me as well, walking through the camp for the first time without my protective journalistic cover and without any Israelis in immediate calling distance. But equipped with prior experience, I responded to the inquisitive and suspicious glances with *"Asalamu aleikum."* *"Aleikum asalam"* came the replies to my greeting.

Abd Al Karim Lubad's home wasn't far from Fat'hi's. From the alley three steps led to a patched wooden door with green paint that had faded over the years. To unlock it Fat'hi used an enormous key, the kind that in the occupied territories is crafted to this day by smiths who proudly term it an "Arab key." Living quarters in the camp were clearly based on the traditional form of housing that existed in agricultural countryside villages. Lubad's house was built around a small inner courtyard, two rooms on one side and a kitchen and toilet on the other. Abd Al

149

Karim Lubad, who had agreed to host the "brother from Balata camp," wasn't at home when we arrived. It was midday and he was still away at work in Israel. Fat'hi showed us around a little and then he and Hassan went their way. As they left, Fat'hi gave me a conspiratorial wink.

Soon afterward Abd Al Karim arrived, a smiling, short, slightly balding young man. He was expecting a guest from Balata, of course, and he readily accepted the presence of an additional guest, an Italian photographer interested in documenting life in the refugee camps. We exchanged greetings, which involved a handshake and tapping one's own chest with a palm, as if to say "with all my heart."

Our host excused himself and went into his tiny kitchenette, reemerging after a few minutes with some glasses of strong and very sweet tea. Then we engaged in polite conversation. Yisrael didn't actually know any Italian, but then neither did Abd Al Karim, and I was kept busy translating from Arabic to English and vice versa.

"Why are you so interested in living here?" Lubad asked. "Everyone knows that Jebalya isn't exactly a luxury hotel."

"Well, they all say that our situation in Balata is better than what's going on here, and I wanted to check it out for myself," I replied.

Later on, after making sure that we wouldn't go to bed hungry, Abd Al Karim fetched some blankets from a room which seemed generally out of use. I asked him where he was going to sleep. "There," he said, indicating the desolate, unfurnished room. I knew better than to try to dissuade him, for the tradition of hospitality is still taken very seriously in this part of the world, and Abd Al Karim spent that night on the concrete floor with only a thin blanket for comfort.

The next day around noon I accompanied Yisrael on his way back to Palestine Circle in the center of Gaza. There we separated, and as he stepped into the taxi going to Tel Aviv, he turned around to have a final word with me. "I'll stay near the phone from now until the moment you get out of Jebalya," he said with concern. "Anytime you feel you need to, Binchu, just call."

150

When I returned to Lubad's house I heard unfamiliar voices inside, and a sudden wave of panic swept over me. I thought to myself; "This is it, there's surely someone here who'll recognize Yoram Binur the journalist. Or else the camp activists have decided to examine more closely the identity of the guest from Balata who has volunteered to spend his time in the lousiest refugee camp in the whole of the occupied territories, and now they're sitting around drinking tea and discussing whether they should interrogate me with a wet towel wound around my neck, which they will alternately tighten and loosen, or whether a simple, straightforward threat with a knife will be sufficient." I stood before the door and my first thought was to simply turn around and get out of there. True, my personal belongings were inside the house, but I had enough money in my pockets to get me to Tel Aviv or Jerusalem. There was a prolonged moment of wavering resolve and then I suddenly found myself standing in the middle of Lubad's small inner courtyard without knowing how I got there, and with several pairs of eyes fixed upon me.

"*Marhaba ala ibn allajiin* [Welcome to the son of refugees]," came a voice, jolting me out of my paranoid reverie.

"*Marhabtein, ya jamaat albir* [Bless all those present]," I answered.

Then, according to custom, the young men raised themselves from the mattresses on which they were seated and I went from one to the other, shaking hands. After each handshake my partner and I would tap our chests with the palms of our hands. This extremely polite welcome calmed me down. Because of Abd Al Karim's bachelor status and the fact that he didn't live with his family, his friends visited him relatively often. The presence of a guest from Balata who was also an occasional journalist, and who was familiar with the Palestinian diaspora in America, was reason enough for them to come and meet me.

The company, six in number, resumed their conversation where they had left off. I gathered that they were talking about the Israeli officers of the Shin Bet, who were in charge of Jebalya.

"Hasona, who worked for the military administration, was an idiot and it's a good thing they replaced him," said a bearded fellow by the name of Munir. "When I came to him and asked for a permit to visit Jordan he used filthy language and shouted at me that until I agreed to work with them, the Jews, I could forget about traveling."

Another fellow agreed with him. "Hasona was really stupid and was always trying to be intimidating. When he called someone in for a *mukabala* [an interview—in this case referring to an interview initiated by the Shin Bet in order to maintain contact with local residents], he would curse and didn't even mind giving a slap here and there. But his replacement, Abu Tomar, seems much more intelligent. He remembers the names of most of the young people in the camp. When I had an interview with him, his attitude toward me was reasonable and he even offered me a cup of tea. Of course, the whole thing was for show and very soon he was trying to find out if I would be willing to give him any information."

As I followed the conversation, I found out the meaning of the strange signs I had seen painted on electricity poles on almost every street corner in the camp. The signs were sprayed in red or black paint and depicted various geometrical forms, usually triangles, with numbers inside them.

"Since Abu Tomar arrived the patrols have been painting more signs for agents in the camp to come and meet their contacts," said Munir.

"How exactly does it work here with these signs?" I asked him.

"When the *muhabarat* [the Shin Bet] want to meet a particular agent they instruct the soldiers who are on patrol to paint an agreed-upon sign. The number within the sign stands for the serial number of that person or it may mean a special instruction such as 'Come and meet me this evening at the central administration.' The painting is out in the open and everyone can see it but it doesn't mean anything to them. Only that particular agent understands the coded message."

Munir works for the Africa Israel Co. "Yes," I said to him, "I've heard that it's a large Zionist construction company." I knew about the company mainly from ads in the Israeli papers; it was a prestigious company that had built what could be considered the extreme opposite of Jebalya—the wealthy suburb of Savyon, near Tel Aviv.

152

As we were talking about working for the Israelis, Lubad, my host, burst into the conversation. "When I go to work as a painter for the Jews, the house is already wired for electricity, and then in order to feel good I have to spoil something in the wiring, so at least the Zionist boss doesn't make a profit off my back."

The men's speech was liberally sprinkled with Hebrew words, especially those commonly used in a work situation or interaction with soldiers at the roadblocks—Hebrew words meaning "O.K.," "fine," "come here," "stand straight." According to my cover story, I had never been employed outside the West Bank and didn't understand a word of Hebrew, so I was frequently obliged to stop them and ask for the meaning of such words. I suddenly became conscious of the tremendous number of Hebrew words that had infiltrated the Arabic language.

Next to the mattresses on which we were sitting lay a pile of old magazines that Lubad had picked up in Israel. Someone picked up a pamphlet and began leafing through it, and soon the others looked at it with him. It was a brochure for Club Med extolling the virtues of their resorts around the world. The young men looked with shamefaced curiosity at the pictures of suntanned and bare-skinned girls which filled the pages of the brochure. "What is this?" they asked, passing it to me so that I could explain its contents to them. "It's a kind of hotel," I replied uneasily. I thought to myself that the moon was no farther from the reality of Lubad's home than the nearest Club Med, which was a mere fifteen minutes away by car, in Ashkelon.

After about an hour of conversation Hassan came in. He apparently knew that a gathering of friends was going to take place at my host's home and wished to see how I would fare in action. Hassan gave me his sly look and it took him only a few seconds to satisfy himself that all was going well. He sat down and thankfully accepted a cup of tea which Lubad served him.

Munir continued telling us about his experience working among the Jews. "Once I was picking fruit on some farm near Ashkelon. We worked like donkeys from morning to evening and slept in a stinking run-down shed in the orchard. After a week, payday came around and the boss brought in some thugs at night armed with guns who beat us and chased us, yelling, 'You're all terrorists!' We had to get out of there and a whole week of hard work went to hell. We didn't get a shekel." The anti-Israeli sentiment was very strong and I was forced to concur with every word that was being said.

Abd Al Karim erupted for a second time. "Those Zionists are getting money from America all the time. Like a flock of sheep, they just stand with mouths open and ask for more. And they're always talking about what Hitler did to them in Europe. I don't believe that Hitler killed the Jews, they just killed each other."

This wicked assertion made my blood boil. The young Palestinians in whose company I found myself were intellectuals. Abd Al Karim, my host, had completed his studies at the university in Gaza. The others were educated as well and knew—or should have known—the truth about the Holocaust. The problem was that, considering all the pent-up anger and frustration that resulted from growing up in a miserable refugee camp, it would have been hard for me to protest against the hatred they felt toward anything that even faintly smacked of Zionism. I hastened to join Lubad and cursed the Zionists who had deprived my parents of their home in Wadi Nisnas in Haifa and had brought so much grief to the Palestinian people.

Someone asked me about the circumstances of my stay in Jebalya. I proceeded to tell about my family, who had been forced to leave their home in Haifa in 1948. "My parents reached Shatila in Lebanon, and after a few years my father emigrated to the United States, where he set up a garage. A few years ago," I lied with great conviction, "I returned to Palestine. I have uncles from the Awad family, on my father's side, who live in Balata and that's where I live now. I came to Jebalya with the intention of learning more about the life of my people in the occupied motherland and maybe to make use of my knowledge of English in order to write some articles about the Zionist occupation."

□ □ □

When I created my Palestinian identity, I deliberately chose to hail from the Balata refugee camp and not from some Palestinian town in the West Bank. The *abna almuhayamaat* (sons of the camps), as they are called, share a common language among themselves and their ease and openness with one another are relatively high. Had I introduced myself as a resident of one of the West Bank cities, such as Bethlehem, Nablus, or Hebron, I would have had to spend a lot of time and energy convincing refugee camp dwellers of my loyalty to the Palestinian cause, since I would be regarded as one who had suffered less under the occupation than they. I also figured that Balata was far enough from the Gaza Strip so that the chances of someone from Jebalya knowing people from Balata were slim. In my cover story I also used as many details as possible from my actual life. I mentioned that my father had a garage because I have an extensive knowledge of car mechanics and could easily answer any question on the subject. My ostensible intention to write about life in the camp gave me a good excuse to meet a variety of people and converse with them while they believed that they were talking to a Palestinian reporter.

Among those present that evening there was one young man who expressed a point of view which was different from that of the others. His name was Nasser, which means victory in Arabic. When the company discussed politics, he was the only one who heatedly defended Anwar Al Sadat's peace agreement with Israel and the Israeli policy of appointing Arab mayors for the various municipalities in the occupied territories. The others argued with him for hours. In their opinion Sadat was a damned traitor, and the mayors appointed by the Israeli military administration served the interests of Zionism. In the heat of the argument Abd Al Karim brought out one of his paintings that normally hung in the other room, above the bed in which I slept. The painting portrayed a Palestinian octopus strangling a dove which symbolized the Israeli-Egyptian peace, regarded by Lubad and his friends as a betrayal of their cause by the Arab nations. In contrast to the others, Nasser didn't make frequent comments expressing hatred for the Jews. Nor did he boast about interrogations he had undergone or about obstructing the routine activity of Israeli soldiers on duty in the camp.

When I questioned Nasser how it was possible that a "son of the camps" would hold such opinions as his, he stated quite simply that he was from Beit Lahiya, a town near the camp. This meant that Nasser wasn't a refugee but a villager whose family was never dispossessed of its land. I was surprised to see that despite Nasser's unpopular views, all he got in response were heated remonstrations and strident arguments. According to the rumors I had heard regarding extremism in the refugee camps, he should have feared for his life.

As the evening progressed, we drank many liters of sweet tea and locally bottled Coca-Cola, a drink especially favored by the people of the Gaza Strip in the summertime. I was engaged in criticizing Nasser for his views when Abd Al Karim left the room and returned a few minutes later carrying three large trays in his arms. A small boy came with him, bringing hot pita bread. I shifted my position in order to sit more comfortably on the straw mattress and joined the others, dipping a pita into yogurt combined with a spoonful of *mujadara* (an inexpensive but tasty mixture of rice, lentils, and onions), a few slices of tomato, and some very hot green peppers.

It was around ten o'clock when the company decided to call it a night. I stood beside Abd Al Karim as the guests filed past, politely thanking the host and wishing us both a good night's sleep. After they had all gone, Lubad brought his blanket back in from the room where he had spent the previous night. We settled into our respective beds and exchanged views on his friends. "They're all people whom I love and respect except for Nasser. His uncle was appointed by the Jews to be the mayor of Beit Lahiya, which is the reason for his defeatism. It's all a question of narrow personal interests." Having thus summed up his opinion, Lubad turned out the light. *"Tisbah bil heir* [Wake well in the morning]."

I didn't dare fall asleep before he did. I have a tendency to talk in my sleep, which under the circumstances could be rather embarrassing, to say the least. I was exhausted, however, and before long a deep sleep came over me.

Some hours later, in the middle of the night, I was awakened by someone shaking my shoulder. It was Abd Al Karim, who was sitting on the edge of his bed with a scared expression on his face. "What's the matter?" I asked. "Shh," he hushed me, "there are soldiers in the streets." At this point I could distinctly make out the sound of marching boots. The steps stopped right outside the house we were in. The wooden shutter, made out of crates and painted green, was open, and against the sky I could see something waving about in the wind, something like a long thin wand or a fishing pole. It took me a moment to figure out what it was, and then I recognized it. It was the antenna of a radio, the kind that the Israeli infantry uses. I could even tell that it was tuned to the "squelch" mode, which silences all signals being received or transmitted, so that an invading force can reach its destination without being overheard by the enemy.

"If they enter," said Abd Al Karim, "then remember, I just invited you to stay the night and apart from that I have absolutely nothing to do with you."

His fear must have been contagious, for I felt a chill creep up my spine. Although my personal history gave me reason to identify with the soldiers outside, who had to spend their nights fulfilling their unwelcome duties, under the circumstances the threat that they posed seemed far more relevant. It is not unusual for soldiers to invade the privacy of a refugee's home in the dead of night, so the possibility that Lubad raised wasn't farfetched. If a guest was found in his house during a night search, he'd have to explain exactly what that person was doing there, and the method of interrogation could be extremely humiliating, not to mention downright uncomfortable.

We waited in suspense to see whether the soldiers would decide to enter the house. Perhaps someone had informed on my presence in the house? After some whispering and murmuring outside the window, the patrol moved on. We both heaved a sigh of relief.

The next morning Abd Al Karim left the house at four, as he would almost every morning during my stay in Jebalya, to work as a housepainter in Kiryat Gat, which is in the south of Israel. I woke up hours later, stretched, and went out to buy some groceries at the store. When I returned and opened the refrigerator to put the things away, I found the shelves and freezer filled with notebooks, paints, and various paraphernalia for painting. Food seemed to be Abd Al Karim's lowest priority, if it was a priority at all.

As a university graduate who was forced to earn his living as a day laborer, Lubad suffered a high level of frustration. He expressed himself by painting motifs depicting the Palestinian people's struggle for national liberation and their life before the great evacuation of 1948. He loved to paint at night. On days when he didn't find work, he'd come home early, sleep for a few hours, and then set up his canvas. More than once I saw him take the tubes of cheap oil paints from that refrigerator and draw Palestinian figures against peaceful rural backgrounds.

A few years earlier Lubad had graduated from the Islamic university in Gaza with a major in geography and with a grade average of *jayid jidan* (excellent). He then joined the twelve thousand university graduates from the occupied territories who cannot find employment in their chosen fields; the Israeli job market absorbs them only in the capacity of manual laborers.

Abd Al Karim nurtured a venomous hatred for the Israeli occupation. "If one day there are a lot of speeches in the Israeli Knesset about peace, then you can be sure it's a sign they're going to attack another Arab state," he declared, expounding the principles of his attitude toward Israel. "The Arab states talk about war all the time and when there is a war they're not worth anything, but when the Israelis last spoke about peace they invaded Lebanon and murdered Palestinians there. Victory will only come by means of the gun. All the rest is idle talk."

"But in order to win we need leaders," I ventured.

Lubad replied, "The leaders can only be those who have fought and sat in the Zionist prisons and not people like Rashad Al Shawa [the former mayor of Gaza and one of the city's wealthiest men] who don't have anything to do with the Palestinian cause."

One morning I woke up early and joined Lubad when he left the house. At 4 A.M. the camp was bustling with activity. It was

158

amazing to see almost the entire working population of Jebalya on their feet at such an hour, still groggy and bleary-eyed, their night's sleep cut short because of the cruel necessity of earning a living. Each man was clutching a plastic bag which contained his meager fare for the workday: bread and onions, for instance, or a spicy liver sandwich. They were all going to Palestine Circle in Gaza or to the camp exit that led to the road connecting Gaza with the Erez roadblock. The main mode of transportation was private Peugeots that had been converted into gypsy cabs. In the Gaza Strip they have even invented a special verb to describe it—to "go Bazhena" (derived from the Arabic pronunciation of *p* as *b*).

Occasionally, when Lubad couldn't find work and came home early, I would make the rounds with him, visiting his friends in the camp. My desire to become closely acquainted with life in Jebalya aroused much sympathy and on our visits we were deluged with cups of coffee and Coca-Cola.

On other days I wandered about on my own. From many of the houses in the camp came the ticking sound of sewing machines. Some of the residents who had formerly been employed in sweatshops in Israel had purchased a sewing machine or two for themselves and had become independent subcontractors for the Israeli factories.

"I get the material from a factory owner in Tel Aviv and sew *bantalon kaboi,*" said Rafik, one of Lubad's friends. "Every week I send him the finished merchandise and get money, but soon I'm going to have to quit. The income tax of the occupation demands sums from me that are as large as if I had a factory here."

I nodded my head in commiseration but hadn't the slightest idea what *kaboi* were. *Bantalon,* I knew, was the Arabic word for trousers. But when Rafik showed me his merchandise I understood that *bantalon kaboi,* in the local idiom, were jeans, and that *kaboi* was simply a distorted version of the word "cowboy." Rafik displayed for my benefit an array of labels that said "Made in America," "Made in Hong Kong," "Made in" any place on earth that one could think of. "These labels," he said proudly, "are also manufactured in Gaza."

Friday is market day in Jebalya. Like markets everywhere, it serves as a social gathering place where people can pick up the latest information. The only discernible difference between this market and others lies in its poverty. Vendors bring their wares to the clearing in the camp center and many of them simply spread the merchandise on the ground. An old woman, for instance, will bring a few tomatoes that she has grown in her yard, set them down, and then wait apathetically until someone shows an interest. Once this happens, however, she will cling to the potential customer and will not let him or her go until a purchase has been made, even if the price has to go down by fifty percent. One fellow, who works for the Tel Aviv municipality as a street cleaner, supplements his paltry income by picking up old toys from the garbage. On Friday, which is his day off, he sets up shop in the market of Jebalya. A doll missing an arm or a leg, toy trucks without wheels, and all sorts of broken playthings are granted a second life in the refugee camp. "Whenever I have a plastic gun for sale, I get a customer right away," he told me.

In another corner of the market a merchant from Gaza unloads several dozen chickens, still alive in their cages. "The Palestinian woman, may she be blessed by Allah, won't buy a chicken if she hasn't seen it walking about and pecking the dirt with her own eyes. Then she'll slaughter it herself or else supervise the butcher as he does his job. Finally, she'll pluck its feathers and clean out its innards. Not like the Jewesses," he added with contempt, "who buy their chickens wrapped in plastic." Once an unsuspecting fowl was selected its fate was sealed. The vendor would set it on the scales with a swift movement and after gaining the customer's approval he would cut its throat and throw it to the ground. There the chicken would expire, with much flapping of the wings and headless running about. It was a bloody, messy affair, national pride notwithstanding.

Despite his relatively advanced age of twenty-six, Abd Al Karim was a bachelor, which was a main reason why Fat'hi Raban, my contact in Jebalya, had chosed him to be my host. For Moslem Arabs to entertain a guest who is a bachelor in a household where there is a woman could pose a rather delicate problem. Fat'hi's knowledge that the guest was actually an Israeli Jew must have added to his concern, and led him to the decision to have me stay with a bachelor. This prevented me from enjoying a firsthand view of family life in Jebalya, but as it turned out, I was amply compensated by the intimate acquaintance that I struck up with Fat'hi himself and with his own family.

Fat'hi, a tall thin man of thirty-nine, would come and visit me on every possible occasion. He would check to see that all was well, and often he would take the opportunity to pour his heart out to me, as one is wont to do when there is a visiting stranger about whom one possesses a critical piece of information. Over the course of time we developed a close relationship that went well beyond what was required by the purpose of my stay.

Fat'hi was employed part-time as an art teacher at a primary school for the children of refugees that was run by UNRWA. He received a monthly salary of 60 dinars ($180). He spent his free time wandering about the streets in the camp and painting. These paintings, for which Fat'hi had already spent some months in jail, deal mostly with Palestinian themes, often supplemented with a heavy dose of nationalist sentiment. The style of the paintings is naïve. A picture titled "To Freedom," or "Al Muhararun" in Arabic, features a thoroughbred Arabian stallion, the symbol of the Palestinian resistance. The Palestinian flag is cleverly (and illegally) worked into the picture so that it forms a part of the horse's neck, around which a heavy iron chain is locked. From among the masses, who are dressed in the traditional garb of the *falahin* (the Arab peasants), there emerge two arms, which are crisscrossed with prominent veins, just like Fat'hi's own. One of the arms is raising a fist and the other is giving the "V for victory" sign.

Fat'hi Raban's family had come to Jebalya from Harbiya, a small village near the city of Ashkelon. His father, Ismail Raban, had been the village butcher and had the reputation of being the best *debka* dancer around. (The motif of *debka* dancing still appears in many of Fat'hi's paintings.) In 1948, with the entrance of the Israeli forces into the area, the villagers had to leave. Fat'hi related his father's description of the event in these words: "The Jews fired on the village for several days. A lot of people were wounded or killed until the situation was totally unbearable and we left."

161

Like many other refugee families who believed that their departure was temporary, the family settled in a tent camp that was hastily erected on the Egyptian side of the new border with Israel. A year later UNRWA constructed the Jebalya camp, which was intended to absorb of the uprooted population. "After a year we lost our hope of a speedy return to our village, and my parents moved to Jebalya. That's how it was—when hope ended Jebalya began," said Fat'hi.

His insistence on using my adopted name, even though he knew my real one, added an odd dimension to our conversation when we addressed each other. "Fat'hi," he said to me one evening.

"Yes, ya Fat'hi," I answered.

"You know, the fact that I sat in the Israeli prison for six months because of my subversive paintings calling for action against the Israelis—that fact helped me in life. Journalists from abroad started visiting me, and my status within the camp greatly improved. In jail they wanted to humiliate me so that I would stop painting after I got out. The wardens received special instructions to keep me in a cell with criminal prisoners, drug dealers, and pimps, not with other political prisoners. The authorities hoped that the criminals would harass me and break my spirit, but very soon our cell received a strict warning from the leaders of the political prisoners that the *shabab* would punish anyone who so much as touched a hair on the head of Fat'hi Raban. After that the criminals showed me respect. I was always given the best food and had plenty of cigarettes."

Fat'hi actually started his career as a nationalist Palestinian artist in the Jewish city of Bat Yam, near Tel Aviv. "In 1972 I was working there for a Jewish contractor and after hours of construction work I used to draw pictures for his children. He saw the pictures, bought me paints, and asked me to make a few for him. These were commercial paintings of landscape scenes and of figures, not nationalist pictures. Within a short time I was sought after by his friends and later I began painting and selling on my own. My work is hanging in many living rooms in Bat Yam.

"Later I began drawing subjects that were more political and I was invited to participate in Palestinian exhibitions in East

162

Jerusalem. Afterward the military authorities decided that I was a subversive and they put me in prison."

Fat'hi's paintings were exhibited in East Jerusalem on several occasions. He once told me how he managed to get through the military roadblocks with his subversive cargo. "When I transport my paintings I cover the frame of the picture with a blank canvas. When the soldiers at Erez ask me what I've got, I reply that these are frames with canvas that I am going to sell to artists in Tel Aviv. They find it easy to believe such a story from a Palestinian."

The relative fame that Fat'hi Raban had acquired was the cause of deep frustration. He'd had some degree of contact with life outside the camp, and this exposure to a completely different world made his humble everyday existence more difficult to bear. "Someone like me, under normal circumstances, would have been free of the problems of earning a living. I only want to paint all day."

Fahti's wife, Miriam, knew the truth about my identity and it amused her. The first time I came to their house dressed in a galabia she clapped her hands and laughed with delight. "Ya Fat'hi, now you look like a real Arab."

"God bless your words," I answered while trying to shake off her two youngest children, who were trying to find out how quickly they could stain my galabia.

Despite her youth (she was only thirty), Miriam was prematurely aged, having already given birth to eight children. This was by no means unusual and was in keeping with the stated policy of the Palestinian leadership. Arafat and others have proclaimed that "each Palestinian woman who brings children into this world is participating in our struggle." The names of the children reflected this perception of children as a demographic element of the struggle to achieve national liberation: Shuala (Flame), Thair (Revolutionary), Kifach (Struggle), and a little baby girl by the name of Falastin (Palestine).

"A few months ago the children painted the word 'Falastin' on the outside wall of our house, in Arabic and in English," Miriam told me. "A patrol of soldiers came by—they pass here at least twice a day—and their commanding officer entered our house and asked who had painted the word 'Falastin' on the wall. He said that it was a nationalistic and subversive slogan and that whoever wrote it would be tried by military court. I told him that it was the name of my daughter, as Israelis call their sons and daughters Yisrael or Yisraela, and that it was my right to write the names of members of the household on the entrance to my home. It made sense to him and he left." Miriam laughed over the small victory she had won over the forces of occupation.

Miriam, unlike her husband, stays at home all day, endlessly busy, taking care of the children, doing the laundry, cleaning the house, or cooking. Because she spends her entire life in the immediate vicinity of her house, she has a thorough knowledge of the soldiers who patrol the streets of the camp. Like most of the local population, she can tell, by the color of their berets, by the type of weapons they carry, and by their age, to which unit the soldiers belong. She knows which units are tougher and which there's a better chance of winning an argument with. "The worst are the border police. When one of their patrols goes by, it's not a good idea to be anywhere near them, and during a curfew there's no point in trying to ask them for permission to go out and get food for the children. They beat you right away. The best are the older soldiers doing reserve duty." The people of Jebalya scarcely knew about Operation Moses, which brought a large number of Ethiopian Jews to Israel. A few months later the first dark-skinned soldiers appeared in the camp. "They patrolled here in uniform, wearing those eggplant-colored berets and toting guns, but anyone could see that they didn't understand what was expected of them. When our boys walked up close to them they would raise their arms in order to protect themselves from flying stones and begged them not to hurt them. In a few months they'll learn how to give out blows as well. For sure, just like the Zionists."

One of Fat'hi's nephews, an eight-year-old by the name of Suheil, was shot and killed, apparently by mistake, by Israeli soldiers during demonstrations which took place in the camp in April 1982. According to the Moslem faith, the boy was *shahid*, one who had given his soul to God. "We wrapped his body in the Palestinian flag and brought him for burial," said Fat'hi. "His funeral turned into a mass demonstration and, as in other cases when we have expressed ourselves, the military administration shut down the camp and refused access to journalists and nothing was published."

I had met Suheil's father and he seemed to be a man whose spirit was broken. For me, as an Israeli, it was difficult to come face to face with such a tragic outcome of the occupation. I couldn't help reflecting on the way in which circumstances can transform an innocent boy into a national symbol.

Some of my days in Jebalya were spent in the company of Hassan Jibril. He would come from Shati to visit and often introduced me to various people in the camp. This cunning journalist knew the purpose of my stay and regarded his work with me first and foremost as an ideological mission.

His views, at least as he presented them, were those of the Marxist organization, the Popular Front for the Liberation of Palestine (PFLP), led by George Habash. The Front's ideology with regard to the situation in Palestine favors, among other things, a collaboration between all the "progressive" elements in the area, including "non-Zionist" Israelis (by which they mean any Israeli Jew who accepts that a Palestinian state is necessary for a peaceful solution to the conflict), in order to eventually create a popular revolution that will bring the proletariat to power in Israel and also the Arab states.

I noticed that Hassan made a special effort to introduce me to activists of the PFLP, rather than to supporters of other organizations, such as Al Fatah (led by Yasir Arafat). Thus, he hoped, I would get the impression that this was the dominant organization in the refugee camps and in due time would say so in anything I might write. To confirm my suspicion that this was his motivation, I confronted Hassan directly on the issue. He didn't deny my assertion.

One of the families whom we visited together was that of Muhammad Musalem, who worked as a janitor at the Quaker school in Gaza. Two of his sons had acted on behalf of the Popular Front and were now in prison: Rafik had been sentenced to five and a half years for a security offense, and Muein was given a life sentence for hurling a grenade at an army patrol.

The family's house had been demolished by the army as part

of the retaliatory policy adhered to by the Israeli authorities to this day. If a Palestinian from the West Bank or the Gaza Strip participates in a serious act of aggression, his house is destroyed. Because most of the saboteurs ("terrorists" or "freedom fighters," depending on which side you're on) are young men who live with their parents, or rent a place which isn't their own, this amounts to collective punishment, causing damage to the families of the accused. The destroyed property is taken over by the army and the family is forbidden to rebuild the house. Generally, they receive a reasonable sum of money from Jordan or from one of the Palestinian organizations for the purpose of relocating. This practice is known to the Israeli authorities but they prefer not to interfere with it.

The Musalem family had lived for a number of years in a large tent supplied to them by the International Red Cross. Although they had already built a new house next to it, the tent remained standing, and served as a sort of pilgrimage site for journalists and others who wished to express their solidarity.

The deeds of the two sons were a source of pride for the family, which has taken its place among the "fighting families" of the occupied territories, families that have contributed something to the struggle. The framed portraits of the sons, wearing shirts on which the initials of the Israeli Prison Authorities were sewn in big letters, were proudly displayed to me. Like any good father interested in his son's acquiring an education, Muhammad Musalem showed me Muein's student card. The document seemed somewhat grotesque to me and I wrote down its details. Name of student: Muein Muhammad Musalem; name of school: Central Committee of the Gaza prison. A few weeks later, when I arrived with Yisrael Cohen to take a "souvenir snapshot" of the father of the family, he had his picture taken with the photographs of his sons in his hands and a white dove perched on his shoulder.

Walking through the narrow streets of Jebalya, I began feeling a certain discomfort. The women who sat in the doorways would send darting looks in my direction and start whispering. I didn't attribute any importance to this until one day Abd Al Karim Lubad said to me, "Those women, may Allah set their tongues on fire, talk too much."

"That's in the nature of women. They sit at home all day and gossip," I answered.

But Lubad persisted. "Because of those crones, the entire camp already knows that I have a guest, and they want to know who he is. One of them asked me point-blank and I told her to go rot in hell and not to shove her nose into other people's business, but she said that everyone was talking about it." Lubad was clearly nervous and seemed to prefer that I not extend my stay much longer.

I was thinking about these matters when I heard a whisper— "*biu, biu.*" This whisper was a warning pronounced by small children who were familiar with the routes of the patrols. Giving warning signals had been the task of children in the camp ever since the early seventies. The word *biu* means "sell" and is a short form of *biu silahkum*, or "sell your weapons." To say such a thing to a soldier, especially by the Arabs, was a daring insult. Over and above the usefulness of giving a warning, the children must also have felt great satisfaction in being able to insult the soldiers straight to their faces without the latter understanding what was being said. I imagine it was the same sort of pleasure I used to feel when I lived in Italy, eight years earlier, and used to pay my monthly rent to my mean and miserly landlord with a big smile on my face, all the while cursing him with a steady flow of Hebrew and Arabic oaths.

Upon hearing the children's warning, people in the street, myself included, made themselves scarce. No passerby was interested in risking an interaction with the military. As I put some distance between myself and the projected route of the patrol, I found myself near the center of the camp, at its lowest point, where an offensive stench filled the air. It rose from the cesspool, where all the sewage of Jebalya gathered and was gradually absorbed in the sand.

☐ ☐ ☐

In the early seventies it was generally at this site that suspected collaborators were summarily executed by members of the Palestinian organizations.

Someone who had actively participated in the events of that period described it to me. "The Israeli soldiers used to lie in ambush at night around the cesspool in order to catch us, but it was no use. In the morning corpses would be floating in the foul waters. Like the sewage, the blood of our traitors was soaked up by the sand."

These executions were part of a more generalized violence in the Gaza Strip at that time. By the seventies, just a few years after the Israeli occupation, the refugee camps had become practically an autonomous territory ruled by the Palestinian organizations. Members of these organizations had large quantities of arms at their disposal. They picked up hand grenades and automatic weapons of Russian make (Kalashnikov submachine rifles) which had been left behind by the retreating Egyptian army during the war of 1967. Hiding places were prepared as caches for weapons and as shelters where people on the "Wanted" lists could take refuge.

During that period there were many attacks on Israelis who wandered into the area. In one incident a hand grenade was thrown at a civilian car with a family of Israeli tourists, the Arroyos; the mother and two of her children were killed. At the peak of Israel's war against the organizations that ruled the camps, forces were sent in, under the command of Ariel Sharon, to restore order to the turbulent Gaza Strip. Israeli secret agents had infiltrated the Palestinian organizations, which as a result began a systematic purging of their own ranks through the elimination of suspected collaborators. Thus, the blood spilled in the camp was both that of Israelis and that of local residents who were suspected of being traitors to the cause of national liberation.

☐ ☐ ☐

Not far from that cesspool stands the central military compound. The locals call it the Center. The army patrols depart from here and those who are arrested are brought here for preliminary interrogation. The stronghold is surrounded by a massive fence topped by coils of barbed wire, and despite its small area it includes no fewer than three watchtowers which overlook the camp. The majority of young men from Jebalya have already seen the compound from the inside.

Years ago, a crazed Australian by the name of Michael Dennis Rohan set the Al Aqsa mosque in Jerusalem on fire. The Moslems did not believe, and to this day do not believe, that the fire was the result of the Australian's derangement. They thought it was a deliberate Zionist attempt to take over the Haram al Sharif, the mosques of the Holy Mount. The local populace staged a demonstration and stormed the Center. That demonstration etched itself on the collective memory of Jebalya and has been recounted to me over and over again.

The stormy mob advanced on the Center, the nearest symbol of the hated Zionists. There were only a few soldiers there at the time, and the mob advanced to the fence while hurling stones and shouting, *"Allahu akbar!* [Allah is great!]." The soldiers opened fire and several demonstrators were wounded, but a few bold youths managed to enter the compound and with a few rags and some kerosene they set a part of it on fire. "Too bad you didn't get to see it, ya Fat'hi," one of my informants told me. "It was a true jihad [holy war]."

☐ ☐ ☐

Hassan came to me one day bearing a message: "Al Wahsh has heard about you. He respects your desire to learn about life in Jebalya and is interested in making your acquaintance." I agreed to a meeting on the spot. Al Wahsh means "the Beast." It is the nickname of Muhammad Abu Al Naser, one of the boldest fighters to come out of the camp. Al Wahsh had spent many years in Israeli prisons, where he had been recognized as a leader among his fellow inmates. Because of his intelligence and his daring past he was widely respected and enjoyed a privileged status in the camp.

That the Beast had already heard about the curious stranger from Balata did not surprise me. I didn't doubt that a leading figure in the community would want to meet me in person, just as a tribal chieftain would want to pass judgment on a newly arrived guest in his territory. I also realized that Al Wahsh was capable of deciding the future of my stay in Jebalya.

Muhammad Abu Al Naser, a short, heavyset, muscular man, received me at his home in Jebalya with a firm handshake. Although he lived in the center of the refugee camp, there was no feeling of poverty or deprivation in his house. A massive metal door separated his place from the miserable scene outside. The Abu Al Naser family had done its best to create a pleasant nest shielded from the filth and the poverty outside. Clean, spacious rooms surrounded the inner courtyard, which was partly shaded by an overhanging grapevine. The rooms were built out of concrete blocks and were modestly but not poorly furnished. On the wall of the small guest room hung photographs of the kind I had often seen in the homes of Jebalya. Two of Muhammad's brothers, Ziad and Jihad, were serving prison terms in the Nafha prison in the Negev after being tried and sentenced for security offenses. As in the portraits of Muhammad Musalem's two sons, the men sported the most prestigious clothing a refugee can wear, the uniform of the Israeli Prison Authorities.

Muhammad Abu Al Naser's younger brother Hosni was present, as well as another friend, Omar, an elementary school teacher who lived in the camp. After we had sipped chilled 7-Up, Muhammad asked what brought me to Jebalya. I told my story once again: "In 1948, when the Jews came, my family fled from Haifa to the Shatila refugee camp in Lebanon . . ."

Muhammad's many sessions with Israeli security agents, and those that he himself had conducted in his prison cell when he questioned other prisoners who were suspected of collaborating with the authorities, had provided him with a lot of experience in interrogation, and added to my discomfort. He barely reacted to my story, and each time I finished telling him about something he would merely nod his head or grunt, without disclosing his opinion on what I was saying. Only when I told him about Haifa did he respond, asking me which neighborhood my parents came from and whether I had already visited their house there.

"No, I haven't been there yet. My father told me he was sure that there were Jews living there now and I prefer not to see that."

Hassan was sitting by my side, listening silently to our conversation. He was monitoring Muhammad's reactions with the alertness of a hunting hound, seeking to identify the slightest sign of mistrust on his part—a mistrust that could cost me, and Hassan, dearly.

Muhammad's friend, Omar, entered the conversation and

asked, "So, Fat'hi, how do you see the solution to our problem?"

The sudden question confused me a bit, but I recovered and
answered in the most ordinary fashion that a Palestinian could.
"The *awda*, the return to Palestine, is what will solve the problem."

"We've long ago forgotten about returning to the homeland,"
Omar answered me. "Let the Jews just allow us to establish an
independent state in the West Bank and the Gaza Strip."

Omar's opinion, which was considered by some in the occupied territories to be moderate to the point of treason, indicated that he was a supporter of the Communist party. My
knowledge of this allowed me to overcome the strained atmosphere that had formed. I retorted, "So you're one of the people
of the Hizb Shuyui [the Communist party], eh?" My response
was clearly approved of by Muhammad, who despite his
friendship with Omar did not share his political views.
Muhammad gave me a reassuring smile and upon my request
began to tell me about himself.

On September 6, 1970, Muhammad Abu Al Naser left the Gaza
Strip with a pistol and a hand grenade in his possession. At the
Erez roadblock his taxi was stopped for a routine check. To
avoid arousing any suspicion, he got out and asked one of the
soldiers where he could find drinking water. The soldier
showed him where the tap was and then finished checking the
documents of the taxi, at which point Abu Al Naser, who had
drunk his fill, returned and continued on his way to Jerusalem.

At that time, Muhammad was employed as a construction
worker by a Jewish building contractor in Jerusalem, but his
real mission was to study the layout of the city and the location
of military stations, in preparation for an attack he was supposed to carry out. "The boss was actually a good person, ya
Fat'hi," Muhammad said, studying my reaction to his praise for
a Jew, "and that caused me to hesitate about the mission which
the PFLP had entrusted me with. But every week on my day
off I would return to the camp and when I saw how Ariel
Sharon's soldiers were treating us here I'd be filled with rage.
Then I'd go back to Jerusalem prepared to carry out any mission.

"The same day I arrived from Gaza I went to Herod's Gate in the walls of Old City. We had instructions at that time from the organization to try to harm only military targets. Some Israeli soldiers, apparently on leave, were parked there in their military vehicle. I waited on the other side of the street, covering the grenade which I held in my hand with a newspaper. A boy, one of ours, was there and I waited until he left. After he'd gone a woman soldier came up to the vehicle, eating ice cream. She had a dark complexion; her family must have come from a Middle Eastern country. I would have preferred to throw my grenade at a male soldier but I couldn't wait, because the Jews would have caught me. I threw the grenade at the vehicle. I walked away from there toward St. Stephen's Gate, where a taxi was waiting to take me back to Gaza." A few days later Abu Al Naser returned to Jerusalem with another grenade and threw it at a police car.

By the time Abu Al Naser returned to Jebalya he had earned a reputation as a fearless hero who had succeeded in committing two acts of sabotage against the Jews. He became an active member in a cell of the PFLP which was operating in the camp at that time. "We had a hiding place in every nook and cranny," said Muhammad. "In this room, where we are sitting right now, there was a double wall, plastered over, with an entrance to it through a tunnel which we had dug in the yard and camouflaged with a bush. My immediate superior was Che Guevara."

Muhammad looked me over and I gave a silent whistle of admiration. Che Guevara, also known as Guevara of Gaza, was one of the boldest of the terrorists who operated in the Gaza Strip. His real name was Muhammad Al Aswad, and every Palestinian youth in the refugee camps has heard of him. Legend has it that when the Israeli security forces succeeded in killing him, Moshe Dayan, who was Defense Minister at the time, arrived on the scene and honored the dead man with a salute. It's a curious story and it is probably not true, since Israelis regard the Palestinian fighters as abominable terrorists, but it paradoxically illustrates the esteem in which Dayan was held by the Palestinians in the Gaza Strip.

"At first the secret service knew me only by my alias, Al Wahsh, but quite soon they discovered my true identity. You know, ya Fat'hi," Muhammad said, looking me straight in the eye, "there are a lot of traitors among us."

"Yes, I've also marked some of the people in Balata with a big X," I answered.

Muhammad's mother peered into the room where we were sitting and said, "The meal is ready, son." In the courtyard, on a paved clearing beneath the grapevine, mattresses were laid out in a square. In the middle sat a huge round tray, about one meter in diameter, piled with yellow rice on which lay three whole chickens, roasted to a juicy brown. Next to the enormous tray there were plates with slices of tomato mixed with hot green peppers and a plate of fresh yogurt.

After washing our hands, we removed our shoes and sat down to the feast. Muhammad picked up a chicken and deftly tore it apart with his bare hands. He spread the choice pieces on the pile of rice, and handed one to me. Then he pushed the plates of salad and yogurt toward me. *"T'fadalu,* help yourself." I immediately began eating the chicken, whose flavor was greatly enhanced by a liberal sprinkling of *sumak,* those ground red seeds which lend meat a refreshing touch of sourness.

The customary silence which accompanies a meal among Arabs was broken by my host. I lifted my gaze from behind my chicken leg; Muhammad was calmly seated, holding a long kitchen knife and whetstone. "Ya Fat'hi," he addressed me, "how well versed are you in the Koran?"

"All right, *alhamdullah* [praised be the Lord]."

"So then, if you don't mind, please recite the *fatiha,* the opening *sura* [chapter] of the Koran."

Hassan, who was sitting at Muhammad's left, threw a quick glance in my direction, as if to say, "We're in serious trouble, and the only one who can get us out of it is you." Omar, the Communist schoolteacher, stopped chewing his food altogether and looked at me with his mouth full. Muhammad, with a thin smile on his face, kept running his finger over the blade of his knife, lightly and deliberately, like a ritual slaughterer who is checking his *halaf* [butcher's knife] to make certain it isn't disqualified, God forbid.

I looked around and noticed that the door leading from the yard to the street outside was shut, and in any case Muhammad was positioned between me and the exit. I leaned back uncomfortably against the wall behind me. Where was Feisal Al Husseini's letter now that I desperately needed it? I'd stupidly left it behind at Abd Al Karim's house, carefully hidden in my bag. But a memory of Professor Kister's class in first-year Arabic at the university flashed through my mind. I took a deep breath, and with as proper an accent as I could muster, I began reciting the holy chapter which practically every Moslem believer knows by heart: "*Alhamdu lillahi rab alalamin, malik yaom aldin, iaka naabudu wa'iaka nasta'in* [God be praised, ruler of the universe. Thee we worship and thy assistance we seek]."

To my surprise the quote was accurate and I passed the test. I nonchalantly wiped the sweat from my brow and we continued our meal.

After the visit was over, Hassan escorted me to the center of the camp, where we parted ways. I found myself taking the quickest route back to Lubad's house. The alleys had become familiar and I felt as if I was hurrying back to a safe haven after the ordeal I had undergone. It was seven o'clock; I could see the owner of the chain-saw store closing up shop. Officially, no curfew had been imposed, but no one was outside.

In the evening hours the streets in the camp fall silent. The local nightlife amounts to watching TV, usually the Egyptian broadcasts. A camp resident who is found wandering in the streets at night is almost sure to be detained and questioned.

The only activity is that of the army patrols and the passing of an occasional car. The car may not be a model used by the army but it may bear a military license plate nonetheless: it is a vehicle of the Israeli Shin Bet, who are busy carrying out their silent and never-ending task of planting agents and recruiting informers.

When I returned I found Abd Al Karim Lubad pale and extremely nervous. He didn't smile in greeting when I entered and he immediately accosted me, saying, "You should have told me the truth. I wouldn't have made any difference and I would have treated you in exactly the same manner."

Apparently Lubad had wanted to find out who his guest was. In my absence, he had searched my belongings and discovered Feisal Al Husseini's letter. Ironically, the document that was supposed to be my last resort in case of an emergency turned out to be the one that disclosed my identity as a Jewish journalist. The revelation shook Abd Al Karim to his foundations. I tried my best to convince him that my posing was essential for me to be able to learn something of value about the lives of the refugees. He cut the conversation short and angrily left the house. Later he returned with Hassan and said to him in my presence, "Take him by the hand and leave, and don't let go until you're out of Jebalya."

TEN

Sumud

BEFORE ONE CAN SPEAK of the Intifada, as the Palestinians call the current uprising, one must first understand how the Palestinians have coped with life under the Israeli occupation up to this point. The key concept in this respect is *sumud*. *Sumud* means "sticking with it," "staying put," "holding fast" to one's objectives and to the land—in a word, it means survival. *Sumud* is an attitude, a philosophy, and a way of life, which maintains that one must carry on in a normal and undisturbed fashion as much as possible. As compared with organized civil disobedience, or passive resistance as preached by Gandhi, *sumud* is a more basic form of resistance growing out of the idea that merely to exist, to survive and remain on one's land, is an act of defiance, especially when deportation is the one thing the Palestinians fear most. *Sumud* also has a political dimension. The term was officially coined during the Baghdad summit in 1978 to refer to the one and a half million Palestinians living under Israeli rule. A special fund, the *amwal sumud*, was established under joint Jordanian and PLO supervision for the purpose of lending financial support to the population in the occupied territories. A man who has received a building permit from the Israeli military administration, for instance, can go to Jordan with a photocopy of the permit, present it to the *sumud* fund, and receive financial assistance to build his house. The goal is clearly to assist the Palestinian population in acquiring ownership over as much land and property as possible.

Although *sumud* is essentially passive by nature, it has a more active aspect, consisting of gestures that underscore the difference between surviving under difficult conditions and accepting them. During the course of my posing project, I was several times presented with examples of this active *sumud*. On one occasion, I was talking with a group of Palestinian youths in the Jelazun refugee camp, about twelve miles to the north of Jerusalem, when one of the young men, whom I shall call Abed, told me about his version of *sumud*. "Despite the fact that I am a university graduate," he said, "I can't find work in my profession, so I earn my living as a construction worker."

"Where do you work?" I asked.

"In Beit El, up there." He pointed at the hill that overlooked the refugee camp. On the hillside one could see scattered houses, with the European-style slanted red-tiled roofs, that are characteristic of the Jewish settlements in the West Bank and that look so incongruous in the dry, dusty landscape of the area. The barbed-wire fence that surrounded the settlement could not be seen from where we were, but I had seen it earlier when I drove past the settlement. "That means that you not only work for the Jewish but work for the worst of them, for the settlers," I said in an admonishing tone of voice.

Abed exchanged glances with his friends, who were sitting around, as if to ask them whether to include me in their little secret, and replied, "True, we work for the settlers. The money we earn allows us to live here, to be *samidin* [practitioners of *sumud*], but that isn't all. For us, in this camp, *sumud* isn't just bringing home money and buying a sack of rice and a few bags of sugar. When I work at the settlement I take advantage of every opportunity to fight them."

"What can you do as a simple laborer?"

"Quite a bit. First of all, after I lay tiles in the bathroom or kitchen of an Israeli settler, when the tiles are all in place and the cement has already dried, I take a hammer and break a few. When we finish installing sewage pipes, and the Jewish subcontractor has checked to see that everything is all right, then I stuff a sackful of cement into the pipe. As soon as water runs through that pipe the cement gets hard as rock and the sewage system becomes blocked."

We were sitting in a coffeehouse in the center of Jelazun, a small building constructed out of cement blocks, just one room with four bare walls. There were about eight low tables in the room and around them some of the locals were gathered, a few of them just conversing while others played *shadde*, a popular card game. It was obvious, at that time of day, that the men there were not employed. In one corner, behind a stone counter whose surface was worn from all the trays of coffee that had slid across it, stood an enormous copper kettle heating over a kerosene burner, and a small sink for washing the cups. A bunch of fresh nana leaves lay across the counter, giving off their sweet smell of mint. The old man who owned the place and doubled as the waiter threw some leaves into each glass of tea that he served. A wide gap in the southern wall of the room opened up onto a small terrace overhung by vine leaves. As we sat on this terrace, beat-up old cars went by on the main street below, raising light clouds of dust that mingled with the sweet tea I was sipping.

I had presented myself to the youths in my usual posing fashion, saying that I was originally from Balata and that after a long absence I'd decided to visit my native land. The youths naturally accepted this as a reason for my inquisitiveness and started describing the conditions of their lives in the refugee camp. One of them pointed to a shop in the center of Jelazun that sold electrical appliances. Black-and-white TV sets could be had there for a song, the youth told me. "We have become the garbage dump of Israeli," he complained. "We buy their secondhand cars which they don't want to drive anymore. We're the ones who load their broken furniture and damaged household appliances onto garbage trucks. Then we bring the stuff here, instead of transporting it to the municipal dumps."

The young men were eager to tell of their participation in the Palestinian struggle. The youngest was a boy of sixteen and, encouraged by his companions, he told about being detained in the Faraa prison, located in the vicinity of Nablus. This "installation," as the army prefers to call it, was formerly a military camp and had been transformed into a detention and interrogation center for those who are too young to be sent to regular prisons. The staff at Faraa expends a good deal of effort in trying to break the spirit of the youngsters and get them to sign confessions in which they admit to having committed various acts of violence and sabotage. They also concentrate on recruiting informers. The youth of the prisoners and the severe interrogation techniques that are employed have given the place an evil reputation and the locals have dubbed it *maslah lashabab* [slaughterhouse of the youth]. Having done time in Faraa serves as a sort of badge of honor for the post-'67 generation, those who were born under the occupation. It is a sign that they have actively participated in *sumud*.

As the young boy who sat with us began to tell his story, everyone else fell silent. "I was taken from my home at night, tied to the floor of an army jeep and blindfolded. By counting the curves in the road and judging by the length of the ride I knew I was headed for Faraa. The reception there was the usual. I had to stand outside, with my hands bound together, until morning came. Then I was interrogated and they demanded that I admit to throwing a Molotov cocktail at an army patrol. I didn't want to suffer too much and so I signed a confession. Then they wanted me to admit to throwing a hand grenade. They told me they had witnesses against me and that it would be best for me to confess, but I stood my ground this time, and it wasn't easy at all. I didn't confess and in the end got five months in prison."

"For the Molotov?"

"Yes."

"And the grenade?"

"I didn't confess to the grenade and so they couldn't do anything."

"That means you didn't throw it?"

"No, my friend, it doesn't mean I didn't throw it. It just means I didn't confess." The youth went on to list the enemies for my benefit, ranked according to priority. First the soldiers; then the Zionists; then the Jews. What he meant by Zionists, I found out, were Israeli nationalists, Jewish settlers, and anyone who opposed the establishment of a Palestinian state.

Two older men who were sitting at a table near ours joined in the conversation. Abu Adnan and Abu Ibrahim represented a generation of Palestinians that is haunted by the stinging defeat of 1948, when they either fled, leaving behind their villages and land, or were forcibly deported. But the younger generation, which is more active in resisting the occupation, owes its nationalistic education and inspiration to these elders. It is they who nurtured and sustained the Palestinians' identification with the villages of their origin. Every youngster who has never known any other existence than the miserable shanties of the refugee camp, when asked where he's from, can proudly name the place of his family's origin, which is often a village that ceased to exist long before he was born. True to form, Abu Adnan, a wrinkled old man of about seventy, told us that, only a short while ago, he had gone past the citrus grove that used to be his in Beit Naballah, near what is today Ben-Gurion International Airport. "I asked the driver to stop and I got out of the car. I wanted to pick a few oranges from the trees in the grove that used to be mine, but the Jew who apparently owned the place noticed me and chased me away." The old man sighed and drew a long sip from his cup of tea, resigned to a life of trial and tribulation, the purpose of which was known only to Allah.

The *sumud* of the older generation is basic and is more in the original spirit of the term, with no connotations of violence or activism for its own sake. But I noticed that some of the young men clenched their fists upon hearing Abu Adnan's tale. Abu Ibrahim, his friend, a stocky man with a mustache, blessed me for undertaking my journey among the refugee camp dwellers. He invited me to join him on his weekly visit to the big livestock market in Nablus the next day, which was Thursday. We agreed to meet in the morning, there at the coffeehouse, and on that note I politely took my leave.

The route from Jelazun to the Ramallah–Hebron road runs uphill. At the very top of the slope, an improvised roadblock had been erected. A few soldiers, new recruits from the military base where I once had the honor of being a platoon commander, manned the position. A man in civilian clothes, who

181

must have been a member of the Shin Bet, stood nearby, leaning against a white sedan. As I pulled up, a rifle was poked through the open car window and I was ordered, along with the passenger who was riding with me, to step out of the car and stand in the glare of its headlights, which I was instructed to leave on. A young soldier performed a body search on us and took a long, hard look at my ID. He opened the car trunk and went over its contents with the aid of a flashlight, then he ordered us to be on our way. It was merely a routine procedure.

Abu Ibrahim was already waiting for me when I showed up the following day in the center of Jelazun. After enjoying cups of black coffee which was strong enough to revive the dead, we got into an old beat-up VW van that belonged to Abu Ibrahim's business partner, and set out for Nablus. As I looked back on Jelazun from the Ramallah–Nablus road, the camp seemed to be blessed with a pastoral calm. It is situated in a small valley surrounded by open fields. From afar, one cannot perceive the squalor of the living conditions and the pervasive poverty. What one sees are the goatherd taking his flock out to pasture, the women hanging laundry on the flat roofs of their homes, and the cheery bustle of life.

Along the way, Abu Ibrahim told me more about himself. He worked as a night watchman for the offices of UNRWA in the camp and his monthly salary of about two hundred dollars was insufficient, he said, even when measured against the humble living standards of the refugee camp. He had a large family to support and thus had to supplement his income with an additional occupation. Every Thursday he would drive to the livestock market in Nablus, buy a few head of sheep, and sell them later, at a small profit, to the butchers in Jelazun and the surrounding villages. Abu Ibrahim turned his attention back to the narrow winding road. The twenty-year-old van was desperately chugging along in the wake of a large truck, unable to overtake it. The truck was laden with horses and mules, headed for the same destination as we were, and so we were obliged to stay behind it all the way to the market.

The market in Nablus is the largest in the occupied territories. Like markets elsewhere, it has traditionally served as a meeting place. Bits of information and gossip are exchanged there. The condition of the crops and livestock is analyzed and business in general is discussed. Apart from the active trade in livestock, various craftsmen such as saddlemakers and blacksmiths offer their services, and grain merchants come to do business. In recent years Israelis have come to the livestock markets in the West Bank, mainly to purchase donkeys, a cheap animal which can be fed to the carnivores in the Israeli zoos.

At the entrance to the market there is an enormous door. Near the door sits the "weigher," a man who arrives at the market carrying a pair of huge scales and for a few pennies weighs the sheep to verify and determine their precise worth. A continuous procession of trucks and vans kept arriving and unloading their cargo of cows, bulls, calves, and sheep. The animals, instinctively knowing what was in store for them, refused to get off the transporting vehicles without a fight. Several men, built like wrestlers, hopped into the compartments and forced the beasts to get out by means of the cruel, painful technique of twisting their tails. Other men, in bloodstained aprons, came out of a building and loaded great chunks of fresh meat, still hot and steaming, onto vehicles that had just brought in a live cargo.

I was mesmerized by the bloody spectacle and the stench of death and for some reason I decided to enter the slaughter-house. "Who is the brother?" a butcher inquired, some sharpened knives dangling from his belt. "I'm from here, from Balata. I've been away for some years, studying. Now I've come back and I'm just looking around." I was willing to retreat at this point, but the butcher grinned and invited me in. He introduced me to the entire staff, starting with the veterinarian, who stood behind a table and examined the intestines of the animals, making sure that they weren't diseased. Toward the back of the hall, where blood mixed with water flowed endlessly into two cement canals that ran along the sides, stood a calf. He sniffed me with his damp nose and seemed oblivious to all the commotion, to the streams of blood and the death rattles of slaughtered animals. I couldn't bear to stay, but the amiable butcher insisted that I watch him demonstrate his considerable skill as he skinned a cow that had just been slaughtered. Within minutes the carcass was relieved of its natural covering, and I was free to go and rejoin Abu Ibrahim.

Abu Ibrahim was engaged in a bout of fierce bargaining, in the best Oriental tradition, with some bedouins who had brought a flock of sheep to the market. He examined the sheep one by one, feeling their fat tails, before stating the price he was willing to pay. The other side feigned shock upon hearing his ridiculous offer and swore by the name of Allah that it was no less than an insult to the excellent sheep, which had been nurtured with such care, like members of his own family, even sharing his bread.

Onlookers, myself included, now entered the bargaining process. Some convinced the bedouin to lower the inflated price that he had set and others persuaded Abu Ibrahim, "for the sake of your honor" and "for the sake of Allah," to raise his offer somewhat. Finally, Abu Ibrahim and the bedouin shook hands and concluded the deal with the traditional sentences, the seller saying to the buyer, "Bless you," and the buyer replying, "Allah bless you." The heated argument that had been raging only a few moments ago was gone without a trace, as if it had never occurred. Five unhappy sheep bleated loudly and with heartrending pathos as they were separated from the rest of the flock and roughly bundled onto the van. It was a reasonable assumption that by sunset that day a butcher's knife would have slit their throats.

I thought about Abu Ibrahim, who had remained a *falah* (peasant) in spirit despite forty years of living without land and without a flock of his own, both of which he'd had in his village before becoming a refugee. In the market of Nablus one could see he was on his natural turf, much more than in the dismal office of some UN-sponsored welfare organization for refugees. It was enough to see his practiced hand run across the back of a sheep to gauge its weight, its health, and the amount of meat that it could provide to understand that forty years as a refugee hadn't changed him in any fundamental way.

When I returned to Jelazun, to the coffeehouse as usual, one of the men I found there told me that a group of people from the camp were going that evening to Deheishe, another refugee camp, near Bethlehem, to attend the wedding of Hamdi Faraj. Hamdi happened to be a good friend of mine and I very much wanted to be at his wedding. The only problem was that I hadn't seen him for a while and consequently he knew nothing about my posing project. I was afraid that he would greet me as Yoram and the men from Jelazun would discover my true identity. So I hastily took my leave and drove to Deheishe.

Hamdi was at home, as indeed he was obliged to be because of administrative orders that forbade him to leave the camp area. I congratulated him, and questioned him about his bride-to-be. With his usual candor Hamdi told me that there had been another girl, from Hebron, whom he had wanted to marry, but when he asked her father for her hand he was told that because of his political activity he was sure to end up in prison or with a bullet through his skull. The father wasn't ready to have his daughter marry such a man. "Then I met a local girl, from Deheishe, whom I also liked very much. Her family has a greater awareness of our situation and didn't object to the match." I told Hamdi all about my posing project and asked if he'd be willing to identify me as Fat'hi from Balata when I came to his wedding that evening. He readily consented, as I knew he would.

Hamdi, about thirty years old, is a journalist and one of the ideologues of the Popular Front in Deheishe. I first met him at the military court in Ramallah, where he had been brought in order to have his detention extended. His lanky, somewhat ascetic figure, bound in handcuffs, caught my attention and I asked the photographer who was with me to take his picture. I got a few details from his lawyer and sent my newspaper a brief item about him. When he was released he contacted me and we became very friendly. The charges brought against him amounted to "incitement," which, when applied to the occupied territories, means any expression of ideas that are not compatible with the official policy. According to the official policy, Palestinian Arabs are supposed to work, eat, and sleep and collaborate with the authorities. At the very most they are allowed to express support for Jordan and King Hussein. As far as I know, Hamdi was never accused of any terrorist activity or of committing any act of violence against Israelis.

That Friday evening I returned to Deheishe. It seemed as if almost the entire population of the camp was coming to the *zaffa* (wedding celebration). The narrow alleyways were jammed with vehicles bearing license plates from practically every town and city in the West Bank. A large empty lot in front of Hamdi's house was furnished with hundreds of stools and benches. Hamdi, with some of his close friends, sat in the first row, facing an unfinished construction which had been turned into an improvised platform decorated with ornamental rugs, palm branches, and large posters depicting Karl Marx and Che Guevara. Hamdi sat there calmly, as if the whole ceremony had nothing to do with him, dressed in his ordinary clothes and sandals, which he wore, I knew, in summer and in winter. There was no strict separation here of men and women as there traditionally is at Moslem weddings. The women sat together as a group, next to the men. The guests were dressed in simple everyday clothes as well, and had for the most part brought practical gifts, suitable for a young couple who were lacking in means: sacks of flour, rice, or sugar. Also unlike other *zaffa* ceremonies which I had attended, no calf or sheep was slaughtered for the occasion, nor were there trays laden with rice and meat. Only tea was served. The other weddings I'd been to were held in the cities. This was a wedding of refugees. "As long as we live under such conditions there's no need for ostentatious celebrations," said Hamdi.

Onto the platform stepped a man of about forty. He addressed the crowd through a microphone: "Good everning, *ya shabab*. We hereby announce the beginning of this revolutionary wedding which is an important event in the life of our comrade-in-arms, Hamdi Faraj. The ceremony will be dedicated to comrade Hassan Abed Al Jawad." Hassan Abed Al Jawad was one of the residents of the camp who had been deported to Jordan a few months earlier by the military administration after he was charged with being active in the PFLP. His mother was among the guests at the wedding, and the speaker pronounced her the guest of honor.

It took me a little while to realize that this was not a wedding in the ordinary sense of the word, but a political rally of PFLP sympathizers. The words spoken on that stage, with Marx's bewhiskered face in the background, gazing out on the proceedings, had nothing and everything in the world to do with the wedding of Hamdi Faraj and Hiam Shahin, both of them refugees, whose families came from the former village of Zakaria, near Beit Shemesh, nowadays known by its Hebrew

186

name, Zeharia. Each speaker or performer, as he or she went up to the platform, would pick up a red keffiyeh that was placed there and wind it around his or her neck like a bandanna.

The master of ceremonies continued: "I hope you all remember the most recent meeting between Shimon Peres and King Hussein, a meeting that was designed to sell us down the river." And again he sent greetings from the *samidin* of Deheishe to the dear comrade Hassan Abed Al Jawad. The volume was turned up on the improvised public-address system and he began to sing: "Destroy Zionism! / What was taken by force will be restored by force / and Zionism will vanish." The crowd answered: "Even if I shall be put at the bottom of the boiling river of hell / I will not give up my country and my identity." Next, a young boy, eight years old at the most, came onstage and recited: "We are children of the revolution / children of the Molotov and of the Kalashnikov!"

The master of ceremonies took the microphone back from the child. Now he settled accounts with those whom the refugees regard as worse than the enemy, as traitors to their cause. "There will be no mercy for traitors like Rashad Al Shawa [former mayor of Gaza and one of the city's wealthiest men] and Elias Frej [mayor of Bethlehem, well known for his conciliatory stance with regard to Israel and his close ties with King Hussein]. Our people have already foiled the enemy's plans in the past. We shall be capable of dealing with such characters!"

This last was a clear reference to the assassination of the mayor of Nablus, who had been appointed to his office by the military government, with Jordan's assent. Zafer Al Masri had been shot at the entrance to the municipal hall by a hit squad belonging to the Popular Front. I had interviewed the man one day before his death. He was a figure of dignity and not at all treasonous; his murder shocked me and was, in my opinion, proof of political immaturity on the part of Palestinian society.

Hamdi tapped me lightly on my arm and suggested that I take a good look around. On all the surrounding rooftops one could see armed soldiers posted on the lookout. From time to time a patrol went by in one of the neighboring streets. I was sure that among the soldiers, maybe even among the guests, there were members of the Shin Bet, who knew Arabic and understood exactly what the ceremony was all about. Even for someone who didn't understand the language the posters of Marx and Che Guevara conveyed a sufficiently clear message.

The wedding at Deheishe was also a form of *sumud*. For city and town dwellers, and villagers as well, *sumud* is more a private matter of survival; at the very most they will resist land seizure by the Jewish settlements. Among residents of the refugee camps, however, political consciousness is more highly developed, and there is a keen sense of loss and of the trauma of having been uprooted. For the refugees, *sumud* has a more active nature, and functions as a communal and political affair. I expected that at any moment the soldiers would interfere and put an end to this celebration, where the participants were openly showing their solidarity with the outlawed Popular Front, in an area that was supposed to be under control of the Israeli army. But no one around me seemed particularly concerned and the festivities continued. The soldiers kept their distance and didn't intervene. The general feeling was that here was an extraterritorial zone in which the camp residents could do as they pleased. Whoever was looking could plainly see, at the wedding in Deheishe, and no doubt in other places throughout the occupied territories, the germinating seed which later blossomed into the fully active popular uprising, one notch above *sumud*—the Intifada.

ELEVEN

Intifada

THE ARABS CALL IT the Intifada, which means "the Shaking" (in the sense of shaking oneself free or awake). Israeli officials prefer, as always, to speak of "violent disturbances of the order" or just plain "riots." The Palestinian popular uprising began in the Jebalya refugee camp at about noon on December 8, 1987.

A few days earlier, Shlomo Sakal, an Israeli salesman who had come to conduct business in Gaza, was stabbed to death. A couple of days after his murder, there was a horrendous road accident, not far from the Erez barrier. An Israeli driver lost control over his truck and smashed into a car filled with Jebalya residents. Four people were killed. In the camp the rumor spread that the driver was a relative of Sakal, who had deliberately caused the accident in order to avenge his blood. In the tense atmosphere of Jebalya such a claim was all that was needed to bring the majority of the population out into the streets in angry protest.

On the first day of demonstrations a young man was killed

by the soldiers' gunfire and about thirty were wounded. One day after the demonstrations in Jebalya there were demonstrations in Nablus, a relatively well-to-do city in the West Bank, which on the face of it bears little relation to the destitute and conservative Gaza. The next day, a woman and two youths were killed by military gunfire in the Balata refugee camp, and what had seemed to be another few scattered demonstrations (perhaps only a little more serious than usual) took on the proportions of a popular uprising.

Workers from the occupied territories almost completely stopped commuting to work in Israel, and the reverberations were soon felt by the Israeli economy. Foreign workers of other nationalities were recruited to replace the absent Palestinians, who normally constitute an overwhelming majority of the cheap labor force. The young people organizing the Intifada occasionally used force to gain cooperation. In the few cases where Palestinian workers tried to get to work in Israel, their vehicles were stoned, both at their point of departure within the refugee camps themselves and along the roads leading from the occupied territories to Israel. In Tel Aviv, Palestinian youths went from one restaurant kitchen to another and issued warnings to the Arab workers that if they knew what was good for them they would quit their jobs.

But for the most part participation was voluntary. The inhabitants of the cities in the West Bank and the Gaza Strip and East Jerusalem went on strike, and most of the people adhered to a self-imposed curfew, going out only for a limited number of hours to purchase necessary provisions. The villages, among them some extremely isolated ones that had never shown much concern with the occupation, had their access roads blocked with stones. Palestinian youngsters taunted the soldiers who were sent to suppress the demonstrations and threw stones at them. Some villages declared themselves "independent entities," no longer recognizing the authority of the Israeli administration.

In Jerusalem, the bubble of coexistence burst all at once, after twenty years of painstaking cultivation. Arab youths hurled stones at neighboring Jewish residences. The police had to raise roadblocks on the streets that connect East Jerusalem to the rest of the city, along the approximate path of the pre-1967 international border. Armed sentries were posted, ready to repel Arab youths who threatened to storm the Jewish neighborhoods. A senior police officer defined it as an "emergency measure so as not to completely forfeit the East city." A month later, the police established a special new unit for controlling and suppressing demonstrations.

The Israeli authorities in charge of security greeted the outburst with what seemed like total surprise. One had to have been either blind or stupid not to see what was coming, but the fact is that they were caught unprepared. This was reflected in the confused orders which the soldiers received when they were briefed on the situation in the occupied territories, before being sent to quell the "disturbances." The soldiers' confusion, in turn, quickly found expression in instances of extreme brutality against the demonstrators.

To Israel's dismay, such brutality is photogenic, and the international electronic media had a field day. (Citizens of "the only democracy in the Middle East" see just a fragment of the whole picture, after the material has been thoroughly scrutinized and censored by the director of the Israeli TV.) The intensive news coverage has done Israel's image a great deal of harm and has served well to convey a damaging indictment of the occupation; this alone can be chalked up as a victory of sorts for the Palestinian cause.

All in all, there have been hundreds of deaths and casualties. Through the first eight months of the Intifada more than 230 people had been killed, according to Israeli sources. Foreign sources quote higher figures, and so do alternative methods of calculation (such as including elderly people who suffered heart attacks as a result of inhaling tear gas and cases of involuntary abortion).

The main actors on the stage of the Intifada are the youth, members of the post-'67 generation. The identity of the leading instigators remains an absolute secret, which so far the Shin Bet has not managed to uncover. These leaders are young, and many of them have done their share of time in the Israeli prisons, which are a good place for learning how to handle the type of covert operations they are now engaged in; the military administration had generously provided them with this schooling for free.

Behind the scenes, the Intifada is directed, with impressive success, by local and national committees that operate without any visible coordination. These is, however, a central committee which distributes leaflets in which the population is given instructions: when to strike, when merchants may open their shops in order to allow the people to replenish their food supplies, and so on. Another source of information is the radio station of George Habash's PFLP, which broadcasts from Syria. A Palestinian friend of mine told me, "We no longer recognize the police or the army, but only the 'Voice of Jerusalem.' Their word is sacred with regard to instructions on how to act. If they were to tell us to go when the traffic lights are red and stop when they are green, we'd do it without hesitation."

The most dramatic change resulting from the Intifada, and one which poses a serious problem for Israel, is the fact that segments of the population who until recently had practiced a very mild form of *sumud* (meaning that they got as rich as they could, while maintaining good business relations with the Israelis) have become active resisters. Strikes against commerce have been continuously in effect, and the wealthier residents are compelled to assist their needy brethren, who are hurt by the strikes. Furthermore, the Israeli arm that wielded a club was not sensitive enough to differentiate between a demonstrator and an ordinary civilian, between an instigator and just another local resident, and many Palestinians who had never been involved in any form of active resistance now witnessed representatives of the occupation breaking into their own homes and felt its "iron fist" on their own skins. Quite naturally, they chose to join the circle of resistance.

At two in the morning, one Thursday, a few weeks after the outbreak of the Intifada, I received a phone call from an acquaintance of mine, whom I shall call Abu Halil, who lives in a small crime- and drug-infested refugee camp near Jerusalem. In a voice choking with anger Abu Halil told me about an operation that the Jerusalem police had conducted in the camp in the wake of recurring disturbances carried out by the local youth. "Some three hundred policemen and members of the border police arrived in the camp. They called through the loudspeakers for everyone to come out into the camp center. The announcer promised that no harm would come to anyone who came to the central square and that whoever stayed indoors would be punished. People started coming out, and already in the streets on the way to the square the police attacked some youngsters and beat them with clubs. We were instructed to sit in the square, and a security agent who knew Arabic addressed us, saying that he knew that most of the camp residents didn't participate in demonstrations and that it was only a case of a group of young hotheads. But we, the general public, pretended we were blind and didn't tell the police who the demonstrators were, and unless we did so, we would suffer. As he spoke, the soldiers walked through the rows of seated men and beat people with their clubs, and took some youths aside and beat them even harder. After two hours they left, and we brought about twenty wounded persons, some with broken arms, to the hospital."

I've known Abu Halil for some years now. He is certainly not an exemplary Palestinian nationalist; in fact, in my opinion, he's somewhere between being a potential collaborator and an ordinary opportunist. He always spoke of peaceful coexistence and his great ambition was to obtain an office in the municipality of Jerusalem. The camp he lives in belongs to the Jerusalem district, and the job he dreamt of would guarantee him a regular income, as well as providing him with some moderate influence and status among the other residents—in the relative terms of a refugee camp, of course. I never thought of him as someone who would engage in any sort of action against Israel, not even participating in a demonstration. "You know me, ya Yoram," he said in his good Hebrew. I didn't want to tell him that I thought he was no more than a miserable opportunist, and answered diplomatically, "Yes, ya Abu Halil, I know that you're one of those who believe in coexistence and peace." "Well, you Jews should know that if you have a list of enemies who hate you and are willing to fight you in every way, then you can put me, Abu Halil, in the number one spot on that list. Now your army and police have shown their true colors. They hit people for nothing and shoot tear gas into the homes of law-abiding civilians. I had to take my baby girl to the hospital because she almost suffocated."

The Intifada took Israel by surprise. During the first few weeks people still tried to believe that it was merely a question of isolated incidents, and various experts argued among themselves whether or not the demonstrations and strikes could properly be viewed as civil disobedience. Many have asked, including those whose job it is to know, how the Intifada came into being precisely when it did and what the reasons were for its having prevailed. This element of surprise was undoubtedly one of the causes for the Palestinians' success.

For twenty years Israel had neglected to give serious attention to what was happening in the occupied territories and to the processes which the population was going through. There existed—and still exists—a gap, both in information and in communication, between the military administration and the vast majority of the Palestinians in the West Bank and the Gaza Strip. Instead of dealing with this problem, Israel concentrated on intensive (and necessary) intelligence-gathering efforts aimed at preventing sabotage, terrorism, and any kind of subversive political activity by identifying possible targets in advance and apprehending potential perpetrators. To this end the Shin Bet used all the means at its disposal to establish a far-reaching intelligence network and develop effective detection and interrogation methods. Many people owe their lives to the successful operation of the Shin Bet.

But this sort of intelligence work is essentially localized. Its task is to pinpoint potentially harmful individuals and to conduct in-depth investigations to ensure that nothing remains unknown about a particular group or organization. The Shin Bet wasn't engaged in making assessments of mood and orientation among the population at large. It was focused on important figures, leaders in the occupied territories, who were affiliated for the most part with the PLO. Feisal Al Husseini, for instance, one of the more important leaders in the occupied territories and an unofficially acknowledged PLO figure, was arrested about half a year after I completed my posing project (long before the Intifada began) and was put under nine months' detention by administrative order without a trial.

The arrest and deportation of the indigenous Palestinian

leadership left a vacuum that was quickly filled on the local level of the refugee camps, neighborhoods, and cities. The local leaders, most of them graduates of the Israeli prisons, are conversant with Hebrew as well as with Palestinian political doctrine. Even in the absence of their "superiors" the new generation is able to conduct the Intifada with considerable skill.

There are several aspects to the occupation, of which the Shin Bet's mission to prevent subversion and sabotage is only one. There is also the administrative aspect of it. But the administration doesn't really keep in touch with the broad base of the Palestinian population any more than the Shin Bet does. It deals primarily with members of the local population who are willing to collaborate with them. The administration hardly ever meets with PLO supporters of various stripes and colors who make up the overwhelming majority in the occupied territories.

Thus the young leadership, which is connected to the PLO in an idcological though not in an operational sense, was able to develop undisturbed by either Israeli intelligence or the administration. While the Shin Bet's microfilm files were being filled with the names of collaborators and subversive elements, new organizations were established which were not directly associated with terrorist or other anti-Zionist activities. These organizations took advantage of Israel's readiness to allow a free flow of foreign funds into the occupied territories, as these funds bolstered its own distressed economy as well. In this way a sturdy infrastructure was established, in terms of organization and human resources. In all the West Bank cities and in Gaza, voluntary youth committees were established, most of them under the aegis of the *shabiba*, the PLO youth movement whose leaders acted as informal regional coordinators. (It was three months before the authorities decided to clamp down on the *shabiba* and proclaim it an illegal organization.) Charitable societies sprang into being, strong unions were established, and newspapers managed by PLO sympathizers began to be published. Almost any inhabitant of the occupied territories could find an outlet for legitimate nonviolent activity, with the support of one of the numerous Palestinian organizations.

Daily contact with the authorities taught the Palestinians how to avoid the mistakes of the past. They learned to compartmentalize their underground activities and to keep a tighter hold over their secrets. These are among the reasons why the Israelis still don't know who the leaders are, though it is manifestly clear to everyone that there are leaders. In addition, there is an open exchange of information. I attended some lectures at which Arab lawyers explained to a young and militant audience what their rights were, how to withstand interrogation by the Shin Bet, and what tactics the interrogators used in order to extract a confession. Uncensored information on what was happening in the occupied territories has been distributed in recent years almost uninterruptedly through the kind of underground leaflets that now serve as one of the major means of directing the Intifada. One such leaflet found its way into my hands quite some time before the Intifada. It spelled out the names of Arab agents who were collaborating with the Israelis and the code names of their Shin Bet contacts; it also listed the cases of nine disappeared and murdered persons in the occupied territories who had been active members in the Palestinian organizations.

In the age of the Intifada, Palestinians are making use of the knowledge they've acquired over the years about the operational methods of the Shin Bet. In several villages the residents who were known to be collaborators received anonymous instructions to return the weapons they had received from the Shin Bet for purposes of self-defense. Some of them agreed to return their weapons, swore by the Koran that they would no longer be in contact with the enemy, and won pardons from the popular tribunals. One collaborator, Muhammad Ala'id, a fortune-teller by profession and a resident of the village of Kabatya in the north of the West Bank, refused to comply with the demands of the young militants in his village. His home was attacked and set on fire by an enraged crowd; Ala'id himself was strangled to death and his body was prominently hung on an electricity pole as a warning to other collaborators.

For twenty years the Palestinians have lived among us. During the day, we were the employers who profited by their labor and exploited them for all they were worth; in the afternoon we were the police; in the evening we were the soldiers at the roadblock on their way home; and finally, at night, we were the security forces who entered their homes and arrested them. While many Israelis regarded the Palestinian Arabs primarily as cheap labor and a potential security risk, the Palestinians studied (sometimes unconsciously) Israeli society with all its characteristic weaknesses and vulnerabilities. They know exactly how the average Israeli thinks and feels; they know what is important to him and how he can be hurt. They know how to identify the military units that are sent to suppress their demonstrations, and can tell which are tougher, which more lax, and what the human profile of each unit is. A curious demonstration of the intimate knowledge that the young Palestinians have of their oppressors' sore spots is the kind of insults that the children hurl in the face of the soldiers to accompany the barrage of stones. "Your sister fucks an Arab!" they shout. As intended, this infuriates many of the soldiers, who are apparently unable to appreciate the irony of an Arab referring to himself in a derogatory way as a means of wounding the enemy's pride.

The young Palestinians work in Tel Aviv, Jerusalem, and other Israeli cities. They identify with the values of Israeli society at least as much as they do with their traditional backgrounds. They get a whiff of the democratic privileges that Israeli citizens enjoy, but they cannot share in them. The young man who spends his workweek among a people living under democratic rule returns to his home, which is only an hour away but which has (in fact, although not officially) been under curfew for twenty years. Any Arab who walks in the streets at a late hour can expect to be detained and questioned about his actions, even during periods of relative calm. He sees and recognizes the value of freedom, but is accorded the sort of treatment that characterizes the most backward dictatorial regimes. How can he be anything but frustrated?

The Israeli approach to dealing with the Palestinians in the occupied territories follows the same routine as the policy which was implemented with respect to the Arab minority within the State of Israel after the War of 1948. In 1967, as in 1948, a population census was taken in all the occupied territories. Whoever was present received an ID. Whoever was away from home at that moment, for any reason, was declared an absentee by the Israelis. The absentee's property was then transferred to an Israeli caretaker, and his right to return to his home in Jerusalem, in Nablus, or in Hebron was denied, even if his wife and children were there at the time of the census and had received identification documents from the military government. The absentee was allowed to enter the area only as a visitor. There were a few exceptions where families were permitted to reunite, most of them in exchange for some promise of collaboration or because of a strong economic incentive.

This is exactly how Israel took over much of the Arab-owned property and how it dealt with the Arabs who remained within Israeli borders after the War of 1948. Like the West Bank Arabs of today, they were placed under strict military rule for a period of thirteen years.

One mustn't fail to take into account, however, the differences that exist between the situation in 1948 and today. The Arab population that remained in Israel then numbered only 156,000 left out of 700,000 before the 1948 war, far less than the one and a half million Palestinians in the occupied territories today. They were weak and divided, and stunned by the trauma of defeat, making it possible for Israel to impose its rule over them.

Today, it is a different story altogether. The population in the occupied territories is organized; there are Palestinian organizations that serve as standard-bearers of the struggle for independence and as a source of identification. The media are much more prominent than they were in 1948 and carry their message to all the corners of the world; there are fewer dark recesses where government agents can operate in the interest of maintaining the discipline of the civilian population using tactics that are best kept under cover of secrecy.

Just as the Israeli authorities never made a sober and realistic assessment of the political situation with regard to the Arabs in the occupied territories, so too they refused to address the human dimensions of the problem. This book has sought to emphasize how, on the level of day-to-day interaction, Israeli Jews have exploited and humiliated their Arab neighbors. The Palestinians were employed in a variety of low-paid jobs, often under demeaning conditions. Many thousands of acres of land were seized from the Arabs for the purpose of establishing Jewish settlements. The land seizures turned an entire generation of West Bank inhabitants into industrial workers, usually in Israeli-owned factories.

Whether justified by security concerns or not, the Palestinian people were turned into victims of arbitrary action on the part of the police and the Shin Bet, and harassed by the ubiquitous roadblocks. A car from the occupied territories traveling on Israeli roads is more than likely to be stopped several times, not only by soldiers conducting security checks but also by the traffic police, who will closely examine the driver's papers and slap him with a fine for the slightest offense. Not long ago, a book of photographs was published which contained shocking pictures of policemen in Tel Aviv harassing Arab prisoners, most of whom were workers who hadn't been convicted of any serious crimes. The police high command looked into the question of how the photographer, Joel Greenberg, had managed to get this insider's view. There was no parallel investigation into the incidents of police brutality that had been documented and published for all to see.

On every occasion when the average Palestinian came into contact with the authorities, he encountered an attitude that was rigid and inflexible. The policies were singularly unimaginative and those who carried out these policies gave them such names as "the carrot and the stick," "the iron fist," "we help those who help us," etc. The way in which Arabs were, and are, treated in Israel reflects a narrow-mindedness and the lack of any desire to deal directly with the political, diplomatic, and human implications of the issue.

The Intifada, in my opinion, can be understood as the anguished cry of a minority trying to call attention to the discrimination that is being practiced against it, as much as it can be viewed as a demand for national liberation. Throughout the events of the last few months, Palestinian friends have continued to call me on the phone. They all know that I'm not working as a journalist at the moment and that if I were to visit them it wouldn't be a guarantee of media coverage. They simply want someone to pour their hearts out to. For a long time I've had the feeling that the Palestinian population has despaired of the ordinary contacts it has with representatives of the Israeli administration, and that it is trying hard to bypass the establishment and address itself directly to the Israeli public. I have heard Palestinians say more than once, "Israelis don't have any idea what's going on here. If they did, things would look different"—a naïve sentiment, in my humble opinion.

☐ ☐ ☐

About three weeks after the Intifada broke out, I drove to Nablus to visit a few friends and gain a firsthand impression of the events in the West Bank. All the shops were closed, and except for frequent military patrols, Nablus was relatively quiet that day. I visited with my friends, listened to their explanations of how they and their fellow Palestinians were handling the situation and about the ways in which the Intifada was being directed, and then set out on my way back to Jerusalem. I should mention that the trip to Nablus was an ordinary one and that I wasn't posing as anyone but myself.

Approximately ten miles south of Nablus, on the road to Ramallah, there was a serious traffic jam. A long line of cars was parked along the roadside, and no one showed any signs of moving up ahead. I was sure that the traffic was being stalled by a roadblock, or that a Molotov cocktail had been thrown at a passing vehicle, or something of the sort. From a distance I could see that a crowd had formed farther up the road. I parked my car and walked over to the scene of the action.

As I drew closer I noticed that the crowd was a mixed one: there were Israeli soldiers, Jewish settlers running all over the place, carrying arms as usual, and a crowd of local Palestinians. On the left side of the road, facing toward Jerusalem, was a small Peugeot car with military license plates, or what remained of it after it had apparently swerved over to the opposite lane and collided head-on with an Arab bus. Trapped in the driver's seat of the mangled car was an army officer of immense girth. There was blood everywhere, yet it kept on bubbling out of his mouth. The officer mumbled incoherently; he was in a coma.

An army ambulance that happened to pass by stopped at the scene of the accident and some young aides tumbled out. But like all the other soldiers and settlers who were standing around, they seemed rather helpless. One of them asked the assembled crowd if there was a doctor among them. An Arab man of about thirty stepped forward. "I am a doctor," he said in English. The aide asked him to insert an intravenous needle into the wounded man's vein, an operation that aides are not qualified to do on their own. The officer was writhing and squirming in agony, and I went up to help the doctor. I wound a rubber tourniquet around the injured man's arm while the doctor felt the arm, searching for a vein. It wasn't easy to find —the man's obesity and his state of shock obscured any trace of his veins—but the doctor succeeded in locating a suitable spot. He murmured the traditional Islamic incantation which must be said prior to performing any act of significance: *"Bismillah Al Rahman Al Rahim* [In the name of merciful and gracious Allah]," and pushed the needle in. A thin trickle of blood slowly climbed the rubber tube connecting the needle to the IV sac, confirming that the needle had found its mark.

The officer's M-16 rifle was inside the car, twisted out of shape but still loaded. I checked the firearm and handed it to one of the soldiers, instructing him to double-check it in case a bullet had lodged in its barrel as a result of the impact of the collision. Then, together with a red-bearded settler who was toting a loaded Uzi submachine gun, I began sawing off the front part of the car in order to have better access to the pieces of metal that had trapped the injured officer's leg. Next we managed to remove the roof of the car, and then someone else joined us in our efforts to get the car out from under the bus. This newcomer was standing on the opposite side of the vehicle, and when I raised my head for a moment, our eyes met and we recognized each other: it was Nidal Taha, a lawyer from Nablus and an acquaintance of mine. He stretched out his hand in greeting over the officer's bleeding head, and we chatted as we resumed our task of trying to pull back the car metal. Finally, a military jeep equipped with a steel cable and hook arrived. First we used the heavy hook to bang some of the metal outward, then we attached the cable to the car and the driver of the jeep towed the misshapen Peugeot back away from the bus as the red-bearded settler, the Palestinian lawyer, and I all shouted instructions at him.

A military helicopter arrived, bringing medical personnel, who removed the injured man from the wreck and flew him to

201

a hospital. I stayed on and talked with some of the Arabs who were there. "He was probably a high-ranking officer," one of them said to me.

"No way," I answered. "You can tell by his long hair that he's a reservist. Yesterday he was sitting at home with his wife and kids and today he was sent here to fight the Intifada, and this is what happened to him."

"May God speed his recovery," said the Arab, and then he hastened to inform the others: "He's not a high-ranking officer, but a reservist. Just yesterday he was watching TV with his wife at their home in Tel Aviv, and today he got hurt here."

I listened for expressions of antagonism among the Palestinians, most of whom were commuters who had been on the bus that was involved in the accident. But all I heard them say to one another was: "I hope that he gets good care at the hospital and that, inshallah, he'll recover."

As I began walking back to my car, I was approached by a young soldier who was returning to the military jeep he had parked farther up the road. In slightly broken Arabic, he said, "You know, today I've changed my opinion about you. It was very human of you to help an officer of ours despite all the trouble and rioting." I looked back over my shoulder to see whether perhaps he was addressing some Arabs standing behind me, but there was no one there. For a moment I was at a loss, then I pulled myself together. Most of the time I was at the scene I had been talking with the Palestinians, and he apparently thought that I was one of them. I could now pass as an Arab even without making any effort to pose.

□ □ □

Several days after I returned from Nablus, I received a call from Hassan Jibril from the Shati refugee camp near Gaza. "Everyone here asks about you and wants to see you." Hassan's invitation included a list of items which he needed and which weren't to be had in the refugee camp or in the city of Gaza because of the strikes and the curfew. Despite Hassan's advice to take an Arab taxi from the old City of Jerusalem, I decided, out of laziness, to go in my own car.

After I got past the Erez roadblock I spread my red keffiyeh across the dashboard, and out of respect for the Intifada I added a black-and-white keffiyeh as well, which I tied on the outside as a sort of flag. When I reached Omar Almukhtar, the main street of Gaza, I saw that all the traffic was turning into a small side street to the left. I searched for a "No Entrance" sign on the main road, in case one had been set up there recently, but there wasn't any, so I proceeded to drive straight ahead, toward the seafront. Two youths, their faces covered by their keffiyehs, were burning a rubber tire on the roadside while a group of youngsters sat on a nearby fence watching them. One of the youngsters saw my car, and within seconds they were all hurling rocks the size of oranges in my direction. Fortunately, they noticed me just a moment too late; I hit the gas pedal and sped out of their range.

Next I encountered a convoy of military jeeps leaving the military administration building of Gaza at breakneck speed and with their headlights on. Armed with clubs, the soldiers riding the jeeps beat the windows and doors of the few Arab cars they passed in the street. This willful damage was apparently a local version of the warning sirens that certain vehicles use in an emergency. These actions were a warning.

The southern entrance to Shati was blocked by piles of junk. A gang of children stood there slinging stones at the roof of a four-story building. I backed up and parked my car in a safe place behind a wall, then I walked in the direction of the children. A few rocks landed by my feet, but their main target was an army lookout post on top of the four-story building, which is relatively tall for Gaza and which commanded a good view of the surroundings. Two bored-looking soldiers manned the position. One of them saw me and, noting that I was a stranger, he yelled out, "Hey, you!," tapping his forefinger against his temple to indicate that he thought I was crazy.

I tried to get close to the kids, but they ran into an alleyway, where they continued flinging rocks. Residents of the camp casually passed through the shower of stones, as if the entire affair had nothing to do with them.

I addressed a young woman who walked by with an older woman, probably her mother. "Excuse me, madam. I'm a journalist and have come here at the invitation of Hassan Jibril and Ibrahim Abu Giap." I mentioned Ibrahim's name because I knew the respect which he was accorded in Shati. "Maybe you can go over and have a word with the children so they'll let me through?"

"Follow us and don't be afraid," they answered. So I took cover behind the two Palestinian women and ventured close to the demonstrators. The women called to the oldest boy in the crowd to come over and take charge of me. The elderly woman continued on her way, but the younger woman remained behind to see what the boys were going to do with me. I repeated my request and again mentioned the names of Hassan and Ibrahim.

"Hand over your press card," the lad ordered brusquely. He glanced at my card without really reading it. "Are you a Jew or an Arab?"

"A Jew."

"Are you armed?"

"Go ahead, search." I raised my arms but the lad didn't bother to search. At this point the young woman who had escorted me intervened: "Take him to Hassan Jibril and see who he is. If he's not a journalist and a friend of Hassan, don't let him leave this place alive." She did not intend for me to hear these words, and I was convinced of their sincerity.

We entered the camp. The streets were charred black and the air was filled with the smell of burning rubber. Junk was piled up everywhere, obstructing the narrow streets. The kids, who up till then had been occupied with throwing rocks at the soldiers, now had a new source of amusement—me. They walked behind me, put little stones into my bag, tripped me up with their feet, and sprayed me with pebbles. *"Sahayuni wassah* [Filthy Zionist]," they cursed. Now and again I would feel a thump on my shoulders or the back of my neck, and I grew tired of turning around each time to try to catch sight of who was jostling me. I soon got used to the situation and just proceeded to walk straight ahead.

Then I heard someone call from behind, *"Ahalan,* ya Fat'hi." It was Hassan. It turned out that he'd been following me for a few minutes, and it was he who had been tapping me on my back, trying to catch my attention. We planted our lips on each other's cheeks, in the customary fashion, and this acted as a

204

sign for the rough company escorting me that their job was over. They dispersed and left us in peace.

The first thing that Hassan asked me was what name I had used in introducing myself. When I told him I had used my own name, he became angry. "This is impossible. There are too many people here who remember you as Fat'hi, so you'll have to go on being Fat'hi. If not, I'll be in trouble." Once this was settled, we returned to my car, taking a detour in order to reach it safely. The young demonstrators who were crowding the entrance to the camp were so drunk on power that even Hassan wasn't able to prevent them from attacking my car with a volley of rocks and stones. In these days of the Intifada, any car with yellow (Israeli) license plates is liable to be demolished. In a sudden reversal, cars bearing license plates from the occupied territories had become safer than Israeli ones.

We managed to drive through stone barriers and burning tires into the camp, where some of Hassan's friends had to surround my car to shield its windows from being smashed by the children, who ruled the street. The children ranged in age from three to twelve. I could foresee the day when people in their twenties, like Hassan, would stand helpless in the face of a mob of children, unable to guarantee the safety of a Jewish Israeli guest like myself. Finally we made it to the garage of one of Hassan's friends, where we parked the car and covered it well.

Shati is a miserable place to live in even in ordinary times; now, the chaos was unprecedented. The sewer had run over, flooding entire streets. The large garbage cans were being used as road barriers, and the sand in the alleys was covered with a black layer of burnt rubber, the residue of all the tires that had blazed there over the past three months. The children, rulers of the Intifada, could be found on all points of the perimeter of the camp, armed with improvised slingshots and creating an atmosphere of apocalypse and anarchy. In the alleys, one could see evidence of the self-imposed idleness that was the result of the strikes. On an old mattress that lay in front of the entrance to one of the houses, a grandfather played with his grandson, who laughed happily. The young men, those who were twenty and thirty years old and who would ordinarily have been off working someplace in Israel during these hours, wandered around in small groups. Well dressed, clean-shaven, with their hair washed and combed, they chatted among themselves and read the newspapers. At their age they were too old to join the daily demonstrations.

We went over to the Shifa hospital, which was located near the camp. There, among others, we visited Muhriz Hamuda Al Nimnim, a young victim of the recent violence. His brother, who was at his bedside, said, "If they had done it to me it would at least have made some sense, because I throw rocks and Molotov cocktails. But Muhriz is a sick person who never participated in a demonstration." He then told us as much of the story as he knew.

People in the camp saw Muhriz being arrested by the soldiers who manned the lookout post I had passed on my arrival. Eighteen days later he was found unconscious, in front of the entrance to the Shifa hospital. In addition to the usual injuries inflicted by the Israeli troops—broken arms and legs—Nimnim had been hit on the head. He was now a vegetable, incapable of speaking, unable to tell what happened. The palms of his hands and his fingers were badly burned, as though he was forced to grasp a red-hot metal object.

I asked his brother if they were sure that the soldiers had done it. He replied that there were witnesses who saw him being beaten by soldiers upon his arrest, "but not in such a way." The brother spread out the contents of a sack which had been found next to Nimnim at the gate of the hospital. In it were the clothes that Nimnim had apparently worn throughout the period of his absence. To my dismay, I discovered a damning piece of evidence among the foul-smelling rags: a strip of flannel cloth, of the kind used in the army for wiping weapons clean of grime and oil. The rag was tied in the shape of a loop the size of a man's head. As soldiers commonly use these strips of cloth for blindfolding suspects, the chances seemed good that the criminal act of sadism committed against Muhriz had indeed been carried out by members of the Israeli Defense Forces.

I asked Hassan to take me over to Jebalya because I wanted to visit Fat'hi Raban and Muhammad Abu Al Naser. We drove there in a Fiat which was dented all over and had shattered windows. Its owner, a teacher from Gaza, apologized, explaining, "I drove it on the day of the general strike and the children bashed it up."

On the way, Hassan told me that during the early days of the Intifada, soldiers had entered the home of Muhammad Abu Al Naser. "They went from house to house, searching for kids who had participated in the demonstrations. When they saw in his identification papers that he was a released prisoner, they took him outdoors and broke one of his legs with their clubs." Fat'hi Raban was luckier. He had succeeded in fulfilling an old ambition of his—he had purchased a relatively spacious apartment for himself and his family in a neighborhood close to the refugee camp.

We entered Jebalya without attracting attention, since we were in a car with local license plates. As we arrived, we heard a burst of gunfire very close by. (Later that evening we heard that two armed men had attacked and seriously wounded a Jewish drilling contractor.) Within minutes, a mass commotion broke out. A military command car carrying a loudspeaker announced a curfew and the local residents all hurried to their homes. My attention focused on a small girl who in the midst of all the bustle ran over to a pile of garbage, where some ducks were waddling about. She grabbed them by the wings, tucked them under her arms, and hurried away—a little girl carrying three squawking ducks off to safety.

Under the circumstances, we couldn't enter Jebalya, so we made an about-face and returned to Gaza. The visit would have to be postponed for an indefinite period of time.

Conclusion

WHEN I FIRST SET OUT to pose as a Palestinian Arab, my major concern was to examine the relationship between Jews and Arabs in Israel from as close a vantage as possible. Instead of dabbling in intellectual politics and adhering to a dogmatic ideological stance, I preferred to meet the situation head-on, under conditions that would probably be as close to the actual state of affairs as any Israeli could hope to experience. In particular, I was looking for the personal dimension, which is lacking in so many learned articles that analyze the Arab-Israeli conflict.

In the end, my experience has not left me with any far-reaching conclusions. To state that Arabs are discriminated against in the Jewish State of Israel is hardly an earthshaking revelation. What I learned that I hadn't known beforehand were mainly details, rather than generalizations of an abstract and theoretical nature.

Posing was a tactic that enabled me to see the conflict in a different perspective and to experience it with a greater intensity. As an imposter, I was able to understand, for the first time, what it means for a man to feel afraid and insecure inside his own home when a military patrol passes outside his window. I had heard Palestinians tell of such things many times, and I had always regarded it as a slightly wearisome example that they were prone to give in order to embellish their arguments against the occupation. But when I was gripped by that paralyzing fear myself, when I felt it in my guts, I grasped a dimension in their lives in a concrete fashion, in a way that I never really could as an Israeli journalist, however understanding I was of their situation. It wasn't a question of discovering new facts, but of discovering what it meant to feel the facts. My imposture didn't alter my political perception, but it served to increase the depth of my awareness and it considerably strengthened my ability to communicate my understanding of the situation.

A second advantage in adopting the device of posing, apart from the intensity and intimacy that it lent to my experience, was the unguarded openness with which I was addressed by the Palestinians whom I encountered. The residents of the occupied territories are well versed in how to deal with journalists and generally present a standard line. As a journalist it is highly unlikely that I would ever have witnessed the sort of conversation which took place among the young men in Jebalya, in which one of them openly disagreed with the others. When I slept in Abu Naim's flophouse in Tel Aviv with the boys from the Gaza Strip, one of them told me what he was working for (to add another square meter to his new home) and what made him jealous (that the girls from Nablus were more liberated than those of Gaza), and when he told me, "May there come the day when we'll settle accounts with the Jews, just one day," I had every reason to regard his words as an unselfconscious and authentic expression of his thoughts. He said them to me as if he were saying them out loud to himself; it was not a pose for the benefit of some journalist who had come to interview him.

Now that the posing part of my project was over, the time had come to convey what I had experienced to the world at large. During the time when I was engaged in writing it all down, I was also invited to appear as a guest lecturer on various occasions. The one instance that attracted the most attention on the part of the Israeli public was, of course, when I appeared on TV. Several newspapers carried a commentary following my appearance. The reactions among Israeli Jews in general ranged from vehement scorn and angry criticism on the one hand to benign curiosity on the other.

Some of the accusations leveled against me were absurd. One columnist, writing for the newspaper *Ha'aretz* (considered liberal and progressive), blamed me for being a "professional justice seeker." Now, just what did she think was wrong with seeking justice? Or did it bother her that I was doing so as a "professional"—that is, getting paid as a journalist and reporter? One may as well accuse a medical practitioner of being a "professional health seeker" or blame a mechanic for being committed to fixing every car that is brought to his garage.

Those of my Jewish audience who did exhibit interest were unfortunately not so much concerned about the Palestinians and how they manage their lives under extreme adversity; mainly they were curious to know how I "did it." My appearance isn't Middle Eastern, and a native speaker of Arabic would have been able to tell that I wasn't an Arab myself had we discussed issues that required a measure of sophistication. However, one's appearance is determined not only by what nature has provided but also by a whole array of props, instruments, and items of clothing that characterize different groups of people, as well as their typical modes of behavior. I have already explained how I prepared myself carefully in this respect.

One of the things I learned was that as long as I didn't upset people's expectations it was very easy to mislead them. The risk of being discovered was much smaller when I was posing as an Arab among Jews. The moment they saw me with an Arabic newspaper and wearing ragged clothes, I was an Arab as far as they were concerned. With Jews I scarcely ever engaged in a conversation that went beyond rudimentary work-related speech. But even when I was more intimately involved with Jews, such as with Miri or on the kibbutz, I did not arouse any suspicion. On the kibbutz, one may recall, I hardly had to make any effort to pose. Perhaps it just shows that people are naïve. They take things at face value, and having formed a first impression, they tend not to change it.

But then, why should a Jew suspect an Arab of being a Jewish imposter? Obviously, nobody is interested in posing as someone inferior, and in Israel an Arab's status is inferior to that of a Jew. There might be a case where an Arab worker living in Israel would pose as a Jew in order to make life a bit easier for himself, but no one of sound mind will suspect that an Arab employee who is performing hard physical labor for very low wages is not actually an Arab.

The Palestinians had more reason to suspect me, for they live in an environment which encourages subterfuge and undercover activity. Yet I found it relatively easy to establish myself as an Arab among them. The ritual greetings, for instance, that take place upon every encounter may serve as an authentication of the persons involved as much as a recital of passages from the Koran. When two Palestinians cross each other's paths they promptly exchange blessings, even if they are not acquainted: "*Asalamu aleikum* . . ." This is an authentic expression of their cultural identity, and anyone capable of conforming to the relatively elaborate customs and etiquette of the Arabs will be accepted as one of them.

Another reaction I often encountered was that of the apologists who attempted to deflect my arguments by means of a comparison which would put Israelis in a favorable light. Their claim is a familiar one: an Arab among Jews is much better off than a Jew among Arabs. "Let's see you pose as a Jew among Arabs," they challenged me. "You would wind up dead." Pose as a Jew? The nature of their argument is revealed by this absurdity. I had no need to pose as a Jew—I happen to be Jewish by accident of birth. What's more, it is interesting to note that the right-wing Gush Emunim settlers were themselves those who repeatedly claimed that they enjoy peaceful relations with their Arab neighbors. Gush Emunim and their like raised this claim as "proof" that the settlements don't cause any undesirable friction with the Arabs.

In fact, of course, there is considerable animosity on the part of both the Jews and the Palestinians, and the situation in Israel and in the occupied territories can often be dangerous. But a lot depends on the circumstances. An Israeli civilian who visited a refugee camp as a guest (in the days before the Intifada) was less likely to be regarded as a representative of the occupation than one who shopped in the open market of one of the West Bank cities, even though it seemed the other way around in the imagination of many Israelis. For three years I had been going around as a journalist among the West Bank Palestinians, often encountering people who were sworn foes of the Israeli regime. Yet not once during that time did I feel any particular threat or danger. To the best of my knowledge my colleagues, who have spent days on end among the Arabs as Israeli journalists, feel the same way.

In any case, the attempt to draw an analogy between ruler and ruled, between an occupying force and a subjugated population, is misguided, if not downright unjust. Anton Shamas, the Israeli Arab writer, responded to this interpretation of my posing project when he commented that one cannot in good faith equate the position of a Palestinian Arab in a Tel Aviv restaurant with that of a Jew in a restaurant in Nablus. I believe that anyone who has read the description of my experiences as a laborer in Tel Aviv will not fail to see his point.

As for the response of Palestinians to my project, most of those who heard about it seemed to regard it with mixed feelings. On the one hand, they were skeptical about what it could accomplish, while on the other, they expressed something that could perhaps be defined as gratitude. At least, they realized, I was making an honest effort to achieve a closer understanding of their situation. Immediately after the project was over I sent to the various Palestinians whom I had misled a copy of Feisal Al Husseini's letter of endorsement, usually accompanied by an apology. Their reactions were almost always the same. At first they were furious that I had deceived them, and then they gradually came around to appreciating my motives and understanding my actions. Thus, the first reaction of Muhammad Abu Al Naser from Jebalya, the released prisoner who had forced me to quote the Koran, was: "You have done a very ugly deed. How could you drink coffee in my home and dine at my table and lie to me at the same time? Besides, it was unnecessary for you to pose. If you had told me that you were an Israeli Jew, I would have received you in just the same fashion." I asked his forgiveness and eventually he acceded.

213

Both Jews and Palestinians asked me why I didn't go all the way, though "all the way" meant something different to each group. Jews wanted to know why I didn't try to join one of the Palestinian organizations. Perhaps I would even have been requested to commit an act of terrorism. In response I would say that while terrorism is one, very real, aspect of the situation in the Middle East, the overwhelming majority of Palestinians do not participate in terrorist activities, and it would be a harmful misrepresentation to imply that they did. Also, I must admit that there are certain "thrilling" experiences that I am inclined to do without.

The Palestinians had a more valid objection. They argued that my project lasted too short a time to allow me to experience what a Palestinian really feels in living under the occupation. Despite my well-intentioned effort, I was no more than an Israeli who had played a game for a short while. There is a great deal of truth in this claim, but again, one has to bear in mind that when I first began the project I was already very well informed about what was going on in the occupied territories.

Then why, some of the Palestinians insisted, didn't I get to see the inside of a prison or undergo an interrogation? These are typical experiences for thousands of young Palestinians. The answer is that I had to impose certain limits on myself. The cover under which I was operating wasn't sufficiently tight to be effective in dealing with the security authorities in Israel, who are equipped to check a person's identity within minutes and with a high degree of accuracy. One has to remember that I was posing in a situation which is extremely tense and in which suspicions are easily aroused in any case. Had I been arrested the truth would have surfaced almost immediately, after which I would have been charged with obstructing the law or else I would simply have been prevented from continuing my project.

In the end, the impressions I received accumulated to form a rather depressing picture of fear and mistrust on both sides. The Palestinians, employed as a cheap labor force, are forced into the role of active observers with respect to Israeli society, whereas Israeli Jews don't even do that much and are satisfied

214

to rule without exhibiting the least curiosity about how the other side lives. My most definite conclusion is that a continuation of Israel's military presence in the West Bank and the Gaza Strip threatens to change Israel into a place which some people, myself included, will find unlivable. Most simply put, I am tired of having to witness the disastrous results of the occupation every day, as well as frightened of the possibility that many people, on both sides, may be doomed to suffer bloodshed and destruction. As an Israeli Jew, I believe that it is too high a price to pay for the messianic and imperialistic aspirations of a small but militant minority among us, all legitimate claims to an independent and secure Jewish state notwithstanding.

When the authorities want to test the strengths and weaknesses of security procedures, at Ben-Gurion International Airport for instance, they periodically plant an agent of theirs who simulates a potential risk, raises a false alarm, and activates the system. This is exactly the tactic I employed.

I had wanted to give a warning signal, to hold up a mirror to the face of Israeli society, of which I am a part. Now, since the outbreak of the Intifada, things have changed in the extreme. The level of distrust among the residents of the occupied territories has very much increased and it would be considerably more dangerous, maybe impossible, to repeat what I was still able to do a couple of years ago. The events which I had intended to warn about are coming to pass even as the warning itself—this book—is being published.